MURDER
UNINCORPORATED

MURDER
UNINCORPORATED

A Windsor Grove Novel

JOAN CUNNINGHAM

ARPress
ILLUMINATING IDEAS.
EMPOWERING VOICES

ARPress
45 Dan Road Suite 5
Canton MA 02021

Hotline: 1(800) 220-7660
Fax: 1(855) 752-6001

Ordering Information:
Quantity sales. Special discounts are available on quantity purchases by corporations, associations, and others. For details, contact the publisher at the address above.

Printed in the United States of America.

| ISBN-13: | Paperback | 979-8-89330-795-5 |
| | eBook | 979-8-89330-796-2 |

Library of Congress Control Number: 2024904716

CHAPTER 1

"You'll never see me in here again! I don't get what people like about this place; that had to be the worst meal ever. I *won't* be back!"

That indignant guest had occupied a table in the middle of our dining room for over three hours and was the last lunchtime diner to leave. Demanding from the moment he walked in, he'd loudly criticized everything on our menu, barking orders at my staff and annoying other diners with constant phone conversations.

I sighed with relief when he turned on his heel and charged through the exit, even though he'd stormed out refusing to pay.

"And goodbye to you, too," I muttered as tires squealed out of the parking lot.

Until I'd begun this short term "management experience" I'd never realized how insurmountable a task it is to keep some people happy. Uneasy in my new position, and unaccustomed to being in authority, I was suddenly supposed to smooth things over and project strength and wisdom (the wisdom part being laughable; I'd never held a similar job in my life).

Could I have handled the situation better? Probably. But I'd been unprepared for his attitude.

Within a few short days I'd look back at this angry guest with a sort of nostalgia, wishing for the days when a disgruntled diner was my biggest headache. But, at the time, dealing with him had seemed overwhelming, almost a deal-breaker in my willingness to remain.

1

"I'm sorry he was so angry. I offered him a different sandwich, but he refused. Do I have to pay for the meal when someone walks out?" Carrie O'Brien, our newest server, asked, reaching into her tip-filled apron pocket.

Relaxing my jaw and unclenching my fists, I attempted to smile. "No, it wasn't your fault; some people just can't be satisfied. When he orders a pesto burger and then remembers that he doesn't like pesto, you know you've got a challenge on your hands. You did exactly what you should have: offer an alternative, adjust his total, keep smiling, and move on."

There was a voice in my head speculating that his furious overreaction may have been an act to avoid paying, or merely a way to express his superiority over a fledgling manager.

"Did you hear him whining because we don't have imported water?" Carrie stood hand on hip. "He almost threw his tap water at me. He wanted something 'better'. But not normal bottled water, oh no, he wouldn't drink that either. He acted like I was serving him sludge from the creek!

"I shouldn't say this, but I'm glad he's not coming back," she said. "I get so frustrated; I have to learn not to take things personally, but that's hard. How could that guy be so rude?"

"Some people feel better about themselves when they throw their weight around. It's sad." I looked Carrie in the eye and shrugged, "You're learning fast, the guests can't tell you're new, so they expect you to handle things as if you've been here forever. In many ways, the better you are as a server, the harder you have to work."

We stood surveying the dining room with its neatly set tables (except for *his*) and the organized waitstations.

"As soon as I clear and reset that last table everything will be back in order. Did I forget anything?" Carrie's eyes scanned the room. Her concern was admirable; she genuinely cared about the details.

"The room looks great." Dark green tablecloths with white overlays and green napkins, sparkling water glasses and shining cutlery should impress even the most critical of guests. "It's ready for a busy evening.

We might get a few more diners this afternoon, but not many. You're here until Dawn comes in, right?"

"Right. She comes at 4:00; I'll be here 'til then." Petite, with naturally red hair, a pale complexion and large blue eyes, she was an enthusiastic learner who was already popular among the staff. Experienced servers know quickly who they can depend on when things get hectic, and Carrie had proven herself within days.

"You seem comfortable in your job. It all makes sense? The menu, the timing, dealing with the public?"

"Some days my biggest problem is keeping track of who's drinking regular and who's drinking decaf!" Carrie laughed. "Now if I could just stop having nightmares about dropping a tray!"

"They say it takes a long time before those dreams stop," I replied.

"Oh my…" Carrie was staring out the window toward the parking lot.

I turned to follow her gaze, and saw a gleaming red and white Wiscon-Trails tour bus pulling in. At first I thought it was simply turning around, but no, the bus stopped and people started streaming out and heading toward our entrance.

"Take a deep breath," I said. "You'll be glad you've got everything organized. It's going to get hectic."

"Bring it on!" she replied, giggling nervously as she grabbed an armload of menus.

Don't get me wrong. I'm thrilled when an extra forty-five customers walk in the door. But sometimes it seems like the basic rules of courtesy have been all but forgotten. Wouldn't you think they could have called first? Especially when they were going to show up at two p.m. on a Thursday? I would have had another server and a fry cook stay longer, had I known.

But I put a smile on my face and said, "Of course. Welcome to Unincorporated," when their tour guide asked if we could accommodate them. I was thankful the tables were set; if they'd arrived an hour earlier we may not have had enough clean tables. On the other hand, we would have had more staff.

One of the first lessons I'd learned about the hospitality industry was to be flexible and make it work…any way I could. In a resort community an unexpected rush isn't all that unusual; I was supposed to take it in stride. *Get over it,* I told myself, *you can handle this.*

"We have a bus. Forty-five people," I said, sticking my head through the swinging kitchen door.

"No sweat." Brad Galenburg, our chef, was alone in the kitchen chopping colorful farm-fresh ingredients for the salad prep table. "I've got it covered back here; I just hope you can handle it out front!" He nodded to himself and adjusted the temperature of the fryers and the grill, eyes scanning the preparation areas. "Why waste time checking on me? It's not like you'd have a clue how to help."

Brad had attended a technical college that claimed to train the "Best Chefs in the Midwest". Unfortunately for him, and fortunately for us, he hadn't been able to market his skills in any large cities. His aggressive personality was probably born of that frustration. The kitchen crew usually bore the brunt of his resentment, but recently he saved his most scathing comments for me and my lack of restaurant knowledge. Being around him with his I'm-better-than-you-are attitude made me feel totally incompetent.

Unfortunately he was correct in his assessment of my skills, so I left kitchen management to him. I'd learned to stay out of Brad's way, trusting him to keep his staff on task. They were in awe of his skills, and willingly followed where he led. Dealing with the front of the house and the ebb and flow of hungry diners was far easier for me.

That afternoon's onslaught of unexpected guests chatted with each other as they entered.

"I only want a sandwich."

"I'm just having dessert…I hope there's something chocolate."

"This place has such a weird name…"

"…wonder if bus drivers eat free."

"What a gorgeous view of the lake. Let's take that table by the window."

"I'm starving…I want a steak!"

"Does anyone know where the bathroom is?" Apparently this was the vital question, since half of the group headed for the restrooms while I led others to the dining room.

After helping Carrie fill water goblets and lay menus on the tables, I took a moment to look into the kitchen one more time.

"Are you okay with the orders all coming in at once?" I realized immediately that it was a stupid question, and it earned me a disparaging look. A sudden influx of guests was the type of thing Brad thrived on. It got his adrenaline flowing and fed his ego.

"Just go back out front. I know what I'm doing, which is more than you can say," was his response. I turned and headed to the dining room where my help might be appreciated.

"They're retirees from up near the Twin Cities, spending several days touring central Wisconsin," their efficient tour guide explained.

"They have a few planned stops each day; beyond that they watch for places that look interesting." Based on the fact that everyone was finally approaching their tables, in this case *interesting* may have meant we looked like a place that would have clean restrooms.

"In addition to those items on our printed menu, our luncheon features today are: a caprese salad with heirloom tomatoes and a portobello pepperjack sandwich," Carrie and I explained at each table. Smiles broke out as we announced the featured dessert, "our famous chocolate crème brule'."

The guests' attire suggested that they were no strangers to their local country clubs. The women also appeared to be familiar with their local jewelers. Hopefully we'd give them the first-rate service they were accustomed to. Even though we might never see any of them again I couldn't ignore the fact that word of mouth is the best advertising.

Thanks to Brad's kitchen skills, and the fact that a leisurely lunch appealed to the group, Carrie and I managed to serve everyone without making it obvious how understaffed we were.

Although Brad had doubtlessly been rushing around in the kitchen like a hurricane, the attractively-plated entrees gave no hint of the chaos involved. The guests left happy, well-fed, and without mentioning slow service.

"I'll be back next time I'm in this part of the state," one after another commented as they paid their bills. "I'm going to tell my friends about this place!"

Carrie stood near the door making pleasant conversation. "You're going to love the Brady Museum...Windsor Gourmet Foods has a great selection of souvenirs...Enjoy the rest of your vacation...What a lovely sweater!

"You don't want to miss Valerie's Boutique and Silversmith's," she whispered to some of the ladies. "Send your husbands over to Rick's Tap while you shop."

"That was fun!" Carrie said as we watched the guests re-board their bus. "That's the best part of this job, the people!"

"You're right. It's exciting to work here; you never know what to expect. You did a great job...waiting on tables seems to come naturally."

"Thanks," Carrie blushed at my praise, and then turned away to begin clearing tables. "I've always loved working with the public. Well, most of the public." We both laughed, remembering the disgruntled diner.

"Guests like him give you something to talk about at the end of the day," I said, "and make the others seem that much nicer."

Carrie had been a real asset, anticipating guests' needs and dealing with the unexpected rush as only an enthusiastic 20-year-old can. At the end of the shift her white tuxedo-style shirt still appeared pressed and clean; several of our more experienced servers would have looked wilted under those circumstances.

"I have a few things to finish in the office; then I'll be out to help put things back in order," I told Carrie.

Contrite for leaving her with the cleanup, I went to my tiny office and sat at the desk, more to rest my burning feet than to attack any paperwork. There's apparently some law that shoes can look good or feel good, but not both. I'd always opted for the fashion effect, but after a few hours on my feet I was regretting that decision. There was serious throbbing going on and I had only myself to blame.

I glanced down at my favorite heels: taupe leather with embossed toe detail. The height slowed me down, but they sure looked good! Fine in the office or when working the podium, they were impractical for rearranging tables or serving guests...not to mention being downright dangerous in the kitchen.

My lack of experience was showing, along with my vanity; I'd rather be trendy than practical. I had to learn to do both at the same time. That wasn't unreasonable, was it? Keeping a pair of practical shoes in my office would doubtless be a smart move.

Painful feet and all, I went back to the dining room to help restore order to chaos. Shortly after we had the tables cleared, Dawn came in to take over as evening head server.

"Thanks, Carrie, for your effort with the bus," I said as she prepared to leave. "Sometimes an unexpected group can totally derail things. Good job!"

Carrie left with a smile on her face and a bounce in her step. I realized that I was smiling too. Unincorporated really did have some terrific employees.

Leaving the front of the house in Dawn's capable hands, I took a chicken salad croissant sandwich to my office, and attempted to make sense of some invoices. Unincorporated had been serving food at this location for over 80 years and right now I was the keeper of the flame, so to speak. Paperwork has always been my enemy, and before long I decided to leave and rest my feet and my brain for a bit.

A few months ago my biggest worries had been whether I had a date for Saturday night, and if my history professor would notice if I skipped his lecture one more time. Now I spent my days thinking about schedules and customer counts and food purchases. It was my first dose of reality, and I wasn't sure I liked it.

Returning that evening I entered the kitchen through the employee entrance, (wearing brown ballet flats this time), to see Chef Brad in a corner laughing with two of our fry cooks. They stopped abruptly when they saw me, and hustled back to their stations. I thought I'd heard "… knows nothing about foodservice…"

Guilty expressions on the fry cooks' faces affirmed that they had, indeed, been discussing my inexperience. I knew I was in over my head, but it hurt to be reminded. It was abundantly clear that I wouldn't get any respect from my chef; I could only hope that eventually the rest of the staff would feel differently.

We made it through the dinner hour without incident. Most of our servers had been waiting table for years so things typically ran smoothly in the dining room. Brad kept things flowing in the kitchen, even with a younger, more unpredictable staff.

"Give our best to Al," I was told over and over as I seated guests, "Tell him we miss him." My Uncle Al, the owner of Unincorporated, was out on medical leave. He was an outgoing guy, and our local guests enjoyed chatting with him when they came to dine. I assured everyone that Al was more than anxious to get back to work.

"I hope he's on his feet soon; it's not the same without him down at the Lodge."

"Bunch of us guys are gonna go visit him next week…see if he's up to playing some sheepshead." The classic Wisconsin card game was a favorite of Al and his buddies; I'd always thought of it as a boring waste of time.

"Remind the old coot he owes me a drink at Rick's Tap. He should know better than to bet against the expert!"

And on it went.

I hadn't said it out loud, but I was even more anxious for Uncle Al's return than he was himself.

After closing, I left through the employee entrance and strolled along a tree-lined gravel path to a rustic cottage, my temporary residence. The short walk was always therapeutic. Moonlight filtering through the trees, the gentle sound of waves lapping on rocks along the shore, the chirping of tree frogs and hooting of owls all combined to ease my stress and calm my tension.

As I wandered I reflected on the day's events. As usual there had been numerous learning experiences, along with numerous times when I'd felt as useless as a pair of stilettos on a hiking trail. My sociology degree hadn't prepared me for the business world, or for much else. During my senior year I'd realized that it takes a Master's degree or better to succeed in the sociology field. But my funds had run out, and a further degree wasn't going to happen.

So here I was, a reluctant restaurant manager, believing that the combination of an angry diner and an unexpected bus would be among the most stressful of days at this job. I'd told myself I could do anything for a short time, and I anticipated that this would be a *very* short time.

Wrong. Wrong. Wrong. Wrong about the duration of my stay. And definitely wrong about the level of stress I'd have to endure.

My name is Ashley Kowalski, and I come from the Milwaukee suburbs. I'm a recent graduate of the University of Wisconsin-Madison, home of Bucky Badger, Camp Randall Stadium built on a Civil War army base, and Babcock Hall where agriculture majors sell superb ice cream. It's also been voted the Best Party School in the country. But none of this does any good if you haven't had any job offers by graduation, and the current job market was bleak to say the least.

"There's something important I want to ask you," Al Richardson, my mother's older brother and my favorite uncle, had said a few months earlier during a phone conversation.

"Your mom probably told you I have a surgery scheduled next month," he continued.

When I replied in the affirmative he explained the reason for his call.

"I need someone to step in as a short-term manager, just until my recovery is complete, a few weeks, hopefully no longer. I hear you haven't had any luck finding a job after graduation, so I hope you'll help me out."

"What will I be able to do?" I was confused at the direction the conversation was taking. "That semester I spent waiting on tables was a lifetime ago, and didn't really teach me much."

"Your title will be 'Manager-on-Duty', but I'll still make the decisions. You'll be my eyes and ears while I'm not there. It's important that it be someone I totally trust, someone intelligent, someone with good people skills, and of course someone currently unemployed," he laughed.

I was shocked. I don't remember replying, but apparently I agreed to his plan.

"Everything will be fine," my parents had encouraged. "It's good work experience. You'll just keep an eye on things; Al's staff knows how to do their jobs."

Maybe so, but the long-term staff loved Al, and weren't at all sure how they felt about me. And no one had mentioned the seasonal employees, just learning their jobs, who were slow at best and undependable at their worst. With me at the helm the phrase "the blind leading the blind" seemed apropos.

I really was as inexperienced in the industry as Chef Brad thought, but I certainly wouldn't admit it to him!

"We'll stay in touch," Uncle Al had promised. "We'll talk daily, making decisions together until you feel comfortable on your own. Don't worry; we're in this together."

His assurances had initially made me feel secure, but in reality weren't much help. He could advise me on how much chicken to order, who to call when a pipe was leaking, and which fry cooks to use on Friday night. But he wasn't there to decide when to cut staffing levels, or to placate annoyed guests.

I'd initially been excited to take on the challenge. I'd pictured myself as a kind of executive greeter, making pleasantries while others did the work. I'd had no concept of what managing a restaurant entailed, but it sounded like fun, like a great way to fill time until I found a *real* job. I hoped that enthusiasm, energy, and a bachelor's degree could make up for lack of foodservice training.

"It will be fine, Ashley," Al had said, echoing my parents when I'd expressed some trepidation. "You have a good head on your shoulders; just use your common sense." I embraced the opportunity, deciding I could handle anything that came my way.

That just goes to show how ignorant I was about what I'd gotten myself into.

CHAPTER 2

On a quiet road in a central Wisconsin forest...

If you could frame one spectacular sunrise and keep it forever this was the breathtaking morning you'd preserve. You'd paint a mural, weave a tapestry and compose a symphony in an attempt to capture the beauty forever. It was Mother Nature at her best.

The June sun rising in a cloudless sky, the birds performing arias in the trees, and the pungent woodsy scent of the lakeside forest brought a smile to Mark Fischer's face as he traveled his delivery route. This shortcut was his favorite part of the daily drive, the time when he felt fully in touch with the blessings of the area.

With an oldies station playing softly on the radio, surrounded by the wonders of the countryside, this was where he was most content, most rejuvenated from whatever life was dishing out. He took a long, deep, refreshing breath, and smiled. The tall grasses did a slow graceful dance; the lake shimmered like a polished mirror. The world was an undeniably wonderful place.

Blond, baby-faced, empathetic and personable, he was content in the community he'd adopted as his new home. People were open and friendly, life was easy, his worries far away. If he could make a few good friends, and get involved in a few local activities, he'd happily spend the rest of his life here. It would all come in time; he felt sure of that. He could be patient.

Suddenly shaken out of these calming reflections, Mark hit the brakes. An acquaintance had stepped abruptly out of the trees onto the dusty gravel road, and stood in front of the delivery van, arms waving to catch Mark's attention.

"Well, hi! What brings you out here?" Mark asked through his open window, removing his sunglasses, flashing an easy smile.

Mark was always pleased to come across someone unexpectedly, but it was puzzling at this early hour on a fire road winding through the forest. During the months he'd driven this route, Mark hadn't seen a single person walking along this road. Ever. It was part of the attraction this path held, the feeling of being alone with nature.

But friendly as always, Mark gladly stopped, curious to learn what brought another human out to a deserted road so early in the day.

"I'm late for an appointment. I decided to take the shortcut, but took a turn too fast. My car slid off the road in a muddy rut. I can't get it moving again." The friend spoke quickly, rushing an explanation. "Can you give me a ride into town? I'll call a tow truck later, right now I really have to get going."

"Sure thing, hop in. It's no problem; it will be nice to have company for a while." Mark was bewildered. The weather had been bone-dry for weeks, he knew the road like the back of his hand, and he couldn't remember any ruts, muddy or otherwise. But no matter; Mark would certainly never question anyone's request. It wouldn't be neighborly.

"Just let me make a quick call, I'll let them know I'm on my way," the friend smiled, nodding, looking satisfied.

Reaching toward a pocket as if for a phone, Mark's visitor suddenly brandished a sturdy wooden-handled knife. Its long, thin, well-sharpened blade glistened in the sun. As Mark sat stunned and staring, his friend leaned forward, stretched an arm through the open van window, and burst into an insanely wicked laugh ending in a shrill howl.

Mark's eyes widened in disbelief. What on earth was happening?

With abrupt moves the knife was brutally slashed into Mark's chest. The left side. The life-giving side. The action was merciless and savage, the act of a crazed being, almost inhuman.

Again and again, with increasing speed, with increasing ferocity, the weapon sliced Mark's rib cage, until one final vicious thrust met no resistance, the sharp blade penetrating deep into the chest cavity. A sadistic *twisting motion enlarged the point of entry, resulting in a haunted sucking sound. That final stroke left no doubt about the desired result.*

Mark's attempts to fight back had been hindered by an initial shock, slowing his reactions. By the time he realized the chilling, deadly gravity of the situation, it was too late. His arms flailed widely as he grabbed for the swift-moving knife, all the while in a state of anguish. He tried to form words, but words wouldn't come.

His shocked expression turned to one of terror as Mark accepted his own mortality. How could everything end like this? His life had barely begun.

A few feeble gasping cries finally escaped, followed by one last, tragic, spine-chilling scream which echoed through the trees. Warm spurts of blood created a sinister red stain, defacing the front of his pressed white shirt, as Mark's body slumped awkwardly sideways. His head tilted to one side. His unseeing eyes stared across the landscape.

For a few moments silence reigned in the forest. Squirrels froze in their tracks, birds stopped singing, and nature took a moment to acclimate itself. It was as if time had stopped for just a second. The sun seemed to stop rising while it readjusted to a change in the universe. Slowly, sounds reawakened, and the world continued on.

With a deep contented sigh the attacker stepped back, ecstatic at the thought of a mission complete. It was a job well-done, a pleasurable experience.

The sun shone brightly as it reflected off the hood of the white Wholesale Wholegrains delivery vehicle, and the well-tuned engine continued to hum. A soft melody played on the radio, as the DJ reminded his listeners of times when life was more simple and undemanding.

Footsteps wandered, unheard and unobserved, back into the forest.

The last thing Mark had seen on earth, as the last bit of breath escaped his body, was the sight of this gleeful "friend" aiming the razor-sharp dagger at his chest and smiling broadly.

The cloudless sunlit sky gave continued promise of a gorgeous summer day. Wildflowers in the area added brilliance to the breathtaking landscape. A delivery van, filled with delicious fresh bakery products that would never be delivered, emitted enticing scents into the surrounding area.

The birds sang more fervently than ever, as if they understood that there was something exceptional about this day.

CHAPTER 3

Friday dawned bright and clear, sunny and in the high 70's with little breeze, an ideal day in a lakeside community, a day that would convince visitors to extend their stay, and should entice families statewide to hit the road heading for a tourist area.

A recent pattern of unseasonably dry weather continued; grass cried out for daily watering and local farmers were dismayed about the state of their crops. But brilliant skies had travelers smiling as they drove into town, and shopkeepers were expecting a weekend of increased sales.

Visions of a good book with a hand-muddled Mojito on a beach, Jimmy Buffet playing in the background, danced through my head. But it was not to be. I had responsibilities now that couldn't be ignored. Even so, the beautiful day lifted my spirits.

I hurried through the woods to Unincorporated, buoyed by the prospect of a busy day serving enthusiastic families. And, I might add, wearing flatter shoes than the day before. I wore one of my favorite outfits, a silky turquoise shirt with a twill skirt in a deep shade of teal. That color combination usually makes me happy. On that particular day my contented feeling didn't last for long.

"What the hell happened now?" Chef Brad Galenburg growled as I entered the kitchen. He gestured with a hand that wielded a meat cleaver, making his question seem overly dramatic. "You forgot to order bread products for the weekend? What were you thinking?"

My stomach sank. I didn't remember ordering any bread that week. Or the week before, for that matter. *Wait a minute…I don't order bread…the deliveryman stops daily to replenish our supply.*

"Very funny. Ordering bread is not part of my job description," I said in what I hoped was a light tone of voice. I wanted to diffuse the situation; Brad's tendency to blame me no matter what the circumstances was wearing thin. *I will not let him get to me*, I told myself, *I will* not *let him get to me.*

"The only reason I can think of that Mark hasn't delivered is that you told him not to come," Brad accused. "He's always here before nine, usually before eight." He was right. Mark was the deliveryman for Wholesale Wholegrains, a local commercial bakery, and his smiling face was always here and gone long before we opened for lunch.

"I wouldn't have done any such thing, especially not before a weekend. I wonder what's up. Has it happened before?"

"Nope. Not once. Not ever. Your uncle would never deal with a company that couldn't deliver on time. Wholesale Wholegrains has always been the most dependable bakery around. Until today!"

"Maybe he's just behind schedule." Even as I said it I realized how lame that sounded.

"Seems mighty odd to me. He'd better get here soon, we're out of focaccia bread, herbal crostini and semel rolls, and we're low on everything else. You probably don't know it, but we keep our supply short so our product is always fresh. We'd better not have to buy bread and buns from some grocery store!"

He sneered the last phrase in a manner implying that local grocery stores were stocking expired inedible bakery products, hoping to pass them off on the next poor schmuck who walked in the door.

"I'll give them a call, see what I can learn," I said as Brad shook his head and muttered. I went to my small cluttered office and picked up the phone, thankful that our regular vendors were all on speed dial.

"Wholesale Wholegrains, Rose speaking." It was a surprise when the customer service number was answered by a living breathing person. Relieved at not having to deal with voicemail I explained who I was, and inquired about our missing delivery.

"I apologize that you haven't received your delivery yet. It's very odd," said the pleasant voice at the other end of the phone. "We've had several calls this morning from customers waiting for Mark. He's not answering his pager or his phone, so we really don't know where he is. It's not like him to get behind schedule or neglect part of his route. We're looking into it; we'll give you a call when we've figured out what's going on."

And that was all I learned.

Now, what to do? We couldn't go into lunchtime without bread products. I certainly didn't know what we needed, or in what quantities. So, as much as I hated giving him the satisfaction, I went to ask Brad for help.

Thirty-something, tall with broad shoulders and a thick neck, Brad had a blond buzz cut, a perpetual scowl, constant five-o'clock shadow and a bit of a weight problem. He was a talented chef who took his position seriously, but working in our small-town Wisconsin supper club was not his idea of success. He wore his white chef's coat, with salt-and-pepper pants and a tall snowy-white toque, as if he were leading a kitchen in a world-class establishment. With Uncle Al out he was working seven days a week, often twelve-hours-plus.

Brad trusted Uncle Al, a trained chef himself, to handle any kitchen duties; but with Al unavailable Brad was reluctant to share even the smallest responsibility.

It wasn't necessary that the chef receive morning deliveries, a retired construction worker handled that. Brad wasn't required to stay late to supervise the dishwashers and cleaning crew, but he often did that chore too. He had a proprietary attitude about *his* kitchen, and was sure that no one could control it like he could. I hated to admit it, but he was probably right.

"Brad, can you please go out and buy the baked goods we need for today? I didn't get any explanation from Wholesale Wholegrains. They don't have any idea where our delivery is."

"I suppose I have to, nobody else around here would know what to buy!" He slammed the cooler door with more authority than necessary. "The nearest decent bakery is in Oak Landing. This excursion you're sending me on could burn most of an hour." Oak Landing is the largest community in the area, and I believed Brad when he said he had to go that distance to get quality products.

"I don't feel good about this…are you sure you can keep things running while I'm away?"

I wasn't sure at all, but didn't seem to have a choice. Chances were good that as soon as we invested the time and money to stock up on bread products, Mark would walk in the door with his huge smile and restock our pantry with the items we'd contracted for.

Thankfully the kitchen staff held things together without incident until Brad returned; I would have been useless if they'd needed assistance.

June business so far hadn't been stellar; I wasn't looking forward to doing my weekly sales report. Numbers had been consistently down since I'd become acting manager, and knowing that the entire community had seen a slow start to the season didn't keep me from feeling responsible.

We had a moderately busy lunch; at one time the dining room was almost full, which recently had been the exception rather than the norm. That day's guests were mostly the locals who were our bread-and-butter throughout the year, but who didn't bring in enough revenue to keep the doors open. Al had explained how badly we needed the seasonal travelers, and the income they provided, to keep money in the bank.

Once schools closed in Illinois it would make a huge difference; that tended to happen a week later than in Wisconsin.

"It becomes a real zoo around here once those Illinois flatlanders show up!" was how some grumpy old guy in the Lounge had described the anticipated busy season.

We'd start seeing better numbers any day now, or so I told myself. I smiled when I thought of how annoyed that old grump would be.

Another elderly man who'd become a fixture in our dining room, Mr. Horner, had occupied his normal table during the lunch hour.

"Far corner, please," he would request, then settle his pudgy body with his back to the wall. From there he could see everything that happened, and everyone who was there. He would sit compulsively pleating and refolding his napkin, making no attempt to hide the fact that he was eavesdropping on conversations. Glancing from side-to-side in agitated fashion, as if concerned that someone might look over his shoulder, he seemed to seek refuge in the corner.

"Broiled Salmon Sandwich with regular coffee?" Carrie asked even before he'd opened his menu. He nodded, handed back the menu, and began creating tiny paper airplanes from scraps torn from a placemat. As long as he didn't try to fly them through the restaurant it was alright with me.

Mr. Horner's dining habits were totally predictable. Three packets of sugar would go into his coffee, a few more disappearing into his pockets. Had it been evening he would have ordered a New York Strip Steak, medium-rare with onion rings, and a Tanqueray Martini, extra dry, with anchovy olives. Portly and balding with thick glasses, he was polite and tipped well, but had little to say.

Someone had pointed his house out to me, a quaint little bungalow on a side road near downtown. He spent hours sitting on a porch swing watching the comings and goings on Main Street. It sounded like a lonely existence to me.

"Is his name Jack?" I had once asked Dawn, our head server, thinking I was clever. (You know, like the nursery rhyme, "Little Jack Horner sat in a corner..."). She didn't get it, and looked at me like I was crazy. Maybe she'd never heard that rhyme.

Mr. Horner was only one of the dozens of regular guests whose meal selection our staff could predict before they'd even been seated. I was learning quickly just how vital *regulars* were to the survival of a restaurant. They added local character, guaranteed that travelers would never sit in an otherwise empty dining room, and kept money coming in the door during the lean winter months.

"The best advice you gave me was on my first day," Carrie had said, "when you said I'd learn to tell which customers wanted conversation and which wanted to be left alone, who was in a hurry and who wanted to relax. You were right, if I watch for the clues, it's easy." For the most part, the regulars came in for relaxation and socialization as much as they came to dine.

After lunchtime I finally got to the duties I should have completed hours earlier. I picked up a change order from the bank to stock up for the weekend, locked the cash in the trunk of my 15-year-old red VW Beetle (complete with racing stripes), and drove to the post office.

Our post office is the town's unofficial gathering place. With no residential mail delivery, people stop in daily to check their boxes, and Windsor Grove news spreads fast in the hectic lobby. This is not considered "gossip"; it is the "sharing of important information".

The postal workers keep a coffee pot filled, set out a "coffee fund" cup, and provide uncomfortable metal folding chairs around an old wooden table, encouraging lingering and conversation for retirees with time on their hands. Despite the characterless acoustic ceiling and a wall color I think of as government-surplus-green, it has a homey atmosphere. It's undeniably the best place in town to learn what's going on; other than Zachary's Lounge of course.

"She's so terribly overweight that when she walks she waddles; and now she needs foot surgery…her little feet can't support her body."

"I hear that Mike Plank's daughter is coming back to help run the shop…no mention of her no-good excuse for a husband…I think he's out of the picture." Shocked faces all around.

"…my left knee is telling me we'll get rain soon…"

"…got caught on the lake without a fishing license…" Much shaking of heads. Fishing was always a popular topic, complete with ongoing friendly disagreements.

"How soon will your uncle be back to work? Is that chef of his getting under your skin?" I was asked this not just once but regularly. It was hard to respond politely after the first few dozen times, but I made an effort to smile and act like those were original questions.

Everyone also seemed to think that I wanted to hear about other restaurants and pubs, sharing tales time and again.

"I had the worst hamburger the other day; I've been spoiled by your Angus burgers."

"Did you hear that Bonnie's Bakery started selling fancy little French pastries? Are they ever pricey!"

"You know that tavern out by the gravel pit? They've got a scrawny new bartender that made a sarcastic comment about Larry's weight. Just because Larry ordered a triple cheeseburger basket!"

"There's a new Italian restaurant in Oak Landing that my sister says has fabulous food."

The discussions would continue throughout the day, the participants changing, but not the topics. It certainly adds to the amount of time it takes to pick up mail.

On that particular Friday there was an additional topic for discussion. "We heard that some places never got a bread delivery today. Know anything about that? Did your bread show up?"

"Ours was one of the deliveries that didn't arrive," I confirmed. "I called Wholesale Wholegrains, but they couldn't give me any explanation, so I don't know any more than you do."

"I hope that new driver of theirs didn't skip town. He seems like such a nice guy." This was repeated several times, by various people, before I could escape. It occurred to me that perhaps I should start sending someone else for the mail...

Windsor Grove is primarily a tourist town, "A Picturesque Lakeside Village" according to our local visitor's guide. With a year-round population numbering in the low hundreds, the majority of businesses don't stay open through the long winter. The historic downtown, stretching lazily along a state highway curving past Windsor Lake, has more shuttered buildings than open ones from Christmas to Mother's Day.

Souvenir shops, gift shops and clothing stores all lock their doors during the quiet season, reopening whenever the frigid winter lets up. Businesses like the Crimson Leaf Gallery, a glass studio operating in the old Evangelical Church, cut their hours; Windsor Gourmet Foods closes off a large section of the 1870's hardware store that it occupies.

"People ask a lot of questions when they visit a community. You'll need to know some history," Al had explained. He'd proceeded to give me some local background.

"Our town board has consistently denied every building application from national chains, so Windsor Grove businesses are all independent, and for the most part locally owned. It gives our town its unique character, like a step back to the time when everyone knew their neighbors and called all the shopkeepers by name. The sort of town you see in Norman Rockwell paintings.

"Tourism is the major industry here, but area orchards run a close second. Windsor apples came to this part of Wisconsin in the mid-1800's, giving the town its name and its personality. With thousands of acres of orchards, we are an autumn destination for apple aficionados. Over the years, a wise planning commission created the guest friendly downtown that extended our tourist driven economy over summer months as well."

The downside to this is the lack of shopping and dining options available when the tourism dependent businesses close for the off season.

Unincorporated is one of the few places for locals to dine during the bitter cold winters that go on forever, so when other restaurants reopen their doors in spring our regular guests are thrilled to have more options. Our competitors spend their downtime sprucing up their facilities, so they seem fresh and new when springtime rolls around. By contrast we're the old familiar stand-by that will always be there, as comfortable as an old pair of shoes that everyone takes for granted.

Business had picked up a bit over the last few weeks as the hundreds of privately-owned cottages, condominiums and seasonal homes were reopened for the summer. As soon as travelers hit the road in full force Unincorporated would see crowds again. Or so I was told. The huge number of resorts, motels, rental cottages and campgrounds would supply us with hungry customers throughout summer. But the tourists had to get here first.

"It's going to be a chilly weekend," the weathercasters had been announcing every week, "with significant rainfall, and threat of thunderstorms. Cancel your outdoor plans!" The rain never materialized, drenching counties to the north and south instead, but the prediction alone was a detriment to business. A guest had told me the name for this: *fearcasting*. Restaurateurs, innkeepers, camp rangers and shopkeepers were ready to scream in protest every time they heard a dismal forecast from the weather service.

Ironically, despite all the predicted precipitation, the weather remained dry, triggering high-risk fire warnings throughout the county. The drought-meter was high, something as small as a discarded cigarette could ignite the forest. The campgrounds posted burn bans and volunteers patrolled parched campsites. Campground occupancy was down as a result; campers could easily go to another part of the state and safely build a campfire, and that's exactly what many of them were doing.

CHAPTER 4

When my p.m. staff began arriving I decided to spend a few minutes back at my cottage, feet up, eyes closed, listening to music. I ordered a dinner salad carryout (locally sourced greens with pomegranate, Swiss and turkey, my favorite), and spent a few minutes opening mail until it was ready.

"Call my phone if you need me," I told Dawn, the evening's head server, and headed into the woods. Some decompression time would clear my brain before we began the Friday evening rush…at least I hoped there would be a rush.

Unincorporated is snuggled into a densely wooded area, and about a hundred yards through towering pines is the inviting cottage I was calling home. It's part of the property that includes the restaurant, the vast parking lot, and one quarter mile of lake frontage.

White wood clapboard with green accents and an exposed limestone foundation, it reflects the style of Windsor Lake's many cottages. This is where Uncle Al sleeps after a late night if he doesn't want to drive the twenty miles to his home in Oak Landing; and this is where my family stays when visiting.

I felt comfortable in Al's cottage after years of vacations, and it had become my current refuge. I'd always enjoyed having time to myself, so living solo was welcome after years of shared college apartments. At the end of a full day at Unincorporated it was a restful escape.

"Ashley, honey, your Dad and I think it's just wonderful that you get to spend your summer at the lake," Mom had said during a recent phone call. She made it sound like I was on an extended vacation, with no responsibilities.

"I haven't actually had time to relax; most of my day is spent at the restaurant. I supervise the staff, manage the dining room, and do a fair amount of paperwork. This job keeps me pretty busy."

"We're coming to visit you someday soon; I'm anxious to see that new art gallery and I love browsing through jewelry stores. We'll have such fun together!"

"But remember, Mom, I'm managing the restaurant. It takes up most of my time. I'll have to be at work when you're here..."

"Just take some time off dear." She hadn't listened to me at all. "If you need to work a little, your Dad can go golfing while I visit with Al. I can relax for a while at the cottage, too; you know I love it there." It was a good thing she enjoyed the cottage; I really did have to work, whether she believed it or not.

Al's sturdy structure is mainly one large room, a kitchen area at one end, cushy seating arrangements occupying the rest. Overstuffed armchairs, several sofa-beds and a few tables suitable for card games invite guests to make themselves comfortable. Large windows provide a lake view through the pines. A screened porch facing the lake features painted wicker furniture, and brings the scents and sounds of the forest into the home. Those earthy elements introduce a serene atmosphere that relaxes even the most stressed of visitors.

A massive stone fireplace covering one end wall is the cottage's focal point. The worker who constructed it had superb masonry skills; everyone who's ever seen it was enthralled by its craftsmanship. With a wide raised hearth, a huge mantel, and various large stones jutting out, it almost begs for a rock-climbing episode up its face.

The huge main room with its high ceiling, timbered beams and no-nonsense furniture emphasizes how tiny the bedrooms are. A person can barely stand next to their bed to get dressed. The word *cozy* was coined for rooms this size. It had never posed a problem in previous visits; there'd been no reason to spend any amount of time anywhere but in the main room.

Suddenly the miniscule closet and narrow two-drawer dresser were supposed to contain my entire wardrobe. Anyone who knows me can tell you that just wasn't going to happen! Consequently, my clothes were spread haphazardly through every closet in the place. Jewelry, accessories and cosmetics commandeered any available shelf space, and shoes took up residence in every corner.

Someday I would make time to organize everything; until then getting dressed in the morning was quite an adventure.

The uncomfortably small bathroom, which seemed to have been an afterthought, felt even more confining. The vintage wavy mirror would have been whimsical, if it weren't impossible to use. The face I viewed each morning was like something by Picasso, with all the proper parts visible, just not aligned correctly.

Each day I looked into that mirror as I twisted my hair into what I told myself was an interesting style. In reality, it was just the quickest way to restrain my hair in a way that would satisfy the health inspector if she showed up.

The undulating face in the mirror had brown eyes, shoulder-length wavy brown hair that frizzed in humidity, a slightly crooked nose (more so in this mirror than in others), and what I thought was a friendly smile. After a few more weeks I might not recognize my real self. I was reminded of a fun-house mirror, meant to be amusing, not flattering. It wasn't especially good for my ego.

Medium height with a slender frame, I consider myself to be average looking. When I take time with my make-up I hope I'm slightly above average. At any rate, Mom says I am. Applying make-up was an artistic challenge with this mirror; thankfully the restrooms at Unincorporated had good lighting and I always did a quick touch-up before unlocking the doors.

"Jeff was due here an hour ago to finish the prep work!" was the first thing I heard as I walked through the staff entrance later that afternoon. Brad's booming voice continued, "I called his number but didn't get an answer. My guess is he's not coming. What are you going to do about it, Ashley? We need him on dishes tonight!"

Here we go again, I thought. My shoulders tensed…couldn't I ever walk in the door without some sort of drama? Apparently not.

The name "Jeff" didn't ring any bells. Was he the quiet one with the disturbing tattoos? Was he the smart-mouthed one who talked incessantly about his private life? Or was he the condescendingly polite kid who pretended to work harder than he actually did? It didn't matter; tonight Jeff was a no-show-no-call, which is unacceptable.

I wasn't about to let Brad know I wasn't sure which employee was Jeff. No need to give my crotchety chef any more ammunition than necessary. He was undoubtedly aware that I hadn't figured out who all the staff were. Getting to know the kitchen staff was one more thing I had to focus on, and sooner rather than later. I didn't need Brad announcing I was clueless any more often than he already did.

"It's too late now to find a replacement. If the fry cooks pitch in to help with dishes we should be okay," I decided. "If I know you, you've already done his share of the prep work."

"Somebody had to. The tilapia isn't gonna bread itself!" Brad rolled his eyes and walked away.

Brad has a need to excel, an innate drive to work at a higher standard than anyone else. His natural talents make this achievement easy, yet with his superior attitude he scorns any praise. I could tell he was proud of having already handled Jeff's work along with his own, but I was certain that complimenting him would just lead to some snide remark.

I left the kitchen without comment. Brad would keep his crew on task and the work would all get done. He refuses to let his kitchen turn out anything less than an impressive meal, and one absent employee won't change that.

Back in my crowded, cluttered office I called Jeff's number.

"Jeff, this is Ashley. Did you know you were scheduled to work tonight? Call me back when you get this message." I wouldn't have placed any bets on getting a return call, but honest mistakes do happen, so I reluctantly gave Jeff the benefit of the doubt. For the time being.

Any time we went for an entire day with a full staff was a plus; no one had to cover for a position they weren't strong at, and service flowed more smoothly. Thankfully everyone else had stayed *healthy* that day; seasonal staff were known to call in sick any time they got a better offer.

"You mean I have to wait? I can't go right to a table?" The man was totally incredulous. "I never have to wait."

"I'm sorry sir, but our dining room is full right now. I'll call you as soon as we have a table available."

"I can't believe you're making us wait."

His three piece suit and disdainful expression said that he was accustomed to swift accommodation. In this case that just wasn't possible.

"Isn't there something you can do?"

At that point his wife stepped in. "Don't worry, we'll be fine. We'll be waiting at the bar. Come on dear."

As they wandered away I wondered where he'd expected me to seat them. If the dining room is full, it's full. I can't magically produce another table.

He was dressed far too formally for dinner in a resort community. Where did this guy think he was? Was he always this demanding? Did he know how to relax? Some people just don't understand how to fit in; or care. Thanks to his understanding wife a tense encounter had been avoided. It seemed likely that she'd dealt with his belligerence before.

It continued to be an exhilarating Friday evening, with a full dining room and guests in the Lounge. Our strongest servers were scheduled on weekends, which worked well for everyone. More efficient staffers lead to a shorter wait for tables and happier guests; swifter turnover means more money in the till at the end of the evening; and the larger number of guests served significantly increases servers' tips.

The kitchen staff were also at their most impressive on busy nights. Brad organized his team like a well-oiled machine, a thing of beauty. The sights, the sounds, the smells, and the hectic atmosphere combined to create enticing meals for hungry guests. I enjoyed standing back and watching the flow. Until Brad would see me and bellow, "What do you want now? Go do your own job; leave me alone." So much for beauty.

Despite the rudeness of my chef, I was beginning to feel like I belonged, no longer a stranger pretending to accomplish things. The regulars were calling me by name, asking about Al, and sharing local scuttlebutt.

Attempting to hold Unincorporated together in a professional manner, I tried to deal with guests like the accomplished restaurateur Al was. Unfortunately I was more like an amateur playing a role in an off-Broadway play, repeating the same lines over and over, occasionally drawing the audience into the action, but other times just filling space on stage.

"Enjoy your dinner.

"Table for four? Will you need a highchair?

"Tonight's features are spicy seafood gumbo, pan-fried locally-sourced whitefish and braised lamb shank with mint jelly.

"Enjoy the play tonight. Come back for a post-performance dessert or ice cream drink!

"We make all the desserts ourselves.

"Thank you for dining with us.

"I'll call you when your table is ready."

As I repeated those phrases for what seemed like the millionth time, I felt as if everyone else took center stage in the production. I was a minor character, part of the ensemble, hoping for a bigger part. Unfortunately this particular character wasn't ready for that bigger part. My proverbial plate was already full, and was being piled higher and higher. I needed to learn how to balance that platter or the ingredients could meet with calamity.

There were days when everyone could presumably see my hesitation, lack of conviction, uncertainty. This wasn't my fantasy career, it wasn't even a back-up fantasy; but that didn't mean I was unconcerned about the outcome. I was just finding it difficult to translate intentions into action.

Windsor Grove is a community with a lot of pride. If I could develop the right mindset, and assume the prevailing attitude of uniqueness, I was confident I could be accepted, becoming a key part of local hospitality. There were some mental adjustments to be made, that's all. *You can do this, Ashley, you can do this!*

Being aware of community activities and controversies was important if I wanted to belong, so I tried to remain on top of the local chitchat. Recently the main topic of conversation among locals dealt with a well-known attorney who had announced his candidacy for state senate. Everyone had an opinion, of course, and wandering through the restaurant I couldn't help but hear them.

"It will be good for Windsor Grove to finally have state representation."

"He'll never win the election; he's too full of himself..."

"...certainly does have a huge ego."

"I'm sure he'll win, he's such an outgoing young man. And so handsome, too," an elderly woman giggled.

"Never hire him as an attorney, he doesn't know what he's talking about...a lot of hot air if you ask me."

"Anybody who runs for office is crazy." This comment was made in an angry tone that made heads turn.

"He's a Harvard man. Can't go wrong with a Harvard man..."

"I can't believe he went to Harvard. He cost me a fortune, and I've got nothing to show for it!"

"He doesn't even like it here...his grandmother, in Oak Landing, paid for his education...made him promise to return to the area...must be why he wants to move on to Madison..."

"...always so good to my mother, he deserves to win."

It was an unending discussion. I'd noticed the candidate's campaign signs appearing around town. The signs, and the local residents, called him RUPERT. I didn't know if Rupert was his first name or his last, and honestly didn't care.

Many local residents regularly returned to the Lounge after dinner in order to debate his candidacy, and we ended up with more cash in the till because of it, which was the up side of the issue. He dined at Unincorporated occasionally, drawing a crowd of well-wishers around his table; but if he lingered near the bar certain other guests tended to drink up and leave. That was the down side.

Conversations in the dining room swirled around me. I'd become aware that once guests were seated I became the proverbial fly on the wall. No one noticed when I walked past or stood nearby, as if I were invisible. Fine with me. I had no particular desire to get involved in their discussions.

I was especially invisible when I wandered through Zachary's. If I'd cared about local gossip this would have been a prime source. (Some local businessman was having an affair. I didn't even know what the guy looked like, but I'd heard every detail of his life from guests who never realized I was within earshot). If you enjoy knowing intimate details, become a bartender.

Zachary's Lounge was designed for friendly conversation. To the right of the lobby, it is a natural gathering spot for guests waiting to be called to their table, summoning them again after their meal. Dark and welcoming, it has a comfortable ambiance that draws every age demographic to the Lounge as if a home away from home.

The curving shape of the bar itself creates friendly areas that encourage lively conversation among friends or strangers. Pub tables along the walls offer the opportunity for private chats. Another seating option is created by upholstered chairs and sofas surrounding low tables. The elaborately carved oak back bar was original to the building, and a large portrait of Zachary Gellings, grandfather of the restaurant's founder, glares down at our guests. All in all, I considered Zachary's Lounge the most inviting bar in town. Not that I was prejudiced or anything...

As election season got into full swing I was amazed at the heated discussions regarding commonplace issues. Never having cared much about politics, I couldn't believe how agitated people became about issues I considered boring.

Our Lounge business was thriving because of two ongoing debates: whether a local zoning ordinance should be approved, and whether a school referendum should pass. I was happily ignorant about the details. That seemed to exempt me from many intense conversations. I got more work done that way; and had fewer things to be angry about.

Had I only known, I would have welcomed those political diversions as being a crucial part of small-town life; I would have felt invigorated at dealing with a cranky chef; and I would have considered terminating an inadequate staffer a normal occurrence in the hospitality world.

Instead I remained happily unaware that normalcy was going to be illusive for the foreseeable future.

CHAPTER 5

Looking out my bedroom window the next morning, peering through the trees, I could see a Wholesale Wholegrains truck parked behind the restaurant. I sighed with relief. We were getting our normal delivery; no one would make sarcastic comments, and I wouldn't have to ask Brad for help.

It had been another all-too-frequent night of tossing and turning. It wasn't just new servers who had restaurant dreams; on frequent nights I'd learned that new managers have them too. Mine, I was certain, were a result of insecurity and uncertainty. A restless sleep was accompanied by nightmares in which I was criticized by guests, had run-ins with Chef Brad, and made errors in paperwork and ordering. I looked forward to nights when sleep would again become a refuge.

I dawdled over a second cup of coffee, then took my time getting ready, donning a comfortable new dress I'd found in an Oak Landing boutique, the soft blue of a summer sky, A-line with silver button accents. I completed the look with silver earrings and bracelet.

Guests often commented on my jewelry, especially pieces from local boutiques. A simple bauble always seemed appropriate; eye-catching but not distracting...all in the interest of promoting local artists (or so I told myself whenever I succumbed to retail temptation; I made the purchase to support the community, not for any personal satisfaction. Of course).

I remembered to take along practical shoes, so I could start the day in fabulous footwear, another pair of heels I'd fallen in love with. This pair was relatively comfortable, but wouldn't do if we had a busy day.

Choices like that emphasized my inexperience; I had to learn to be more professional…but I loved wearing a great pair of shoes.

Feeling put-together and fashionable, I took a few moments to inhale the lake air. There's nothing like the fresh woodsy scent of morning air near a sunlit lake. Okay, the sun has nothing to do with the scent. Or does it? Either way, I went to work feeling good, carrying my comfy shoes, looking forward to the day.

"They sent some new guy with the bread delivery!" Brad was immediately in my face when I walked in the door. "He didn't have a clue what we needed; I had to teach him how to do our restock. What in the hell good is a delivery guy that doesn't know how to do our delivery?"

There was no answer to that, so I said I'd make a call to find out what was going on. So much for feeling light-hearted.

"And then," Brad was as belligerent as ever, "I said to that new guy, 'Where's Mark?', and he shook his head and turned away. No answer! What a jerk! Not a word! I hope to hell I never have to deal with *him* again."

I expected that the new delivery guy hoped to never deal with Brad again, either. I knew better than to express that opinion verbally; I had learned when to keep my mouth shut.

I went to my office to use the phone. Windowless and cramped, the interior room was a typical restaurant office, almost an afterthought, taking up as little space as possible. If two people were in the room together it was quite an accomplishment to open a file drawer. A large desk that took up most of the floor was cluttered with invoices, inventory sheets, and equipment catalogs. Bundles of visitor's guides were piled in one corner of the room, another corner held a case of carryout containers with a pile of aprons on top.

Ancient dented filing cabinets covered one wall. The remaining floor space was occupied by a visitor's chair (an old wooden dining chair that had seen better days). An extremely inconvenient safe was sunken into the floor, mostly hidden by the desk.

Al said the floor safe was an old supper club tradition, the cement floor being the most secure space any old building had. I'd learned the hard way to close that safe completely even when empty. A stiff ankle continued to remind me that an open safe was definitely not "safe". Nothing about that office was convenient or user-friendly.

Punching buttons on the phone, I wasn't confident about finding anyone in the Wholegrains office on a Saturday. Amazingly, the phone was answered immediately; however any satisfaction from that dissolved within seconds. When I identified myself and asked about the substitute deliveryman the woman on the other end dissolved into tears.

"He's dead, Mark is *dead*!" she sobbed. My heart skipped a beat at the news. "They found him in his truck in the forest. He'd never finished yesterday's route." Her voice broke; she stopped for a moment, and then continued falteringly, "There was still bakery waiting to be delivered." I knew that; Unincorporated's delivery would have been among those still in the truck.

"Sorry...sorry," she apologized in a squeaky voice. "Give me a minute to get my act together." I heard her draw a deep breath, then she continued.

"We're all in shock. He was such a nice guy. I...I just can't talk about it, it's so upsetting...I don't understand why it had to happen," she prattled nervously. Her overwhelming devastation was alarming, seeming overly dramatic.

"That's so sad. Wow, what a shock. We'll miss him. So...um...can you call me with any updates about our delivery?" It seemed inadequate and insensitive, but I was flustered and couldn't be any more articulate. After hanging up the phone I realized that there were many questions I should have asked, but hadn't.

"Mark is dead," I reported to my chef. "Yesterday's delivery was still in the van when he was found."

"Well, that's just great!" As expected, Brad's main concern had to do with the new deliveryman; there were several profane comments made about the work involved in training him. I had trouble working up any sympathy. Mark was dead, and I was supposed to feel sorry for Brad?

The rest of the kitchen staff were stunned, and reacted more appropriately. They all expressed thoughts that echoed my own; Mark had been a nice guy who'd always had a smile and something pleasant to say.

One of our fry cooks said it best, "Everyone was happy to see him come in the door because he made us all feel good." A person really couldn't wish for an epitaph better than that. I hope that someday someone will say something that kind about me.

"He was really cute, too," offered one of our female staff. "It was never a problem to look at *him* in the morning!" Also a great epitaph.

"How did he die?" someone asked, and it occurred to me that I had no idea; I'd not thought to ask. Come to think of it, his death did seem surprising. He'd been young and fit, someone whose name you'd be surprised to see in an obituary column. I tried to do an online search, but with no local daily news source there was nothing available.

The Oak Landing radio station was reporting that, "Mark Fischer, a 27-year-old resident of Windsor Grove, a recent transplant from Plainfield Indiana, was found dead in a Wholesale Wholegrains delivery truck along the fire road in the state forest late Friday afternoon. An investigation is in process." Not helpful at all. The mention of an investigation seemed curious, however.

It soon became clear that word had traveled through Windsor Grove about Mark's death. Local residents visit the post office early on Saturdays, as much to catch up on local scandal as to pick up their mail. The information isn't always accurate, but spreads like wildfire nonetheless. I was happy to say that I'd avoided the post office; weekend mail could wait until Monday.

An unexpected death was always fodder for the rumor-mill. As I walked past tables I constantly heard Mark's name being mentioned with speculation regarding his untimely demise. I didn't need to go downtown to hear the news; this was a day when the news came to me. That can be one of the good things about the restaurant, or one of the annoying things, depending on what's on everyone's mind.

"It's a shame when bad things happen to good people," I heard at one table. "When he came into the hardware store he always asked about my grandkids and enjoyed seeing their pictures."

"After Bob's surgery Mark called to find out if there was anything he could do to help...I didn't even know that Bob knew him."

"Mark was so curious about everyone that he asked constant questions. He was so anxious to be accepted..." said a regular guest. "It was almost sad, how badly he wanted to belong."

"He even remembered the names of our dogs; only a thoughtful person remembers details like that," said one elderly lady with a trembling voice. And on it went, with everyone agreeing that Mark was a good neighbor who would be missed.

There was talk of a heart attack, a collision, an allergic reaction, an engine explosion. The locals wanted answers, but all we had was speculation. There was a rumor that the sheriff's department had been called in, which sounded unlikely. I thought it more probable that an ambulance and EMTs had been dispatched.

"You think he had health problems? He didn't appear sickly."

"Mildred says he was injured so badly that no one could recognize him..."

"You mean it wasn't a natural death? I don't believe it."

"...heard there was a woman with him and she was dead too!"

"I'll bet it was carbon monoxide poisoning...he was renting that tiny apartment above Lillian's old house."

"Not. The radio said he was found in his work vehicle...that delivery truck."

"My cleaning lady said that the coroner was called in. That means something bad happened."

"His poor mother! Does anyone know his mother?"

I knew that eventually we'd all learn the details. In the meantime, business was picking up considerably. Between the travelers in town for the weekend, and the locals who were afraid they might miss juicy details if they stayed home, we had a hectic evening.

At one point, when I'd gone to my office in search of children's activity sheets, I noticed I'd received a text.

"Met a great guy!! Went with him to that new bar on Brady Street. I'll fill you in soon. How's the job going? Have fun!!"

My friend Bekah enthused over every guy she met, always sure that the newest one was *the* one. I felt as if she was part of a different life, my past life when there'd been dating, parties, and excitement. What was I doing here, dealing with staffing and customers and health codes and death? *Have fun?* That could be difficult.

Guests who drive into our parking lot see a sprawling one-story structure of indeterminate style, red brick near the ground, forest green siding above. A burgundy canopy covers the entryway, with lantern-style lights above stained glass windows on either side. A weathered wooden door with leaded glass sidelights beckons to guests as they arrived.

A large sign by the road, designed to mimic a highway sign, announces that this is UNINCORPORATED, with the words SUPPER CLUB below, followed by *and ZACHARY'S LOUNGE* in italics. The burgundy field distinguishes it from an actual highway sign, but the dimensions of the sign and the font of the white lettering were chosen with that look in mind. On the building a similar sign is displayed to the right of the entry. Spotlights illuminate the signs from several directions. Precisely-trimmed shrubbery surrounds the building.

"When guests pull in we want them to see a property that's neat and clean and comforting," Uncle Al had explained. "We want them to feel welcome, to immediately picture themselves indoors. Once we get them inside it's up to us to keep them; but the first thing we have to do is get them in!"

I had learned that when you're talking about lake property, the area nearest the road is considered the back; the area near the lake is the front. Being a city girl I always find this confusing; I expect the front yard to face the street.

The *front* yard of Unincorporated, the lake side, has the comfortable ambiance that the *back* lacks. A large area paved with local limestone is home to welcoming wrought iron chairs, benches and tables, all arranged to offer great views of the water. Guests have access through wide glass doors near the dining room.

"Visitors feel like they've discovered a hidden gem, an intriguing secret space they share only with our other diners," Al said, continuing his narrative. "It gives them a personal attachment to our property, and keeps them coming back."

In good weather the patio is a favorite place for diners waiting to be called to their table. The overwhelming natural beauty of the forested lake area guarantees that few guests ever complain about a moderate wait. Once the tourist season gets into full swing our outdoor space becomes a preferred spot.

Indoors Unincorporated has retained its Old World look throughout the 80-plus years it's been in existence. Necessary updates have been accomplished with a thoughtful eye toward maintaining the original atmosphere.

"Once they're inside they feel the historic character. The huge picture windows add the comforting elements of water, earth, lush greenery and elegant flowers...nature's recipe for relaxation. That's what my decorator said when she convinced me to add so many large windows." Al was obviously proud of the results.

Our dining room features an enormous eye-catching fireplace covering one entire wall, obviously laid by the same skilled craftsman who built the fireplace wall in my cottage.

"Local legend has it that the original owner's cousin was allowed to live in the cottage free-of-charge providing he completed all the stonework in both the restaurant and the cottage," Al related. "Another version says he wasn't a cousin, he was an itinerant mason paying off gambling debts. Either way, he was certainly an artist at his craft."

That spectacular fireplace sets the decorating tone. Dark wood, polished brass chandeliers, dark carpeting, and richly upholstered chairs were all chosen to give the impression of a building unchanged in generations.

Modern bathrooms and conversational seating in the Lounge (I'm supposed to call it that, but it's still a *bar* to me) give evidence that the facility hasn't been neglected; our guests enjoy the century-old atmosphere coupled with modern-day amenities.

"Hey Missy, my low-alcohol light's on over here!" an elderly gentleman wearing a battered fishing hat announced when I wandered outdoors to assure guests their tables would be ready soon. "We're getting mighty thirsty!"

"I'll be right back to take care of you." I hate answering to "Missy", but accepting rudely-delivered commands with a smile is part of my job. I headed to the Lounge and questioned Renata about outdoor drink service.

"You're supposed to schedule someone for outdoor service on summer weekends. For beverage orders, and maybe a few appetizers. I thought you knew," was the answer I got. No, I didn't know, and now I'd found out the hard way.

Couldn't someone have mentioned it during previous weeks? I imagined the staff laughing behind my back, waiting to see what happened when we were understaffed. It was an uncomfortable picture. Every time I thought I was finally being accepted as a supervisor, something happened to make me feel increasingly incompetent.

I went outside and took orders. The guests' reaction was to be expected, a combination of, "It's about time," and, "We thought we'd been forgotten." I handled outdoor service throughout the evening, thankful I'd remembered the sensible shoes. I hadn't given a thought to patio service. I would have to start thinking proactively if I wanted to succeed at this job.

I was thankful I'd recently asked Renata for a crash course in beer terminology. Being able to explain the difference between an ale and a lager, a porter and a stout, hopefully made me sound more knowledgeable than I really was. I'd spent many hours learning details about our entrees; it was time to start learning details about the Lounge.

I'd been amazed to learn that a Brandy Old-Fashioned was almost unheard of outside Wisconsin; I'd always thought it was a common drink. I was so ignorant about the distribution areas of local and craft breweries that I had assumed everyone was familiar with Spotted Cow and Lakefront IPA. There was indeed much to learn.

The sudden-death grapevine was encouraging people to linger longer than usual; we did an impressive amount of business outdoors that evening. Guests who finished eating often wandered back outside to take in the scenery and enjoy casual conversation, after-dinner drinks being an important part of the equation. That evening the patio was exceptionally popular. I couldn't believe I'd overlooked the need for an outdoor server.

I also couldn't believe that no one had told me.

Conversations about Mark's death dominated all others, both indoors and out. By the time the topic had travelled from cocktails on the patio to wine with the meal, then carried on to ice cream drinks in the Lounge, even those who'd never met him were professing shock and deep sorrow in thick-tongued discussion.

When things began to slow I sat at my desk and made a call to Bekah Greene, my best friend since high school, the one who was constantly meeting Mr. Right. We still used each other as sounding boards for all of our thoughts, and I needed a good dose of girl talk.

"Ashley, I'm glad you called! We haven't talked in forever! What's up? Tell me all about your new job," she said when she answered.

"You wouldn't believe what an arrogant rude character Chef Brad is," I started. As I continued I could tell she was struggling to act interested. I needed to vent my frustrations to someone, and she'd asked the question so she got the download.

"…and no one told me about outdoor bar service…" I had to give Bekah credit for continuing to listen, "…and the nice guy who delivers our bread died…"

"Wow. That's such a shame," she muttered in a tone that told me she didn't really understand how frustrating it all was. I couldn't adequately explain the unsettling feeling that Mark's death had given me, so she dismissed my concern that somehow it was going to affect me. But she continued to listen and I continued to talk.

Then, abruptly and with enthusiasm, Bekah started telling me about her newest boyfriend ("His name is Duncan, and he's absolutely wonderful!") and the party they'd gone to the night before. From there we moved on to details of her job search; she was also a recent graduate searching for employment. We finished the conversation making plans for Bekah to visit Windsor Grove, listing the many things we planned to do together.

"With all those interesting shops, and cute little boutiques, and fun places to eat, we'll have an amazing time!" she said. "I hope I have a job lined up by then so I won't feel bad about spending money."

"Even if you can't spend much, it'll be great to have you around. I haven't had a chance to make friends here; sometimes I just need someone to talk to. It's kind of lonely here."

"You make friends easily; pretty soon you'll be too busy to even call me! Are there any cute guys around?"

"All the cute guys in town are college kids here for the summer, working two jobs and living four to a room until school starts again. I'd be more likely to hire them than date them!" Sometimes this job makes me feel old.

"What do you do for fun? I want to spend time on the beach. How many days do you think I should plan on being there? I just bought the cutest new sandals." I'd grown accustomed to the way Bekah changed topics. "You're sure it's okay if I stay at your uncle's cottage? I can't wait!" Her enthusiasm was contagious; I was looking forward to having her around.

Comments I made about having little free time were ignored (it was just like talking to Mom); she promised to call back in a few days with potential dates for a visit.

"Have fun at your job! Gotta go, Duncan's waiting! I'll be in touch," she said as she hung up.

Even though conversations with Bekah could be exhausting when she was enthused, or when I was unable to get a word in, our chats always made me feel good because of how comfortable we were together. During this conversation, however, it had become obvious that for the first time ever we were at different stages in our lives. She was still in full college party mode, and I had become a business manager, however odd that seemed.

It would work out somehow, I told myself. As I became more accomplished at my job I should be able to get away for short periods of time. Maybe we really *would* have a great time shopping, sunning, and dining. And talking. Having a long conversation with a friend sounded like the best thing ever.

I vowed to myself that I'd become very organized, I'd learn to delegate authority, and I'd earn the respect of my staff. Somehow. *Then* I'd be able to relax once in a while.

Restaurateurs around the globe would have laughed uncontrollably if they'd heard my thoughts. Organized? Relax? Words unheard of in the industry. *Frantic* was a word they would have recognized. And *exhausted*. Probably also *overwhelmed*. I had much to learn.

CHAPTER 6

On Sundays our guests dress more formally than usual; some having attended church services, others pretending they had. I tried to choose my clothing accordingly, a flattering dress, better jewelry, and of course amazing shoes. Unfortunately my wardrobe was limited, and my few Sunday ensembles were in constant rotation. *Some new dresses* was at the top of my shopping list, should I ever have the opportunity.

By the time we opened for brunch that Sunday the word "murder" was being used regularly. No one could explain where that information had come from; they'd heard it from a neighbor, or at the grocery store, or after mass, and it was certainly causing consternation. Any accurate facts were magnified by overactive imaginations; an element of excitement was masked by concern.

"There was a murder in town, did you hear?"

"Who was killed? Is that how the bread guy died?"

"My brother said someone was shot behind the Brady Museum…"

"I don't believe it. People don't get shot in Windsor Grove. Must have been a traffic fatality."

"Maybe somebody killed the bread guy?"

"Why would anybody want to kill a bread guy?"

"More likely it was a tourist from Illinois. There are lots of murders in Illinois."

On and on went the conversations; few specific details, but plenty of speculation.

I wondered when, and how, any facts would be disclosed…or if the entire community would spend days imagining far-fetched scenarios. I also wondered, of course, if that really was how Mark, the bread guy, died. But that seemed totally ridiculous in this friendly small town.

Needless to say we had a tremendous crowd that noon. Folks who'd never before come for brunch suddenly considered it indispensable. I felt a bit guilty (but not really all that much) knowing we might be profiting from someone's tragedy. But I had responsibilities, and our numbers would certainly look better this weekend.

The Sunday brunch buffet at Unincorporated requires a totally different room layout than any other meal. Banquet tables line the dining room walls, offering cold, hot, and dessert buffet stations. Featured areas include a meat-carving station and the create-your-own-omelet station, where Chef Brad proudly displays his skills.

Guests fill their plates numerous times, and sit in the dining room or in Zachary's Lounge or on the patio. It's informal, hectic, and profitable. Conversation flows, as does the consumption of our popular Bloody Marys.

Uncle Al was proud of his Sunday Brunch, and wasn't pleased about how many weeks he'd miss it. He would have been amused by the amount of "important local information" being shared that day.

It was much like being at the post office.

My curiosity about when we'd learn details about Mark's untimely demise, and about those murder rumors, was satisfied late that afternoon when Officer Gregg Littner from the sheriff's department walked through the entrance asking to see me.

Tall and tanned with broad shoulders, evident biceps and a commanding presence, Officer Littner had dark crew cut hair and even darker eyes. In his early 30's, he had a physical strength about him that demanded attention. He wasn't handsome in the normal sense, but in his pressed brown uniform with his erect posture he had a presence that couldn't be ignored.

We'd met in the past under more pleasant circumstances (sitting at Rick's Tap), so introductions weren't necessary. He was born and raised in Windsor Grove, in other words he was a *local*, so he had the trust and respect of other locals, who considered him a friend as much as an authority figure.

"Can we talk? Privately?" I'd done nothing wrong, but his words brought a moment of panic. His stony-faced expression indicated that this was serious, and I felt my spine grow tense. Would I ever outgrow the feeling that every officer was watching me, waiting for some indiscretion I could be lectured on? I'd expected that once I was out of college I would be more self-confident than that.

"Sure, come this way." I smiled to myself. Officer Littner was a kind man, just doing his job, and I had nothing to worry about. I hoped.

We went to my office where he wasted no time with preliminaries.

"The Windsor Grove Sheriff's Department is dealing with a criminal investigation. I'm visiting as many businesses as I can today to spread the word about a serious local incident. Rumors are flying rampant; it will be helpful to us if everyone has some facts. The Gazette won't be printed until Wednesday, so we're trying to disburse some specifics any way we can.

"Here's what we know: on Friday morning Mark Fischer was stabbed in his delivery truck, on the fire road south of here that runs through the forest."

"Stabbed?" My voice came out in a squeak.

"Stabbed. Several times. Probably died instantly. We'll know more once the autopsy report is released. He took that shortcut almost every day, and lots of people knew it. The engine of his truck was running when he was killed, but by the time he was found the truck had run out of gas. Some boys playing in the woods saw the vehicle, noticed his body inside, and ran to tell their parents."

"How horrifying for them! Will the boys be okay?"

"A school psychologist has already talked with them, and will stay in contact."

He didn't tell me then, or ever, who the boys were. That detail has never been released.

"We need people to be on their guard; there's a killer out there. I'll spare you the details, but this was the most gruesome crime scene any of us has ever encountered. It's important that everyone be cautious and alert," he continued. "Also, we hope that someone, just possibly, has useful information.

"We're asking people who think they have helpful knowledge to get in touch with us immediately. We're especially curious if anyone knows of someone who had a grudge against Mark, or knows of any person or persons seen entering the woods early on Friday who normally wouldn't have been there.

"We've completed our investigation at the scene. A forensic photographer and several crime scene techs were called in; they've gathered their evidence. Mark's vehicle and other pertinent items have been removed, and the road has been reopened to the public. From this point forward we'll be working with state investigators."

He pulled a notebook out of his pocket and held a pen ready. "Have you seen anything suspicious in the forest? The cottage you're using is located where you might notice unusual activity in the woods. Do you remember seeing, or perhaps hearing, anything out of the ordinary?"

"No, nothing," I muttered. I was stunned. And a bit frightened. The thought that there could have been a killer near my comfortable home was more than a little alarming. Terrifying, in fact.

"Please let me know if you think of anything. One more thing, and this is very important Ashley, we know that you walk into the woods after dark to get to your cottage. Consider this a warning: make sure someone accompanies you, or watches you until you're indoors. Or, at the very least, please call someone to let them know you've made it home safely. Mark was stabbed, and until we close our investigation we won't consider anyone safe."

"Stabbed. Stabbed? Safe?" I was stunned and could tell I was babbling. I had enough trouble absorbing the fact that Mark had been murdered. The thought that I might be in danger just didn't register; it couldn't be real. There were too many disturbing thoughts at once; it was difficult for my brain to process.

"Leave a light on if you might return after dark, and carry a flashlight for your walk. A sturdy flashlight can also be used as a weapon if need be." His serious expression wasn't comforting. Nothing he was saying fit into my comfort zone. A flashlight as a weapon? Yikes!

"What we need from you is to please pass the word among your customers and staff. Ask them to be on alert, and to contact us with any pertinent information," Officer Littner requested.

"This type of thing just doesn't happen around here," he smiled ruefully. "We'll need all the help we can get."

His voice took on a more friendly tone. "We know that restaurants and shops are where the locals go to get their news, so we're depending on Windsor Grove merchants to alert everyone. We'll do what we can to pass the word, of course. But you will, no doubt, talk to more people than we will. A homicide has been committed, and the more vigilant people are, the better."

"Alright," I agreed, but it didn't sound like smart business practice to go up to diners in a restaurant and discuss murder. It wasn't a feel-good conversation starter.

Homicide. The word seemed so alien. Would our guests be pleased to learn the facts, or would they be disturbed by them? So disturbed that they'd lose their appetite?

Should I wait until they'd finished their meals? Probably. But our guests are so nosy they'll start asking questions the minute they get in the door. You can't lie to your customers, they'll never forgive you. What a dilemma.

And what would the tourists think? Would they want to get out of town as fast as possible? This could be even worse for tourism than the drought.

"One other thing," he said, again writing in his notebook. "Can you tell me what you were doing at eight o'clock on Friday morning?"

I was shocked at the question; it was that uncomfortable feeling of panic again.

"I was just getting out of bed. That's when my alarm goes off. Is that when it happened?"

"That's our best estimate, based on when he delivered at The Forest Cafe. That was the last delivery he made; Unincorporated would have been the next stop on his route, and as you know, he never made it. Is there anyone who can verify where you were at that time?"

"No, no one," I shook my head.

I was staying alone in the cottage, so there wasn't anyone who would have known what I was doing. I was asked if I could verify anyone else's whereabouts at that time, and of course the answer to that question was also "no". He made some notes, turned, and headed out the door.

I was apprehensive about this whole situation. After Officer Littner left I got on the phone and called Uncle Al.

Al's advice was to keep a welcoming smile on my face, and make the most of the extra business from curiosity seekers while I could.

"If all they want to do is talk, let them talk, but offer them a menu, and always have a bartender on duty. Nothing brings people out, and encourages them to spend a few leisurely hours, like the desire to be up-to-date on the latest news.

"Everyone is afraid their friends will know more than they do. People learn the basic news at the post office. But they get the down-and-dirty details at their favorite pub. Let them think that Unincorporated and Zachary's Lounge are the places to get the full scoop, even if you don't have any more details than anyone else.

"Remember, you'll have a late afternoon rush today, after the concert at St. Francis Church. Be ready; after sitting in those uncomfortable seats for a few hours everyone needs some comfort food and friendly chatter."

I hadn't known there was a concert scheduled. I wasn't accustomed to keeping track of community events…another thing I'd have to put on my mental radar.

"One more thing," he said. "How are you getting along with our chef? Is he being cooperative?"

"Well, he sure can be rude; he's not an easy person to work with."

"Keep in mind, Ashley, that without Brad we don't have a restaurant. Especially now, with me recovering. Get along with him, okay? I know you can do it."

I agreed, but sighed to myself. That fit in the category of easier-said-than-done.

He laughed at my reluctance. "If there's one thing you learn in our industry, it's to make the best of a bad situation. So these are my two pieces of advice for today: never, ever, alienate your chef; and encourage guests to think of Unincorporated as a home away from home. Keep in touch. Oh, and Ashley, there's a killer out there. Be careful, and be sure to lock up at night; I don't want anything to happen to my favorite niece." And he said goodbye.

CHAPTER 7

Al's expectations were on target; we served far more guests at lunch the next day than on a typical Monday. Many of them lingered after their meal, talking with friends and neighbors, nibbling on the last few crumbs of dessert.

An up-side of being a cluster on the local grapevine was that our staff felt invigorated, and no one called in sick that day. A full staff was on hand to accommodate the rush of information seekers.

"How's your uncle doing? I bet he hates being out when all this excitement is going on," was heard more than once. Apparently this tragedy was considered great entertainment by many of the locals. I thought that was rather gruesome, but there is a lot of morbid curiosity in the world.

"Al's recovering slowly. We talk often, so he's up to date with what's going on," was my standard comment.

"Well, he's an inquisitive guy, interested in everything, wants to know everything, *deserves* to know everything. Give him all the details! Don't leave anything out when you talk to him," I was instructed by a frail elderly diner waggling a bony finger at me. "He needs to know it all!"

I promised to do what I could. I obviously would have discussed the murder with Al anyway, but being commanded to by a guest seemed unreal. Small town life at its most intrusive....

The guests were right, though. Uncle Al would have loved the hectic atmosphere that day. He would have been far better than I at keeping staff on task, and keeping the flow of business moving. Things could easily fly out of control, and I wasn't a strong enough leader to restore calm from chaos. Crossing my fingers, I hoped that chaos wouldn't happen.

The downside to the day's additional business was the guests who seemed to think our staff had nothing better to do than talk. Everyone assumed we had the most recent information; customers were literally asking for details the second they walked in the door. Local residents expected us to provide up-to-the-minute specifics; even vacationers had an insatiable curiosity about the tragedy.

Surpassing incessant chatter in the annoyance factor, however, was the emergence of the media. The first contact came from a kind woman representing the Oak Landing radio station.

"I'm calling to ask a few questions about the recent homicide," she started.

"I really have no knowledge about it," I replied. "We never received our bread delivery on Friday. That's all I know."

"Have you talked with anyone who heard or saw anything suspicious?"

She continued to question, but soon realized I had nothing to report and said a polite, "goodbye".

Recalling a lesson on "Controlling the Message", I instructed our staff to refer all media contacts to me. My stock comment would remain the same for the next several weeks: "Our sympathies go out to the family and friends of Mark Fischer. Beyond that I refer all questions to the Windsor Grove Sheriff's Office." That statement saved me from hours of unwelcome scrutiny; most of the reporters weren't as polite as the woman from Oak Landing…or as familiar with life in our area.

"You gotta hear this…" began a retired truck driver sitting in the Lounge that afternoon. "Somebody was trying to get one of those TV remote broadcast trucks onto the fire lane to do some filming, and the clumsy driver got the dish caught in the trees. The guys from Doc's Towing had to climb up in the tree and cut branches down." Much laughter greeted the story.

Another retired guy replied, "And we all know that Doc's rates change depending on if he likes ya, and where you're from."

"No kidding. That TV crew is gonna pay his 'dumb-ass' rate!"

That seemed to bring great satisfaction to the locals at the bar.

It was easy to pass along Officer Littner's warning requesting that people remain alert. But it was his request for residents to share pertinent information that got the most remarkable response.

It was mind-boggling to learn how many people claimed they saw someone entering the woods, were suspicious of a neighbor, had a conspiracy theory, overheard a whispered conversation, or had a gut feeling that someone disliked the deliveryman.

Whoever was answering the phones at the sheriff's department had my sympathy. All the locals thought they had some important insight, and were anxious to share it with anyone who would listen.

"If guests continue to stick around like this we'll have to invest in more outdoor furniture," I said to Renata, our bartender, as she rushed to fill drink orders. Who would have thought we'd need two bartenders to cover a Monday noon? On the other hand, who would have thought there'd be a murder in Windsor Grove? *Hire more bartenders* got added to a list in my head.

It had become abundantly clear that employees like Renata were a godsend to the hospitality industry. Renata's personality could usually get every guest involved in conversation. Her easy smile lit up the room, and her listening skills encouraged many a guest to linger for the traditional "one for the road".

Our bartenders' work attire was the same as our servers', a white tuxedo-style shirt worn with dark slacks or skirt. Tall, with hazel eyes and hair the color of dark chocolate, Renata had an elegant presence. Gold earrings with an attention-getting pendant were stunning against her olive complexion. Her long hair, pulled back and secured with a hairclip, looked polished, while complying with state health department standards for hair restraint. (I'd learned more about health codes recently than I'd ever wanted to).

"Schedule me whenever you need me," she had offered. "We're trying to work as many hours as we can to put together a down-payment on a house." In her late 20's, she was engaged to a local guy who worked for the highway department.

"TJ has been volunteering to work overtime and be on call most weekends, so I'm available any time. I love my job; I'd rather be here than home alone." Several of our regular bar patrons stayed longer if she was there to chat with; it was a win-win situation all the way around. Uncle Al said a terrific bartender was the best asset a supper club could have, and based on our bar sales I had to agree.

After the lunch rush, when things had calmed a bit, I got serious about polishing off the weekend paperwork. I'd just finished putting together a deposit and had called the bank with a change order, when Officer Littner was back, asking once again to speak to me in private. When we'd entered the office he wasted no time before pulling a clear sealed pouch from a leather case he carried.

"Does this look familiar?" Again his face wore the serious expression I'd seen the previous day.

What I saw in the pouch made my stomach roll. I was looking at a sturdy knife, about 12 inches long, with a worn wooden handle and an ominously sharp steel blade. Encrusted with a thick brown substance, the blade told its own tale. I didn't have to ask where it had come from.

"Could this knife be from your kitchen? Detectives from the state crime lab say it's professional quality. Your restaurant is the closest to the scene, so I'm asking here first. Does it look familiar?" With a blade worn thin from numerous sharpenings, it was undoubtedly a deadly weapon.

"I suppose it does, we have a lot of knives." I gulped and turned to stare at the filing cabinet, unable to continue looking at the crusted bodily fluid. "But, Officer Littner, you have to understand that I've never actually worked in the kitchen, so I'm not even going to speculate if it might be ours."

"You can call me Officer Gregg, or just Gregg, you know. Officer Littner is way too formal for this community. No one else will know who you're talking about," he laughed. The laughter seemed out of place considering the circumstances, but when solving crimes is a person's job I guess a bloody knife is just one more part of a workday.

"Is there someone around who knows your equipment well enough to recognize your knives?" he asked. I called Chef Brad into the office, and the officer repeated his question.

"We use knives like that," Brad said. "That letter K on the handle means it belongs to Kellam Sharpening Services. They supply most of our kitchen knives. We own a few specialized chefs' knives, but none like that; that's a size we rent. I can't tell if that one's from here. Most of the restaurants around here probably use the same type.

"Dewey, the driver for Kellam's, is here every other Tuesday morning. He brings in a box labeled 'Unincorporated' containing three boning knives, four chef's knives, and a dozen paring knives. Early on those Tuesdays I go hunting for all the knives. *My* knives are always where they belong. I let Renata have two paring knives at the bar; she wants three, so she hides them from me." His accusatory tone insinuated that this was a major offense.

"Sometimes I have twelve paring knives for Dewey, sometimes eleven, sometimes thirteen. It averages out. I think our boneheaded dishwashers throw them away once in a while. Who knows where they are all the time? Not me."

He said that last sentence defiantly, as if daring anyone to suggest that missing knives were potentially his fault.

"Of course we own our heavy-handled steak knives, but I don't have any idea how many. And I have my own carving knives, but I take them home every night; no one else touches *my* knives. Also Al owns a few professional knives; but I think he's got them at his house in Oak Landing right now."

It was news to me that Unincorporated didn't own the kitchen knives; once again Brad had managed to make me appear ignorant. Gregg requested contact information for the sharpening service, and left to make a phone call. As he reached the door he turned and reminded me not to walk to the cottage after dark without an escort. Just what I needed: thoughts of personal attack added to all my other insecurities...

Hopefully Brad was right about most restaurants using the same brand of knives. The death of the deliveryman surely couldn't have anything to do with us.

Our front-of-the-house staff has great relationships with local guests and enjoys getting to know the vacationers. That evening a middle-aged man alone at our bar, Zachary's Lounge, was the object of their curiosity. Sitting at the end, away from others, he quietly gave terse answers to questions, offering no information.

"Fine. A good choice," was his response when asked how he liked his micro-brew.

"For a while," was his answer regarding how long he'd be in town.

When asked whether he'd previously been to Windsor Grove he replied, "Nope; never been here." That was the extent of his conversation. He hadn't been out-and-out rude, but it was obvious that he was uninterested in conversation.

Of average height and weight, there was nothing memorable about his appearance. With a gaunt unsmiling face, thinning brown hair and pale eyes, wearing a tan polo shirt with brown pants, he could blend into any background, a man who might move through life seldom being noticed. After a few beers he paid and left without ordering any food. That was not unheard of, but not typical either.

"Thanks for joining us. Come back again," I called as he left. He nodded in response. In my mind I called him Man-in-Brown, because that seemed to reflect his personality as well as his coloring.

"He tipped well, but talked less than any customer ever, even when he was deciding which beer to order," Renata Toriello, our head bartender said. "He kept staring at the wall, or into his drink, but I felt like he was listening to every word anyone said."

Visitors sitting in the Lounge were typically anxious to discuss vacation plans, or had numerous questions about the area. His withdrawn demeanor made Man-in-Brown stand out; this man was an obvious exception to the rule.

I tossed and turned again that night, hearing sounds I'd never noticed before. The creaking of the old wood floors, branches scraping against the siding, a howling animal in the woods. Sounds in the darkness that had always seemed comforting suddenly felt haunted and sinister. What was that shadow passing by my window? Was there someone outside? Had I remembered to lock the door?

Reluctantly I crawled out of bed, checking windows and doors in the darkness, relieved to find them all properly secured. The temptation to peek outdoors was strong, but so was my anxiety. I rushed back into bed and pulled the covers up tightly, trying to ignore the feeling that someone was outside, watching and waiting.

CHAPTER 8

"I just took a phone call about a food purchase, something about a playground? Am I supposed to know about this?" I'm sure I sounded clueless over the phone with Uncle Al, because I was. "The call was from someone named Mary, who assumed I knew what she was talking about."

"Oh, right. I forgot to tell you…you're ordering the food for a community festival. Next month. You know, the fundraiser for a new children's area in Veteran's Park. The one The Marys are planning."

"The Marys?"

"Sure. The three sisters, Mary Lou, MaryBeth, and Mary Rose. They live up on the hill, above the downtown; that spectacular house everyone gazes up at from Veteran's Park." I nodded at his explanation. I knew the house, of course. You couldn't miss it.

"I'm sure you've seen The Marys around," Al continued. "They're involved in almost everything that goes on in town. If there's an event, chances are they helped plan it. I told them months ago that they could depend on Unincorporated to find purveyors to supply the food." Al acted as if there would be nothing to it, but I was panic-stricken at the thought.

"Oh, Ashley, stay on their good side. The Marys are vicious gossips. They're big-hearted and well-meaning, but if they have any complaints about you everyone in town will hear about it! They're the original small-town scandalmongers. If they like you they'll sing your praises.

But woe be unto anyone who incurs their wrath." He laughed as he said it, but he sounded serious all the same.

"Just what kinds of food are we talking about, that will have these sisters raving about us instead of talking behind our backs?"

"Typical Wisconsin picnic foods. You know…brats, burgers, corn on the cob, the things you find at every church festival. And have deep fried cheese curds. They're always popular. And cream puffs, like at the state fair. Get a service club to sell deep fried candy bars. And have slushies for the kids…and popcorn…maybe ice cream cones…all food that's fun to eat. Any of our key restaurant suppliers can help with the planning. Get quotes from them, and remember to ask if they're willing to donate or discount."

It sounded like one huge nightmare. Al was acting like I should just be able to ask a few questions and get everything ordered in no time. Had he forgotten who he was talking to?

"Anything you can't get donated have invoiced separately, so there won't be any questions when you give The Marys the final bill. And in a case like this go for the best price, not the best quality; it's a fundraiser. And I hope they're having a beer stand. Gotta have a beer stand, it's Wisconsin after all. You'd better mention that."

Just what I needed. What if they wanted me to organize the beer stand? I could always plead ignorance. But how can someone who's managing a supper club claim complete ignorance of something as basic as beer? As far as I was concerned this didn't sound like any fun at all.

Uncle Al proceeded to rattle off suggestions of things I could offer to prepare at Unincorporated: bacon-wrapped breadsticks, hot German and cold American potato salads, fruit cups and desserts. Or things *he* thought we could prepare for the festival. Having no experience in food-preparation, I knew that there was no chance it would be me doing the work. I could only imagine the response I'd get when I repeated Al's ideas to Brad. Perhaps I'd put that off for a while.

During our conversation I'd been making notes, and added more of my own afterward. Placing the orders was something I thought I could handle, if only someone would tell me what we needed, and the anticipated attendance. The foodservice sales reps did this for a living, after all; hopefully they'd be ready with suggestions.

My main concern was that I might be expected to do some actual cooking at the event, or line up a crew to do it. And supply the equipment. What if they wanted me to set up stands, or tents, and determine price levels, and handle signage, and publicity, and recruit volunteers....just considering it made my head spin.

Thinking back to fundraisers I'd worked on in college, I remembered hearing about the importance of delegating. I would obviously have to learn to delegate, and learn fast.

Or maybe my concerns were all for naught and The Marys, who were supposed to be such accomplished fundraisers, would carry the load. I could only hope.

Just to show how little experience I'd had in this sort of thing, I realized I didn't even know when the festival was. That was undoubtedly a question I should have asked.

I was preparing to return The Marys' call when Officer Gregg again walked in the door, dressed more professionally than he'd been the past two days. Today a brown tie, almost as dark as his eyes, adorned his neatly pressed tan shirt, and a wide-brimmed Sheriff's Department hat covered his dark hair. He seemed to have more prominent insignia than previously, but I may have imagined that.

His service revolver hung at his waist; I didn't remember seeing it before. A two-way radio, a flashlight, handcuffs, keys and a myriad of other official-looking pieces of equipment now adorned his thick belt.

Gregg's manner, too, seemed more formal than the previous day, as if experiencing an increased level of anxiety.

Did Gregg have a Taser on his belt, I wondered? I wouldn't know one if I saw it. Back home in Milwaukee an officer would not only carry a Taser, he would travel with a partner, might handle a K-9 and occasionally patrol on horseback. In Windsor Grove officers were more likely to hand out trading cards.

Seeing Gregg's grooming and demeanor it was difficult to keep a straight face. I couldn't help but think of the deputy in old sitcoms who spruced himself up any time there'd been criminal activity, the guy whose gun was never loaded, who kept his bullet in his shirt pocket. There really wasn't any connection between the wistful bumbling TV deputy and Gregg Littner, who radiated power and intelligence. But I was amused, nonetheless. Did these guys really groom themselves more thoroughly when there was serious criminal activity?

"I'll need to get a look at the set-up in your kitchen," were the first words out of his mouth. No "Hello" or "How are you doing?" Just an immediate demand to see the kitchen. This sounded serious. I was starting to feel apprehensive, and thoughts of TV deputies vanished.

I led him through the swinging door to the kitchen, where only Chef Brad wore the traditional white chef's jacket with salt-and-pepper pants. The rest of the staff wore matching polo shirts over shorts or jeans. The contrast also defined a difference in commitment to quality foodservice. Much as I hated to admit it, the only kitchen employee who continuously strove for excellence in our food was the same one who valued a professional appearance and a spotless work area.

Uncle Al felt immense pride over the pristine state of his kitchen. Brad shared in this pride and was doing an admirable job of caring for it during Al's absence. The stainless steel counters and equipment were gleaming, the floor was spotlessly clean at the end of every day, and supplies on the wire storage shelves were in precision order. The restaurant I'd worked at in college had a kitchen that was sad in comparison.

Cleanliness, however, wasn't going to help with the matter at hand. With a grim expression on his face Gregg explained what he was looking for.

"The staff at Kellam Sharpening tells me you're the only place in the area using knives with high-carbon steel blades like the one that killed Mark Fischer. It could have been brought to Windsor Grove from somewhere else, but we have to work with the assumption that the weapon came from your kitchen." Ominous words.

Great. I had convinced myself that Mark's death had nothing to do with me, or with Unincorporated. Wishful thinking on my part. Suddenly there I was standing with an officer in my kitchen discussing knives in general, and one knife in particular, a knife used in a brutal killing.

Brad showed Gregg where knives were stored when not in use, along with various other locations they might be found throughout the day. Gregg seemed disconcerted by the number of places a knife could sit during working hours.

He had continuing questions about our knife inventory, but I didn't have any answers to give. I asked hopefully if perhaps someone at Kellam's knew how many knives we may have "misplaced" over the last few months.

"Their records show that each of the last few months you were short one or two knives. Various types and sizes. They say that's higher than normal, but not unheard of," was Gregg's reply.

"Like I said, it's not up to me to keep track of how many knives we have," Brad volunteered gruffly. "I just use them, I don't babysit them." I felt uncomfortable and embarrassed at Brad's uncooperative attitude; he could at least make an effort to be civil.

No one else in the kitchen offered any thoughts about missing knives, but there was no reason any of them would have known. Or cared. They were hustling at their jobs, pretending not to eavesdrop.

"I assume you haven't been able to determine if any other knives, like steak knives, might be missing?" Gregg asked, in a way that indicated he already knew the answer. We shook our heads in reply.

"Maybe Uncle Al can figure it out." I hated the number of times I called him with problems. It was my duty to keep things under control, not run to him with continual questions. The guy was supposed to be resting and recovering, not managing from home.

Gregg pulled a notebook out of his shirt pocket and made a few notes.

"I'll need a list of all your staff, and anyone else who has access to your kitchen. I want the names of anyone who's been in the kitchen during the last four months," he said.

Brad turned and walked away, trying to hide the smirk on his face. Better than anyone, he understood the size of the job I'd just been handed.

Four months! I'd only worked here for one month. I was starting to feel like I was on brain overload. Run a restaurant, plan a community fundraiser, supply information that I didn't have, and smile while I shared details about a murder. This was definitely not the pleasant summer job I'd been anticipating.

"Regarding your staff, I want information about how long they've worked here, where their hometown is, other jobs they have, and anything else that might be pertinent. In particular I need details regarding any disgruntled past employees.

"For anyone else who's been in the kitchen," Gregg continued as if he was asking for something simple, "give me as much information as you can. When they were here, how often, and why. Anything you can tell me about everyone who may have been near your knives."

Finally he smiled, a broad smile that made him seem less intimidating. But his words were just as discouraging.

"Obviously, I need the information as soon as possible. Can I come back for the list this evening?"

"Sure," I said, though I wasn't sure at all. I could never think of suitable replies when he asked questions. It felt as if I were being interrogated every time I saw him. Maybe I was.

A plumber came in the employee entrance, headed directly to the scullery sink and lay down on the floor. At the same time our primary liquor salesman came from the front of the house, asking for our weekly order. I was starting to realize just how many people had routine access to our kitchen, and it wasn't a pleasant thought.

I asked the liquor salesman to come back in a few hours, told the plumber to talk to Brad if he had any questions (I wasn't even aware that we'd called a plumber), and assured Gregg I would work on the list right away.

"I'll be back later today to see if you have it ready," he said. "I've been assigned to take the lead in this investigation, so you should contact me directly with information."

"Oh, um, congratulations, I think..."

"Right now I'm off to a meeting with someone from the Wisconsin Division of Criminal Investigation. They've assigned a detective to assist us; no one on the Windsor Grove force has experience with murder investigations. We mostly handle traffic and domestic offenses; we seldom have to deal with even petty theft, there's so little of it here."

When I starting working here I'd been told that crime in Windsor Grove was almost nonexistent. No one locked their cars in this town. Many residents didn't even bother to lock their homes unless they'd be away overnight.

I knew of several restaurants that used the "key drop" system, making keys available for delivery drivers so that no staff member need be present when deliveries were being made (let's see *their* managers make a list of everyone who'd been in the building).

I was still a city girl at heart, and locked everything, but I sometimes felt foolish locking doors when no one else did. Unincorporated had security cameras that were easy for guests and staff to spot, but they hadn't actually functioned in years, and Uncle Al didn't seem to care. I wondered how many of our staff were aware that the cameras were inoperable. Probably all of them. Probably half the residents, too.

"Is it true that this is the first murder ever in Windsor Grove?" I repeated what guests had been saying.

"No. There was one about 65 years ago. Claude and Erv Schultz, brothers who worked at the big apple orchard, argued over chores that neither wanted to do. Somehow Erv, the older brother, ended up dead.

"Claude maintained that Erv stumbled and fell, hitting his head on a boulder. Claude had a reputation for a hot temper; a jury decided that Claude and Erv had a physical fight and Claude's violent tendencies went out of control.

"Claude was convicted of manslaughter, but the old-timer judge never held a sentencing hearing because the evidence was slim. Claude didn't serve any time, but everyone knew what had happened. No one was willing to employ him, so he left town. It was a fairly typical case; the average murder is just a sad story of people who can't get along.

"When people talk about murder, they don't usually mean family squabbles that went too far. But most fatal arguments take place between loved ones, and family homicides are far more common than you'd expect. Statistics show that almost 30% of murders are committed by immediate family members."

I remembered hearing something along those lines in a human relations class, but I'd pictured an inner city fight over drugs, not an argument about farm chores.

"Well, I'll stop back later. Please try to have that list together by then." Gregg requested as he walked out the back door. Sure thing. Piece of cake. I'd barely figured out who all the staff were. Now I was supposed to just throw together an accurate list of everyone else who'd been here too?

He turned back, saying, "Remember, it's not a good idea to walk alone through the woods after dark. I can't emphasize that enough." As if I needed a reminder.

I started mentally creating a list, beginning with my entire current staff, and anyone who'd quit during the time I'd been here. To that I added all the various repair specialists who were here regularly; the electrician, the plumber, the HVAC guy, and the refrigeration repair team.

Then there were the truck drivers and delivery people, and the suppliers from dairy, bakery, soda and liquor companies. And the sales reps. And the yard care company, the computer repair gal, a local carpenter, and the nighttime cleaning team. Then I remembered the group tours that Al was proud to host: the Girl Scouts, a kindergarten class, the local Rotary Club...

To complicate things further, Uncle Al and Brad were both so proud of the cleanliness of our kitchen that they'd give a tour at a moment's notice to anyone who asked. Kitchen tours were offered to anyone, at any time, and were mentioned on the back of our menu. Guests who were total strangers had toured the kitchen, then told their friends, who'd also asked to see the kitchen.

I'd never be able to come up with every name. There were hundreds of people who'd been in the kitchen recently; this was an impossible task. Gregg and the state investigators were not going to be happy.

I asked the plumber what I thought were some intelligent questions, getting the impression he was knowledgeable about his job, which was reassuring since I literally had to depend on him to keep things running. I asked the bartender, Renata, to put together a list of what bar items we were low on, and estimate how much we'd need to get through the next week. I decided that it was too soon to mention the community fundraiser to Brad. I was avoiding the issue, but I rationalized that it just wasn't the right time to bring it up.

I didn't know if I was learning to prioritize and delegate, or if I was just postponing the inevitable. But I felt overwhelmed, and needed time to process everything that was happening so I wouldn't make ridiculous errors every time I turned around.

The phone rang while I was wracking my brain trying to think of everyone who'd been in the kitchen.

"Unincorporated Supper Club, Ashley speaking, may I help you?"

"Ashley, this is Rose. Rose from Wholesale Wholegrains."

"Rose, I am so sorry about the tragedy. Everyone in town feels horrible about what your staff must be going through."

"That's really what I want to talk about. Well, sort of," she said as her voice broke. "It's hard to keep my brain on track today; we've got reporters standing out on the sidewalk, and the phone is ringing off the hook, and shaggy looking photographers are taking pictures of our delivery trucks, and a TV truck from Wausau is parked across the street, and our employees are all really upset. This is one huge nightmare. I can't get any work done."

She paused to catch her breath, and then continued. "Anyway, why I called is…I'm trying to plan some kind of a memorial for Mark. You see, his body is being shipped to his parents in Indiana for a family funeral." I sighed and closed my eyes, as if that could block part of my brain. I didn't want to think about Mark's body.

"I think we should also hold a service for him here," she continued. "Something simple. He apparently didn't belong to a local church. So I thought I'd ask my minister to say a few words, and maybe someone from the town board, and hopefully Bob or Kathy Winchester, the owners here at Wholegrains."

"I called to ask if we could invite everyone for dessert at Unincorporated after the service. The Winchesters have agreed to pay for a gathering, and Mark always talked about your kitchen staff, saying how much he enjoyed his daily stops there."

Mark hadn't really met many of us, his delivery was too early in the day, but I didn't think it would be polite to mention it. An ironic picture popped into my head of Mark casually chatting in our kitchen while standing next to the knife that would eventually kill him.

"We enjoyed his visits too," I replied. "He was such a kind, friendly guy. Of course we'd be happy to have a gathering here after his service." I wondered if it was insensitive to immediately think of the income the event would bring.

Rose's inclination was on target. In times of stress people gravitate toward foods high in sugar, and feel comforted when surrounded by friends who are also consuming these comfort foods. Serotonin, a feel-good hormone, kicks into gear creating a feeling of calm and much needed relief.

We chatted for a few minutes about Mark, with Rose reminiscing about his outgoing personality.

"He genuinely wanted to get to know everyone, wanted to meet our families, and cared about our hobbies. He's going to be hard to replace."

"What brought him to Windsor Grove?" I asked. "It's not a town that attracts many young single adults."

"He went to college with Todd Braun who owns The Village Flower Shoppe, and they'd kept in touch," Rose explained. "Mark had a bad breakup with a girlfriend and wanted to get away from Indiana, so Todd convinced him to apply for the opening at Wholegrains. Mark rented the small apartment above Lillian Walker's house. He said that coming here was just what he needed."

Rose mentioned a day and time, we discussed dessert and beverage options, agreeing to stay in touch as plans developed. Rose seemed very competent, so I was confident that I could commit our dining room even though it was a loosely organized gathering.

We could handle it easily; a dessert buffet is pretty straightforward. It's a simple way to entertain a crowd, requiring no planning meetings and having little chance of last minute changes. The only real dilemma was having absolutely no idea how many people would attend. Were we talking about a few dozen people? A hundred? More? We would prepare for a crowd of any size. Amanda, our pastry chef, would be in her element. I had nothing to worry about.

CHAPTER 9

fficer Gregg was waiting for me again when I returned to the restaurant late that afternoon. I struggled to avoid rolling my eyes; I understood why he needed to ask questions, but couldn't he get it all over with at once? Was it really necessary that he show up quite this often?

Spending so much time at Unincorporated probably wasn't his idea of a good time, either. I vowed to be pleasant; he was only doing his job, after all, just like I was doing mine.

He wasn't as well put together this time, as if possibly he hadn't taken the time to eat, much less look in the mirror. I decided I liked the casual rumpled Gregg better than the formal Gregg. Rumpled Gregg led the way to my office as if it were his own.

"You seem relaxed this afternoon, for someone in the middle of a murder investigation," was the first thing out of my mouth. *Awkward. Insensitive. I know better than to joke about murder.* Thankfully he didn't seem to find it inappropriate. Uncomfortable situations were a daily part of his life.

"There are a lot of people to question, and there just aren't enough hours in the day," he sighed. "If I look relaxed it's because I'm probably not running on all cylinders. I haven't had much sleep.

"It's a challenge to deal with serious crime when you're not used to it. But, Ashley, now don't repeat this please, but I'm enjoying it. I didn't get a degree in criminal justice in order to set speed traps. This is what

I wanted; and now I've got it. I just have to make good," he shrugged. "There will always be speeders to catch."

"We suspect that this was a premeditated murder, not a random act," he said, getting down to business. "It's unlikely that anyone would so diligently plan a murder, and then wander along a deserted road hoping to find a handy victim. The fact that Mark had stopped and put his truck in 'Park' indicates the attacker was probably an acquaintance of Mark's, not a stranger.

"If it was a deliberate homicide of Mark Fischer, then perhaps no one else is in danger. We can't, of course, be positive that Mark was the intended target, and the only one. Also, we can't overlook the fact that once a killer commits such a heinous crime any natural reluctance to kill is gone, the brakes come off, and there's no telling what they may do next.

"But it should ease everyone's mind at least a bit," Gregg concluded, "to know that it was probably premeditated, not a random killing."

Someone intentionally stole a knife from Unincorporated in order to commit a murder, and it would ease our minds that it was well planned? Everyone in town was on edge, and this knowledge didn't reassure me a bit. A killer is a killer, and if someone wanted to eliminate a friendly guy like Mark, any one of us could be next.

The picture in my mind of a crazed maniac with a violent grudge against society wasn't a pleasant one (I could thank the national news services, and their constant coverage of tragedies, for that thought. People had been killed for their clothing choices, their lifestyle, their political affiliations, and the expression on their faces. No wonder so many people lived in fear).

"I wanted to get this information to you right away, since it happened relatively near your property. Your guests might be relieved to hear that it was most likely a deliberate attack." *Don't count on it*, I thought. But it was kind of him to give me the heads-up. "You can pass the information along."

"I'm making progress on the list of kitchen visitors," I said. It was true, sort of. "I should have it ready by tomorrow morning."

"Thanks, I appreciate that. It might not be important, but we never know what matters and what doesn't." I didn't tell him just how long the final list was going to be. He'd probably figured that out for himself.

"Are there any leads?" I asked, probably too eagerly. I was as anxious as everyone else to know if there'd be an arrest any time soon.

"Sorry. I can't disclose certain details of an ongoing investigation." Gregg smiled and shrugged when he said it; he understood how badly everyone wanted to be kept informed. "But I can give you an overview."

"We're focusing on Mark's personal life. Trying to learn if he's had any disagreements, made any enemies, things like that. There was nothing helpful in his apartment, or on his computer or phone. Since he's only been in town a short while we're looking into his life before he came to Windsor Grove, too. We'll figure it out somehow; we just have to be diligent." He nodded thoughtfully to himself, and continued.

"With the ground as dry as it is there are no footprints, no indication that anyone was present at all. The killer must have had a vehicle nearby, but there's no sign of that, either.

"There's a clearing in the woods, close to the crime scene, where some high school kids hang around after dark, smoking and drinking. There's a chance some of them may have seen something, and are afraid to admit it. We've got our work cut out for us."

I was happy to have even this bit of information. Customer questions were continual, and anything I could divulge would help satisfy their curiosity. If I continued to ask Gregg questions, maybe I'd keep gaining snippets of knowledge.

"Let me know when you have that list ready," he instructed as he closed his notebook.

"And remember to be careful walking to your cottage," was his final comment before hurrying out the door. *Enough with the warnings already!* I was going to scream the next time he mentioned walking after dark.

My capable staff had taken good care of our guests while we'd been talking, no thanks to me. I continued to keep myself occupied, but my mind was spinning in a dozen directions. I couldn't accurately describe anything that happened in the dining room that evening, and when I'd walked around greeting guests my mind was so distracted that I answered questions automatically, probably seeming very aloof. Thankfully they were so caught up in their discussions about the murder that they didn't notice.

Our guests were soaking in every possible detail. Some of them seemed unsettled and apprehensive about having a murder in our midst. Others were intrigued by the investigation.

The prevailing reaction, however, was anger and a demand for swift action. People wanted to know *who*, and *why*, and made it clear that they favored harsh punishment and retribution. They were affronted that this act occurred in Windsor Grove and they wanted justice. And they wanted it soon.

My staff were not only spending a lot of time discussing the murder with the guests, they were also constantly discussing it amongst themselves. It was understandable; it was the topic of the day after all. But it wasn't appropriate work conversation, and it definitely cut into productivity.

"Ashley!" Chef Brad bellowed from the kitchen. "Get those Goddamned reporters away from my kitchen door!"

I checked out the situation. Details about the murder weapon had been released, and a large contingent of media representatives were swarming around arriving staff, rudely shouting questions.

"What can you tell us about your knives? Are more of them missing?"

"Do you think the killer could be someone who works here?"

"Did all of you know the victim?"

Electronic notepads and recording equipment in hand, they'd struck aggressive postures and jockeyed for position.

Oh-oh. That was way beyond my wheelhouse. I rushed inside and made a quick call to Uncle Al, then followed his instruction.

"This is private property, and I'm asking you to leave, or I will have to call the sheriff's department," I announced loudly to the group. To my surprise they meekly complied, as if they'd been expecting just that order.

I realized that Brad had been behind me, arms folded across his chest, glaring as only Brad can glare. No doubt this accelerated the speed with which the crowd disbursed.

"Inside! Right Away!" Brad barked at our staff. Once indoors he laid down the law.

"If I hear that any one of you gives information about my kitchen to those idiot reporters you've just lost your job! Don't even think about showing off any of our knives, or answering any questions! Do you hear me?"

The staff nodded numbly. Word would get passed to those not present, and with Brad so adamant I knew I needn't worry about the staff sharing inappropriate details with the media. No one would risk attracting the wrath of Brad.

The dining room staff, having missed the drama outdoors, were still engulfed in their discussions.

"Mrs. Johnston overheard the most interesting conversation..."

"I shouldn't admit it, but it's exciting talking to our guests about this."

"...and their son, who's a detective in Green Bay, said..."

"Ashley, the five people at the table in the corner want to hear what Officer Gregg had to say."

We were not supposed to be the local information station; I felt the need to crack down on the continual chatter. Sadly, I had no idea how to stem the topic other than giving the staff extra duties to keep them continually busy. This wouldn't make me popular with the employees, but I wasn't there to be popular.

On the other hand, Al had said, "Let them think that Unincorporated is the place to get the scoop."

So all I had to do was encourage conversation and the sharing of gruesome news among guests, keep my staff on task, remain in control of the general atmosphere, and pass along the word about the murder being premeditated. Sure thing. No problem. *Al can't get back to work soon enough to suit me!*

Keeping my wits about me would have to become priority. My mind was swimming with thoughts of a community fundraiser, a post-memorial-service gathering, a list of kitchen visitors, a murder in the woods, and people who wanted to come and enjoy a relaxing meal.

Being a competent restaurant manager was starting to sound like an impossibility. Being appreciated by my staff sounded even less likely. I felt increasingly inadequate for the task.

I started scribbling a list of everyone who'd been in the kitchen recently. I remembered more and more people, thinking of them so fast that my hands could hardly keep up with my thoughts. This list was going to have more names than there were residents of Windsor Grove.

I never did call The Marys back that day. But, once again, I called Uncle Al.

CHAPTER 10

Leaving the cottage Wednesday morning I vowed to stay on track, making good management a priority. It was time for me to own the job, and stop letting the job own me.

Seeing no squad cars in the parking lot, I felt my shoulders relax and I breathed a bit easier. As concerned as I was about the murder, it was my primary obligation to take care of Uncle Al's restaurant. Unrelated distractions weren't making the task any easier.

My list of kitchen visitors had been completed the night before, and was as accurate as I could make it, with many asterisks and etceteras. The sheriff's department and the state department of investigation would just have to work with what I had.

Windsor Grove is a friendly town, and everyone feels a personal involvement in their neighbors' business. There may be only 250-or-so year-round residents, but there are 1,000-plus property owners, and each of them has family, with every member feeling a proprietary interest. A surprising percentage of those people had been in our kitchen; the safety officers would just have to sort it all out. I had more pressing things on my agenda.

I called Gregg's number and left a message, "You can come and get the list. You'll find it on my desk, if I'm not around."

Mark's uncanny ability to judge our bread usage had become legendary since he was gone. His intuition had told him with dead accuracy (oops, I shouldn't have said that) how much Italian bread we needed for the Wednesday night spaghetti extravaganza, and how much rye bread we'd use during Friday night's fish fry.

Try as they might, the Wholesale Wholegrains drivers who temporarily covered our route were either cutting us short, or overcompensating and leaving us so overstocked that our donations to Feed the Hungry made us seem like huge philanthropists.

"Don't give that a second thought," Uncle Al reassured me. "Wholesale Wholegrains is responsible for the cost of overstock. Just make sure it's all documented." Whew! One less thing to obsess about.

Chef Brad was the only current staffer who had a handle on food product usage. So now he was arriving for work early to advise the new delivery driver. Grumble he might, but he voluntarily took on that additional duty.

Uncle Al continued to handle our computerized payroll from home, and I dreaded his questions about Brad's overtime. How could I explain that only the executive chef was capable of ordering hamburger buns? Not for the first time I gave thanks for Al's understanding nature.

When I'd entered the kitchen that morning Brad was the sole employee there. It was a picture I was accustomed to; he spent mornings planning menus, taking inventory, cleaning equipment, and performing numerous other duties our customers never thought about.

Many entrees require advance preparation. It wasn't unusual to see tomorrow's feature being portioned and marinated during Brad's prep time. Our soups, sauces, and salad dressings are all scratch-prepared and time-consuming. Brad was the only staffer allowed to use the efficient but dangerous meat saw. Behind-the-scenes duties were numerous and impressive, and all currently fell on our chef's broad shoulders.

"It really is gratifying to know you're on top of everything that happens in the kitchen." I meant it sincerely; not a moment need be wasted worrying about the back of the house.

"Yeah, that's my job," he muttered without glancing up from the grill where he was browning spicy Italian sausage for that evening's house-made orecchiette with sausage and red peppers. For someone who is so compulsive about his kitchen duties, it is amazing how little he cares about the impression his personality makes. Food is his passion, and few other things matter to this talented but bristly man.

Carrie, the first server scheduled that day, was organizing things in the dining room. I chatted with her for a bit, and then went to take a stab at clearing the clutter from my desk. (It's amazing how many violence-related phrases have become part of our vernacular).

"Ashley," Carrie came into my office minutes later, "Officer Gregg and another officer are here to see you." I tossed a few industry newsletters into a drawer, and walked out front to greet Gregg along with a good-looking stranger who was even taller than he.

"This is Detective Rob Milton, here from Madison to help with our investigation. It was time for us to bring in the big guns." (One more violent phrase in common use. I'd never before noticed so much of this).

"This is Ashley Kowalski, she manages Unincorporated." As we shook hands I had a moment to study Detective Milton, wearing casual clothing as if on vacation; khakis, pale green button down shirt and loafers made up his attire. If he hadn't arrived with Gregg I would have apologized that we weren't yet open for guests.

Well-tanned with softly waving blond hair, in his late 30's with chiseled features and deep-set blue eyes, he had a friendly air that could put anyone at ease. He didn't look like someone who spent his days tracking down criminals, not that I knew what that looked like. No, this guy came equipped with classic movie-star-good looks. That was doubtlessly helpful when questioning witnesses, at least the female ones.

I could picture Bekah turning on the charm for this officer if they ever met. (An age gap never mattered to her; a good looking guy was a good looking guy, and she liked tall blonds).

"Hi, Ashley." He flashed a smile that could make most women swoon. Okay, I admit it; I was breathing a little harder myself. "I'm glad to meet you. Unfortunately when I'm working I meet people under less than ideal circumstances. This seems like a terrific community; I'll have to visit again when I'm not on duty."

Wow. He was gracious too, a guy who'd bring a smile to any gal's face. Or he was trying to win my confidence before interrogating me; one or the other. Time would tell. I glanced at his left hand, trying not to be too obvious. Nope, no wedding band. Not that I had any spare time, but it was important information, nevertheless.

"Believe it or not, we didn't come here to ask questions," Gregg announced, smiling. "I just wanted you two to meet, since I'm sure you'll be in frequent contact. Also, I want Milton to see the set-up in your kitchen. Then we're off to visit other businesses. We'll probably be back later."

"Give me a minute; I have that list you want." It only took a moment to get to my desk and grab a file folder. I produced my multi-page list of kitchen visitors, watching as their eyes widened at its length.

"You're kidding," Gregg muttered. He flipped through the pages, shook his head, then said, "Okay. Thanks for putting this together." I could have been wrong, but I thought Detective Milton smothered a laugh. I considered saying, "Don't shoot the messenger," but that would have definitely been overkill...

"There might be more. But that's all I could think of right now. I'll let you know if I have names to add." I have to admit that I enjoyed their discomfiture. If they thought they could narrow things down by limiting their suspect list to people who'd been in my kitchen, I wanted to show them that it wasn't just people directly connected to Unincorporated who they had to investigate.

"Nice meeting you Ashley," Detective Milton called as they headed to the kitchen. As I watched him walk away, (which was a great view, believe me), I realized that there might be a good side to this whole horrifying mess. Should I have felt guilty for thinking that?

I spent the next few hours on paperwork, paid some bills (now I understood why I was sending money to a company named Kellam Inc. I'd rather not know), went to the bank, enjoyed a bowl of our zesty seafood soup, and in general tried to carry on as if everything was normal.

I didn't yet have control of the paperwork; I wasn't sure I ever would. The state of the office mirrored the chaos in my brain. A more organized office might help me get a handle on the finer details of the job, but the office was only mine temporarily, and it didn't seem right to rearrange Uncle Al's things. Al apparently thrived among the clutter;

it wasn't up to me to change his preferred system. I'd just have to learn to function amongst confusion.

A text from Bekah came in around lunchtime. "Can you get home the 2nd Monday in July? Volunteering at golf outing for Humane Society. It'll be fun!"

"Sorry. No spare time in July," was my short reply.

It did sound like fun, and like part of a life I'd left behind. I tried not to feel sorry for myself, but why was everyone else able to enjoy free time, while I was working and worrying?

Mid-afternoon a woman I didn't recognize, a tall brunette, toned and fit with the erect carriage of an athlete, approached the podium, asking, "Is the owner here?" I explained that he wasn't available, but I was the current supervisor.

"Is there a place that I can post some information? The Windsor Recreation Center is sponsoring an entry-level self-defense course for women on Friday, and we're trying to get the word out." Her athletic attire gave testament to her involvement in the fitness field. Her broad smile said she enjoyed her profession.

"We can display it right inside the doorway," I offered. "Considering the circumstances you should have good attendance."

"We know it's short notice, but that was the only option." She handed me a small sign, black print on basic white copy paper, and hurried out the door, saying, "Hope you can join us!"

"What a great idea," Dawn said, having overheard our conversation. "Especially now. I'll tell all my friends. What time is it?"

We read the notice; there would be two one-hour sessions, one at 8:00 a.m., another at 2:00 p.m. No cost to participants. *Hmm…I should try to make it; I can get to the early class and still be at work on time.* I entered the info in my phone. I tried to ignore my chagrin that self-defense techniques had suddenly become in-demand skills.

Business was booming all day, in part due to the numerous tourists arriving in town, but mainly because it was Wednesday, and the *Grove Gazette* had been on everyone's doorstep that morning.

"Cold Blooded Murder" was the Gazette's banner headline; every possible detail of the episode was reported. Photos of the dusty gravel road were printed alongside Marks' high school graduation picture and a sketch of the Wholesale Wholegrains property. Local residents had been interviewed at great length whether or not they had anything to contribute.

The article ended with the bold command, "Contact us if you have any knowledge about his dastardly crime!"

The Gazette article contained little that wasn't already general knowledge; but the locals felt a sudden urgent need to get out and mingle with friends and neighbors. All of our regular guests dropped in, along with some who seldom came to Unincorporated, and a few who were total strangers to me but seemed to know everyone else. The words "stabbed" and "bloody" had become constant part of ongoing conversations.

No reporter, no matter how experienced, can rival a Windsor Grove resident determined to learn all the local news (by *news* I mean *gossip,* much having little or no basis in reality, but I'm sure you knew that). Zachary's Lounge was bedlam all day. Copies of the Gazette were getting dog-eared from being passed around. I couldn't help but overhear the conversations, covering the same few topics with predictable regularity.

"…says he was 27. Same as my Robbie."

"It makes us look bad, a newcomer getting himself killed here."

"It's those kids hanging around in the woods that worry me."

As with any *sharing-of-important-information*, it continued throughout the day. At least they were spending money.

One item in the article had seemingly caught everyone's attention. It was a quote from Officer Gregg.

"We can't put much credence in an alibi provided by a spouse, or a lover, or a best friend. So there are very few people with iron-clad alibis for that early hour of the morning. Unless they were at work, it's unlikely that they've been completely cleared."

His comments caused much laughter in the Lounge at the idea that the Windsor Grove residents were all suspects. But it was a nervous laughter, and I noticed a few people casting suspicious glances at their neighbors. This was an additional reason to hope the investigation would be concluded soon; suspicions among friends could completely ruin the friendly atmosphere our town was known for.

Wednesday night was softball night. Co-ed teams from Windsor Grove, Oak Landing and several other small towns took the sport seriously, with long-standing rivalries adding to the intensity. The Unintimidated, a team sponsored by Unincorporated, had contributed numerous trophies to the Lounge's back-bar. Discounted prices on beer pitchers, with free bowls of crunchy snacks, guaranteed that the team would visit for "a cold one" after their games.

In their late-20's to mid-30's they're not the most athletically-fit group, but they're a friendly and enthusiastic bunch who are fun to have around The players add some excitement to a summer Wednesday, and many have become year-round regulars.

That particular Wednesday was different. The Unintimidated, plus various followers, crowded into the Lounge after a win, but it was an unusually subdued gathering. They were celebrating a resounding victory over the Wholesome Hitters. The Hitters represented Wholesale Wholegrains, and had played minus one recently deceased outfielder.

"I've never felt so bad about a win."

"We should have forfeited."

"*They* should have forfeited!"

"They really needed to play. They had a lot of tension to burn."

"It's not a very satisfying 'W'."

A few of the Wholesome Hitters dropped in, and Renata extended the pitcher deal to them too. It wasn't much, but it was something we could do in support. I was beginning to realize just how many people were affected by the tragedy.

Throughout that evening Man-in-Brown sat at the end of the bar. He nursed one beer for almost two hours, saying almost nothing, staring at the carvings on the back bar. He made no secret of the fact that he was eavesdropping on conversations, occasionally smiling at a joke or nodding in agreement. He got many odd glances from the softball players, but seemed not to care; perhaps didn't even notice.

The midnight moon cast deep shadows in the forest, giving cover to the dark-clad figure moving cautiously, unheard and unseen, circling the cottage.

To remain unsuspected and undetected it might become necessary to eliminate another threat. Only time would tell. Proper planning and detailed surveillance would be key from this point forward. One must be prepared for all eventualities.

What a delicious sensation...reveling in the nearness to a possible adversary, potential prey. Life was full of satisfying opportunities...the opportunity to destroy supercilious attitudes, to exhibit unexpected strength... an almost heavenly sensation.

Bright stars in the clear summer sky glittered in seeming anticipation of events to come. A person could almost taste the deliciousness of power.

CHAPTER 11

I hate funerals.

There, I've said it. I hate everything about them. I've heard all the justifications; how important they are to the grieving process, how they give closure to the family. Doesn't matter. I hate funerals. I hate attending them, and I'm certain there has to be a better way to pay respects to the deceased than sitting around feeling horrible with other people who are feeling equally horrible.

Either way, it was expected; an obligation that went with my position. So on Thursday, six days after his murder, I sat reluctantly in attendance at Mark's memorial service, along with almost everyone from Windsor Grove. Uncomfortable metal folding chairs, the best our town hall had to offer, added to the misery of the occasion.

The Windsor Grove Town Hall is a stately structure, brownstone and Wisconsin granite, standing like a sentinel keeping watch over the center of town. Its dignified stature made it the pride of the community in the late 1800's. Positioned in a large park-like space with mature trees and colorful flower beds, the town hall grounds have become a favorite picnic spot for visitors and a popular subject for photographers and painters.

An elaborate Victorian bandstand sits elegantly in the center of the grounds, surrounded by park benches ready for music lovers during frequent concerts. When there isn't a concert, there are usually children in the bandstand playing pretend instruments, performing for imaginary crowds.

The land adjoins Veteran's Park, sprawling landscaped acreage with numerous statues memorializing Windsor Grove veterans. When asked, every area resident will claim to be descended from, or related to, at least one of those veterans. No one questions the veracity of those claims.

Evidence of drought detracted from the usual tranquility of the normally well-manicured lawn. Areas that should be lush and green, but were currently various shades of brown, certainly weren't as pleasing to the eye. Flower beds cried out for more moisture than the once-daily watering they were receiving, and yet this was still the centerpiece of Windsor Grove.

Our town hall has undergone several remodeling projects over the years. The plumbing, wiring and accessibility are completely up to current codes; modern bathrooms are situated behind original heavy oak doors; office equipment is disguised behind cleverly placed panels. The overall ambiance of the building makes visitors feel like they've stepped back in time.

Town Hall continues, as originally intended, to be the center of everything important in the functioning of Windsor Grove. Town board meetings, the Windsor Grove Visitor's Center, the local library and local residents' post office boxes all have a home in this historic building. The wooden floor has valleys worn in it from generations who conducted important business and disbursed local news within its walls. It seemed fitting that this is where we gathered to honor the life of Mark Fischer.

Rose's plans called for the Windsor Grove memorial service to be held concurrent with the service in Plainfield Indiana, Mark's hometown. It seemed appropriate that he be held in everyone's thoughts simultaneously, so as the crowd took their seats in the town hall's largest gathering space, family members and friends were entering his childhood church many miles away.

Bob and Kathy Winchester, owners of Wholesale Wholegrains, had traveled to Indiana to attend those services and offer condolences. Detective Milton had traveled there also, intending to remain for a few days to interview Mark's relatives, acquaintances and Plainfield area friends.

Pachelbel's Canon in D played quietly as we entered the hall (I was proud of myself for being able to put a name to it). Residents of Windsor Grove were well represented at the services; the room was filled to overflowing. Officer Gregg and two other representatives from the sheriff's department stood at attention just inside the doorways.

Mark's coworkers were there, having rearranged production schedules and delivery routes in order to pay their respects. Like other commercial bread providers, Wholesale Wholegrains works a 5-day-per-week schedule with Wednesdays and Sundays off, so they can deliver on restaurants' busiest days. This week their day off was adjusted to allow Mark's coworkers to attend the memorial.

Local restaurants, delis and inns were well represented; these were the people who'd had daily contact with Mark. Uncle Al was there, thin and pale, walking with a cane, greeting friends he hadn't seen since his surgery.

Other local establishments had a smaller presence, having the need to keep their shops open for travelers. Several businesses had been left in the care of seasonal staff, leaving owners and year round residents free to put in an appearance.

I recognized numerous regular guests amongst the crowd, including Mr. Horner predictably sitting in the back of the room against the wall. I watched him unwrap a red-and-white mint and pop it into his mouth. He had an unending supply of those mints in his pockets; we all speculated that they came from the bowl on the bar at Rick's Tap.

Members of the town board sat as a group, as did volunteers from the visitor's center. The majority, however, were people I didn't recognize. I hoped there were no curiosity seekers gaining fodder for the grapevine, but I assumed there were, small town life being what it is. I knew perfectly well that if *I* hadn't attended it would have become a topic of conversation.

I imagined I could tell which older mourners had clothing reserved specifically for funerals, and which attendees, like me, had thrown together whatever they could find that looked somber. I wondered what it would feel like to attend so many funerals that you had designated funeral attire. My all-purpose black skirt with a royal purple blouse and a pair of black pumps that were beyond painful was the best I could do. I'd been pleased that I could put together an appropriate combination, given the cheery hues inhabiting my closet.

After surveying the crowd I took a moment to step out to the hallway and call Unincorporated.

"There's a good sized group here," I told Dawn. "We should expect over 150 people, maybe as many as 200." I knew she could take it from there. As head server, Dawn was the best we had at rearranging the dining room at a moment's notice; I knew she'd have everything ready for the arriving throng.

Re-entering the gathering, I admired the fresh displays decorating the space; eye-catching floral arrangements adorned the speaker's platform. The largest was a spectacular display of white flowers: hydrangeas, calla lilies, roses, and many blooms I couldn't name. Another spray was all red, one was done in pastels, and an especially impressive one ran through the entire green palette. I remembered Rose telling me that Mark had been a college friend of Todd who owned The Village Flower Shoppe. Todd's obvious floral design skills added a calming, elegant touch to the gathering.

Rose's minister, Pastor Upton, opened with an eloquent and thoughtful eulogy. In a firm voice that reverberated through the room he quoted the very appropriate psalm 46, "God is our refuge and our strength, a very present help in trouble. Therefore we will not fear..." Tall and slender with white hair and shining eyes behind wire-rimmed glasses, he was the epitome of small-town clergy. He rambled on a bit too long about the sanctity of life, as if determined that the service be of appropriately numbing length. He finished by leading everyone in *Amazing Grace* accompanied by an elderly woman at a piano.

Ron Barber, president of the town board, voiced a thoughtful reflection on the lasting impression Mark's kindness and generosity had on the people of Windsor Grove. The crowd listened attentively as he admitted that he'd seldom spoken to Mark, but along with everyone else he was familiar with Mark's constantly smiling face.

"He was a kind and considerate individual, who had a sincere interest in everyone he met. Windsor Grove is a better place because of the time he spent here," were Ron's final words, eliciting a few sobs from the crowd. Heads nodded in agreement, and I felt deprived that I'd not known Mark better.

A few of Mark's coworkers then read bible passages while a local musician played somber melodies on a harp. The slowly rotating paddle fans overhead added an angelic touch to the proceedings, as if Mark were there comforting us, as we mourned his loss.

I was touched by the caring attitude of this community. The only person who'd known Mark for more than a few months was Todd, yet feelings of genuine sorrow and loss were evident. Despite being a community made up primarily of part-time residents, there was a closeness that larger cities could never duplicate.

I tried hard to concentrate on the ceremony, but found myself surveying the room, wondering if someone in the crowd could have been the killer. I'd heard that a murderer often attends the victim's funeral. Was that an old-wives' tale? Or a fact? Was that why the sheriff's officers were on guard? Or was it merely for crowd control?

It seemed impossible that anyone in the room, or in the community as a whole, could brutally stab someone. The thought that someone here had planned a horrific murder was tough to imagine; people in Windsor Grove were honest hard-working folks, and everyone seemed devastated by the loss. Yet the crime did occur, and Mark was dead. Murdered.

The final speaker was Rupert, the candidate for state office. In his early 30's, broadly proportioned and prematurely bald, his ruddy cheeks and easy smile could charm friends and enemies alike. The jacket of his suit was stretched tight across his belly, his tie slightly askew. He spoke passionately about the trustworthy local population and the friendly atmosphere permeating the community, finishing with comments about how wonderful it is living in central Wisconsin.

It's more of a campaign speech than a memorial, I thought. Maybe I'm too skeptical, but I found it annoying. Others seemed energized by Rupert's comments, as if he'd reawakened a sense of pride. I supposed that being reminded about the integrity of the community could calm the tensions that had existed since the murder. But somehow the word *windbag* kept coming into my mind.

When the memorial was drawing to a close, and the pastor began leading everyone in *How Great Thou Art,* I moved toward the exit. The man who'd recently visited the Lounge, the one I thought of as Man-in-Brown, sat near the exterior door. He didn't seem interested in the ceremony, but there was no other explanation for his being there. Alone, sitting perfectly still and expressionless, he intently studied a brochure about kayak rental.

When I walked past him he glanced up and I nodded in his direction. He looked away, and then glanced back, saying, "Oh, yes, you work at that supper club. Hi." Then he turned to stare at a crack in the wall. Again he wore brown slacks, this time with an ecru button-down shirt. I couldn't put a finger on it, but there was something eerie about that man.

It was aggravating but not a bit surprising to find a few of the ever-present reporters hovering outside Town Hall. It was gratifying that their number had diminished somewhat, but their presence seemed highly inappropriate.

"Hey Ms. Kowalski, do you think customers are avoiding your restaurant now that they know a murder was committed with your knife?"

I ignored the question, bit back a rude retort, and rushed to my car hoping to get to Unincorporated before the other mourners. I needn't have worried, slow and somber was the order of the day, and as I pulled out of the lot no one else had left the building.

Our pastry chef, Amanda, had arrived early that morning to prepare numerous desserts to serve after the service that would also enhance that evening's menu. She'd baked additional cookies and bars that were immediately frozen, could be thawed at a moment's notice, and would be as good as fresh whenever needed. Our coffee was heralded as the best in town, and combined with Amanda's desserts I expected the entire crowd from town hall to attend.

Entering the dining room I paused in awe. While I'd been at the memorial service the room had been transformed. Floral arrangements graced the buffet table at each end, and were complimented by smaller displays on several of the dining tables. The deep green of our tablecloths was the ideal background for the muted tones of the arrangements; the effect was peaceful and comforting.

"I assume The Village Flower Shoppe is responsible for the décor?"

Dawn confirmed it. "The delivery lady just started carrying things in the door and helping me rearrange tables. At first I was annoyed; I was busy and didn't want to change the room layout. But she was energetic, and did most of the work herself. I think everything looks great."

"It's certainly impressive."

Always attractive and stately, the huge room now had an air of elegance. The overall effect was breathtaking.

I'd scheduled two bartenders for the afternoon, which turned out to have been prophetic; several of the first to arrive entered the building and headed directly to the Lounge. Funerals weren't enjoyable occasions in any circumstance, and with murder thrown into the mix apparently many guests felt a need for liquid relaxation. Some found that relaxation in alcohol, some in a strong cup of coffee or in an herbal tea.

Once everyone had their beverage of choice the atmosphere was less tense and conversation flowed. Keeping dessert trays filled and tables cleared kept me busy, and seemingly made me invisible to the guests. (I'd exchanged the painful pumps for a low-heeled version. What a relief!) I listened casually while I worked.

"I hope they find Mark's killer," was a common theme, of course.

"D'ya think the murderer was with us this afternoon? Think he lives in town?" I found it interesting that everyone assumed the killer was male.

As I eavesdropped, I noticed that the specifics of the crime were not being discussed. Everyone knew the details, but acted as if the horror might dissipate if they were denied.

"Did you see what Mary Lou was wearing? Wasn't that the ugliest thing you've ever seen?" This was greeted with loud groans from a group of women at a table in the corner. I hoped that Mary Lou wasn't around to hear. I still didn't know what any of The Marys looked like.

"This torte is delicious. I wonder if Sarah would like to serve torte at her wedding instead of cake…"

"I seldom eat chocolate, but these cookies are amazing. I think I'll have another…and another cup of tea." More than one person was appeasing their grief by giving in to natural cravings.

"I'll bet the killer was abused. I was abused myself as a child. Abuse can cause psychological problems years later," a shrill female voice announced. I struggled to keep myself from turning to see who'd said that, but being said loudly and publicly it apparently wasn't intended to remain secret. "It took years of therapy before I could talk about it." Should her therapist have mentioned that there's a proper time and place for such conversations?

"This is the only place in town with decent single malt scotch. Let's drink a toast to Mark." This comment was met with enthusiasm, and several bar orders were placed. I expected that it had little to do with toasting Mark, and more to do with calming nerves.

"…always enjoy a large funeral…"

"Oh, I know. It makes me feel so good to see people mourning together. I try to make it to every local funeral." I guess it takes all kinds of people to make a world.

It wasn't long before the conversations reverted back to that old standby topic, the weather. "The only good thing about this drought is that there are hardly any mosquitoes."

And to everyone's other favorite topic, personal pain or discomfort. "Did I ever tell you about my gall bladder surgery?" Time to keep walking…

"I can't wait to get my shoes off." I empathized with that lady.

When the crowd started to thin out and leave the dining room many people headed into Zachary's Lounge to enjoy their favorite beverage, and to talk about Mark…or his killer. Several groups also wandered out to the patio to sit and gaze across the lake. Lush greenery partially hid the homes and cottages on the other side making them appear more illusion than reality, either structure or mirage. That afternoon numerous minds took the opportunity to wander happily beyond the recent unpleasantness.

When I approached those guests to take drink orders they were enthusiastic. The tradition of the Irish wake continued in Windsor

Grove that afternoon. All in all, it ended up being an exceptional afternoon for bar sales.

The CEO of the Wisconsin Restaurant Association, Ed Hill, professes that restaurants comfort souls as well as bodies when guests visit to celebrate or grieve; literally a place to restore tranquility and peace (the root word of restaurant is *restore*). Restaurants, according to Ed, help people begin the recovery process after the upheavals of life. This was demonstrated that afternoon, as our guests all began to accept Mark's death and move forward.

Several guests continued to enjoy desserts and conversation until eventually they returned to the dining room for dinner. They weren't tremendously hungry, having enjoyed the overwhelming buffet, but their orders of sandwiches and salads were enough to provide a hectic evening. Not for the first time I had a twinge of remorse at profiting from someone's misfortune. But business was business, and I had to appreciate every guest, no matter what their reason for visiting.

Mr. Horner had arrived immediately after the memorial, claiming his traditional spot against the wall. True to form, he'd parked himself in the back row at the service, nervously wringing his hands. Once he was situated in our dining room he surveyed the crowd, nodding an occasional greeting as he sipped a cup of black coffee. His stony-faced demeanor was out of character, if anything he seemed to have been more affected by the funeral than most. So much so that when dinner hour arrived he ordered Pecan-Crusted Walleye instead of his usual medium-rare steak.

He built little teepee houses from sugar packets throughout his meal, knocked them down, and started again. In many ways Mr. Horner was a 10-year-old in a 70-year-old body. It certainly wouldn't be the worst way to go through life; adding a little childish pleasure to even the worst times. I wondered if Mr. Horner had any real friends. He always ate alone; it sounded like a lonely existence to me. But in general he seemed very content.

"I'm so worried, so scared." An elderly lady alone at a table, frail, with wrinkled cheeks and neck, had begun quietly sobbing. I sat next to her, reached out to touch her trembling hand, and listened to her fears.

"I'm trying to be brave. But I live alone, you see. I've never been around a murder before. It's very upsetting. Sometimes now I can feel my heart beating. I can't sleep at night, I hear every little noise. When I do fall asleep I have terrible nightmares. I don't know what to do. My children aren't nearby; if I try to tell them how I feel they'll think I'm imagining things…becoming paranoid."

"I've been hearing nighttime sounds that I've never noticed before, too." I totally understood how she felt. "Everyone is tense and nervous right now. This is affecting all of us."

I looked at her sweet face, delicate wire-rimmed glasses, softly permed grey hair and arthritic hands, and saw Everyone's Grandma, or Everyone's Favorite Neighbor. In a long-sleeved high-necked dress with a dark tiny print, she seemed very vulnerable, and completely trustworthy.

"There's a lot of evil in the world," she said in a quivering voice, "I just never thought it would come to Windsor Grove."

Hoping I wouldn't regret it, I said, "If it will help, I'll give you my phone number. Call 911 if you have an emergency of course. But if you just need someone to talk to during the night you can give me a call."

"Oh, honey, you're so sweet! That's wonderful. Such a blessing, no wonder your uncle loves you. I feel better already." She hugged me, dabbed at her eyes with a tissue, and smiled. "Do you even know my name, sweetie? I'm Margaret. Margaret Hunter."

"I'm glad to know you, Margaret Hunter. Ashley Kowalski at your service!"

She had relaxed before my eyes. Her face, a picture of pure pleasure, made my day. Having a younger buddy to lean on could do much to increase her feeling of security. Maybe having an elderly buddy to look after was just what I needed, too.

It had been an emotional day all the way around. I was touched by the fellowship and camaraderie I could feel among the servers, the bar staff, the locals, and any visitors who'd come in.

By the time I headed back to the cottage I was exhausted, both physically and mentally. It was only after I had comfy pajamas on and was climbing into bed that I remembered I was supposed to have had someone keep an eye out while I walked through the woods. *Too late now*, I thought. *Tomorrow I'll definitely remember.*

I got out of bed to close the heavy draperies. Somehow that action made me feel safer and less edgy. I couldn't imagine anyone in the woods waiting for another victim, least of all me, but I slept more soundly knowing that no one could peer inside.

CHAPTER 12

The beeping alarm clock disturbed my slumber earlier than usual on Friday. Groaning, I dragged my body out of bed, pulled my hair into a no-nonsense ponytail, and donned yoga pants and a tank top. I drove to the recreation center located just outside town, and was amazed at the number of cars overflowing the lot.

The Windsor Recreation Center was small by most standards, but the gym was large enough to accommodate the dozens of women attending the early session of the self-defense course. I recognized many faces; Dawn was there with several other Unincorporated staffers, quite a few of our regular guests were there, along with many women unfamiliar to me.

It was a friendly gathering, a gathering of people with a shared connection, albeit a connection to murder. Smiles and greetings were tinged by a touch of uneasiness. Clothing choices ranged from trendy work-out wear to tattered tee-shirts. I saw a few Unintimidated jerseys in the mix, along with several from the Wholesome Hitters.

"I'm glad to see a lot of people that I know." Our pastry chef, Amanda, in her early 50's, walked up to me looking apprehensive. "I'm so out of shape, everyone will be staring at me."

"No they won't. People all have different skills and weaknesses." I was trying, probably unsuccessfully, to be encouraging.

Soon Dawn came to join us, followed by other Unincorporated staff. Amanda stood up a bit straighter and threw her shoulders back, saying, "Okay, now that I know I have friends here it's better. This is kind of nice. It's like we have our own special section. Let's do this!"

I was glad to be part of that group. We weren't exactly friends, more like acquaintances, but at that moment I felt accepted, as if I had truly become part of the community. We moved to an inconspicuous spot near the back of the room, hoping Amanda wouldn't be self-conscious.

When most of the attendees had moved expectantly or nervously into the main room, the woman who'd delivered the flyer to Unincorporated took a position at the front, got our attention, and introduced herself.

"Hi, I'm Suzy Warren, your instructor for today." Her bright, enthusiastic smile made the anticipated workout seem less intimidating. "I'm a certified personal-protection instructor from Minnesota. I'm in town visiting an old friend, Ellie the rec center director. She asked me to put this class together for you. I'm leaving for home tomorrow, so I had to organize this quickly. I want to thank you all for coming."

With that, she launched into a fast-paced hands-on training session, overwhelming at times, that left us all feeling drained. Women at every level of fitness were encouraged to do what they were able to, and back off when it became difficult. I'd thought I was in good physical condition, but learned quickly that I'd been away from my gym for too long. Amanda was breathing hard, but for the most part managed to keep up with the group.

Suzy was a good teacher, letting everyone shine at their own pace, so we all had an enlightening lesson. We learned which body parts are most easily damaged (eyes, nose, ears, neck, groin, knee, legs), and which body parts can inflict the most damage to others (elbows, knees, head). We practiced upward thrusts to the face and sideways kicks to the shins.

"There are everyday objects that make good weapons," Suzy told us. "Keys, nail files, pens, hairspray, cologne, even your fingernails. Keep these available; have them in your hands when you're in a dark parking lot."

We spent time practicing effective punching, and learned how to block those same punches. We learned how to break away from a chokehold, and what to do if pinned to the ground. We tried to inflict injury on tackling dummies using quick eye jabs and knee strikes to the groin. We laughingly acted the roles of the attacker and the attacked.

Our lesson ended with Suzy talking to us about the most important thing we could do if we felt threatened…scream as loudly as possible and run away.

"Don't hang around trying to win a physical fight with a criminal unless you have no choice. Never risk your life to try being a hero," she emphasized.

"Don't worry," I heard Amanda whisper.

By the time we headed back to our cars, I was a sweaty mess. Hopefully I was also a bit safer having learned a few useful moves and security tips. Not that I ever expected to need them. No, I definitely didn't intend to need them.

I told myself I'd merely added another category to my life skills. And I'd certainly started the day with a good workout.

Once I'd cleaned up and made it to work, I reluctantly acknowledged my need to get serious about the fundraiser. I sat down at my desk to call The Marys, but was interrupted by Roger, one of our quietest young fry cooks. A dependable worker, he was often the voice of reason when tensions threatened to boil over in the kitchen.

"Um…Ashley…I, um…I need to tell you something," he stammered. "There was some stuff on my application that's not exactly true." His thin frame quivered as he stood in front of me shuffling his feet. He clenched and unclenched his hands repeatedly, then put them in his pockets.

His pale complexion, various facial piercings, and arms covered in tattoo art gave him a persona different than usually seen in Windsor Grove. While we try to be an accepting community, not judging people by their looks, there are few who vary from the norm. Roger came from a different background than most of us, and it showed.

Trying to remember details of an advocacy skills class, I mirrored back what he'd said, "Things that aren't exactly true?"

He took a deep breath, stared over my shoulder at the wall, hesitated for several seconds, and then seemed to make a decision.

"I needed a job, you see, and I knew I wouldn't get one if I told the truth, not at a nice place like this. So I sort of skipped some parts."

"Skipped some parts?" I prompted.

"Yeah…well…I came from central Milwaukee and wasn't from the best neighborhood," he started haltingly, picking up speed as he continued. "Lots of drugs and guns and gangs and trouble. In high school me and my friends got into some stuff that wasn't so good, and I sort of have a police record."

"You *sort of* have a police record?"

"Yeah…well…yeah, I have a police record. But even then I never hurt nobody. Fighting people is for losers. But now everybody's being questioned, so the cops here know about me. So I figured you should know about me too." He inhaled deeply and continued, finally looking at my face, "Things are okay now. I live with cousins up here and it's all better. I learned my lesson. No more jail time for me. That's it."

"Oh, and when I said I graduated from high school, I actually got a GED. But I do have a diploma." He turned to walk away and looked back at me, smiled shyly, and said, "Thanks." His demeanor had changed already and he held his head higher, as if a huge load had been lifted from his shoulders.

"Thanks for being honest, Roger. I appreciate it." I made a few notes to add to his personnel file regarding his revelation, including a comment that he was the best multi-tasker we had, and he stayed calm when other fry cooks became frantic.

I wondered if Uncle Al had been aware of Roger's past when he hired him. I assumed that Al ran every applicant's name through the Wisconsin Circuit Court website, but only crimes committed as an adult are matters of public record, juvenile records remain sealed. A violent past can appear fairly benign on paper. If Al did know details of Roger's indiscretions he hadn't shared them with me, or made any notations in Roger's file.

New facts about Roger's situation were irrelevant at Unincorporated, he'd proven himself here, but could cause difficulties during the investigation. That was something he'd have to deal with himself, a result of poor decisions in the past. Life was never simple; I only hoped that he was telling the truth, and he'd really turned his life around.

After updating his file, I finally got on the phone and called The Marys.

"Can you come over this afternoon? We'll get right to work," Mary Rose said when I'd introduced myself. "Do you know how to find our house?" As if anyone could miss their magnificent home.

Arriving at the imposing house on the wooded hillside, seeing it up close for the first time, I was flabbergasted. It was more estate than home, Italianate in styling, huge and white with a wrap-around porch, balconies and pillars.

The driveway curved past well-manicured flower gardens, winding paths and an octagonal white gazebo. A side drive circled back toward a 100-year-old two-story carriage house complete with balcony, and several fieldstone outbuildings, all totally unexpected in this lakeside farming town. An in-ground sprinkling system sent arched fountains of water across the lush green grassy areas, making it clear that this home would not be affected by drought conditions.

Leaving my dented 15-year-old Beetle in the parking area adjoining a grove of trees (yes, their estate had a parking lot), I climbed the wide veranda stairs. Pressing the shiny ornate brass doorbell produced the opening notes of a classical piece I couldn't put a name to. The view of Windsor Lake was incredible from this vantage.

"You must be Ashley." A personable, fashionably-dressed woman, probably in her mid-60's, slender with well-shaped grey hair and clear brown eyes, answered the door. "I'm so glad to finally meet you. I'm Mary Rose. Come in and meet my sisters." Clasping my hand in hers, she led me into her home. I'm no expert, but her earrings, pendant and bracelet were screaming "the real thing". No faux jewelry for this lady.

Mary Rose's expensively-cut cream linen pantsuit made me feel sadly under-dressed. My denim skirt and brightly striped knit top no doubt looked like someone else's castoffs by comparison. If Mary Rose was put off by my attire, she gave no indication, her manners were impeccable.

I could hear my mother saying, "Never go into a house with strangers." Well these weren't strangers, not exactly. I didn't know them, but everyone else in town did. My brain couldn't get beyond this whole homicide thing. I felt suspicious of everyone.

Mary Rose led me through a three-story chandeliered foyer flanked by sweeping marble staircases into a large comfortable room with a bank of floor-to-ceiling leaded glass windows, an elaborately carved fireplace, gilt-framed oil paintings and impressive period furniture. Massive floral arrangements softened the formal lines of antique marble-topped tables and added a wonderful scent that I inhaled through deep breaths. This was the type of place I live in in my dreams, like a scene from a glamorous old movie.

"I'd like you to meet my sisters. The three of us have been working furiously to organize this event. We're so pleased to have your assistance and support."

I was introduced to MaryBeth and Mary Lou, two women of a similar age to Mary Rose, the three having almost identical facial features and coloring. Now that I saw The Mary's together, I realized I'd noticed them at Mark's memorial service, sitting quietly off to one side. They'd been constantly glancing around, not enough to be obvious, but since I'd been studying the crowd myself I'd realized that these three women didn't miss anything or anyone. I should have guessed that they were The Marys.

MaryBeth and Mary Lou weren't as stylishly dressed as Mary Rose, and lacked her poise and presence. While Mary Rose was gracious and dignified, her sisters seemed quieter and more thoughtful, although just as cordial. Neither had her natural air of authority, or was as perfectly appointed, giving the impression of being subordinate to their more striking sister.

"Welcome to our home. We're so pleased you're willing to help. How is your uncle doing?" the sister introduced as MaryBeth asked. "We saw him at Mark's memorial, but didn't have a chance to talk." MaryBeth wore a coordinated slacks outfit and had neatly combed hair, but there was no sense of style, no jewelry, no makeup. She had a healthy appearance, as if she worked out regularly and was concerned about fitness over fashion.

She sat at a large desk of polished wood, with notebooks and a laptop nearby, pen in hand. Ready to work, she was prepared to take notes, and create lists and work schedules. I felt as if I had arrived late to class and the teacher was anxious to get started.

Mary Lou was yet another story. Looking at her I saw mismatched slacks and sweater, ruffled hair, and a vacant gaze. Not only was she not wearing any jewelry, she gave the impression that she'd never owned any, and didn't care.

"Nice to meet you," she said, staring over my shoulder with a small smile, never looking at my face.

Her hair, though the same grey as her sisters', appeared drier, and not as well-shaped. Lacking the overwhelming personality of Mary Rose, or the healthy energy of MaryBeth, she would be the sister most likely to be overlooked.

We quickly got down to business. An easel displayed an architect's rendering of a magical playground with structures that mimicked everything from a sailing ship to a school bus. There were towers and tunnels, slides and swings. Bright colors made it look like an enchanted land.

"This will be the feature of the town center. We have permission to situate it in Veteran's Park, off to the side beyond the statues," Mary Rose disclosed. "That way it won't be disrespectful to the war heroes, and won't be close enough to the bandstand to cause a conflict during concerts."

"A friend of mine, an engineer, designed it for maximum safety. It will be created with all eco-friendly materials, but we need a successful fundraiser to purchase the best quality. It can be constructed with mostly volunteer labor, however we don't want to start it until we can afford to do it right." The plans made the playground look so intriguing that I almost wanted to play there myself. No doubt about it, The Marys didn't do anything halfway.

"What do you have in mind for food service?" MaryBeth asked, shuffling through some papers. "We have some ideas, but want to know what you think." I was glad I'd consulted Uncle Al about this; otherwise I would have sat tongue-tied and flustered.

Thanks to Al's suggestions I was able to contribute ideas that seemed to fit with The Marys' general plans. My phone held a quickly growing list of foods that would be needed, and I promised to solicit donations before committing to purchases. I didn't admit it, but I was considering asking Al to handle those donation requests; I believed he'd be more successful in that area than I would. He had a long-standing relationship with many vendors who would naturally be more generous toward a long-time client.

The plans called for numerous food stands, each having items not available at any other stand. The brat stand would also have chili fries. The hamburger stand would have deep fried cheese curds. The hot dog stand would have corn on the cob. One small stand would have only ice cream cones and sundaes. Cotton candy, popcorn, and cream puffs would be at another stand. And our list kept growing.

A featured booth would focus on treats from local orchards. Caramel apples, apple cake, apple dumplings, apple cider, and apple wine would lead the list. The Marys seemed confident that these items could be locally sourced even out-of-season. I assumed they were right.

Thankfully The Marys were as organized as everyone said they were. Sources for cooking and grilling equipment, tents, auxiliary power and sign printing had already been contacted.

Other than the food, I was only asked to order the necessary paper products. Cases of paper products that aren't opened can be returned, so I wasn't concerned about overspending on those items. Figuring out how much food to purchase was another story. Hopefully Al and the vendors would have input that would help with those decisions.

"There will be a beer stand, won't there?" I asked, remembering Uncle Al's suggestion. I kept my fingers crossed that I wasn't creating more work for myself.

"We always have alcohol at our fundraisers if at all possible," MaryBeth stated, flipping through a few pages in her notebook. "We're working with Rick's Tap to plan that part of it. A temporary liquor license will cover beer and wine for the day. We don't believe it's wise to offer anything stronger. But we know people do like their adult beverages, and will stay longer and spend more." With a mischievous grin she added, "It's amazing how much more money we raise if people are imbibing!"

Mary Rose nodded as we laughed at the thought. "We wanted to involve as many local businesses as possible, and Rick enjoys being a part of things." She seemed concerned that I was offended at not being asked to handle that detail.

"I'm happy to know that Rick will run the beer stand," I assured her. "You're right that we need to spread the responsibilities around, and he'll do a great job." I didn't admit to The Marys just how relieved I was.

"Can I interest you in a cup of tea?" Mary Rose offered.

"That sounds wonderful," I answered, even though I had never appreciated the beverage.

She reached over to press a button on the wall; a woman entered the room promptly to ask what she could do for us. In a tailored grey dress, with hair pulled back in a large silver clip, she appeared businesslike and orderly. I had the impression that she was in uniform; a simple and practical uniform that would be presentable on any occasion.

"We'd like tea served in the conservatory," Mary Rose requested. The woman nodded and hurried away; we rose and crossed the hall to a bright sunny room filled with large lush green plants. Windows on three sides dramatically framed Windsor Lake, and much of Windsor Grove. I stood in awe, looking down at a breathtaking view of the community that had become my temporary home.

"Wow." Words couldn't begin to express my wonder. I hope my mouth wasn't hanging open.

"That's a common reaction when someone sees this for the first time. I purchased this home because this is the most valuable piece of land in the area," Mary Rose explained with a smile. "No other residence in Windsor Grove can rival this exposure. Never a day goes by that I don't give thanks for how fortunate I am. It's like living in a fairy tale."

The woman in grey entered the room carrying a tray with a silver tea service and dainty china cups that I was almost afraid to touch. I was tempted to turn a saucer over to see what hallmark was on the bottom, but managed to resist. I did make a mental note to do an online search for the pattern; I was sure this was the most expensive cup I'd ever handled, and my curiosity was aroused.

"Earl Grey or Jasmine Tea, both organic," the woman announced as she set down her tray. Also on the tray was a china platter of tiny elegant cookies and pastries. My mouth watered just looking at them, and I wondered how many I could take without being impolite.

The woman poured our tea, and handed us small plates and linen napkins. We each selected a few treats from the platter, and she left the room.

As we enjoyed our tea The Marys filled me in on other details they'd been strategizing. I have to admit that I only pretended to enjoy the tea, but the pastries more than made up for it. I decided to develop a taste for organic tea; I felt so elegant sitting in this lovely home with my dainty cup in hand, it was a shame that I thought the liquid tasted horrible.

"We're calling the event Windsor Day. All the posters and flyers will show the proposed playground," MaryBeth revealed. "If it's a huge success, we can hold a Windsor Day every year, and change the focus depending on what the town needs." I thought it might be overreaching to talk about a yearly event when the inaugural one was still in the planning stage. But The Marys assumed success, and were ready to keep moving forward.

An early morning run/walk, face painting, an apple-pie-eating contest, a variety of concerts in the bandstand, an evening boat parade, and various other ideas were being talked about.

"If you think of anything that people would get excited about, anything that will develop enthusiasm, let us know. It's important to have activities that attract both locals and visitors if we want to raise the money we need," Mary Rose said, "and things geared to every age group, of course."

It became apparent while we talked that, despite having been told that no one in town could remember which Mary was which, the three Marys each had very distinctive personalities. Mary Rose was the most gregarious of the three, with an enthusiastic, energetic, and imaginative personality. MaryBeth was more analytical, more methodical, and more concerned with organization, details and statistics than her outgoing sister.

The hardest sister to characterize was Mary Lou, who mumbled cryptic comments that she seemed to think were funny. Her sisters chose to ignore her statements, rather than reply to them.

Before I left, Mary Lou motioned for me to approach her chair. She smiled slyly, winked, then whispered, "That man was killed with your knife, wasn't he? That must be so exciting!"

I nodded uncertainly, not really knowing how to respond. I found her question unnerving. It wasn't *my* knife, it belonged to Unincorporated. And there definitely wasn't anything exciting about it. It had become apparent that many of the area residents were fascinated by the homicide in our midst. I just wasn't among those who considered this to be grand entertainment.

"Who do you think did it?" Mary Lou pried. "Do you think it was someone who works for you?" She was whispering now, looking up at me expectantly as if I knew the truth and she hoped I'd reveal the guilty party. I shook my head, wondering if others in town also thought I had inside information.

She gave me another conspiratorial wink, as if assuming we shared some special secret. What was up with her, I wondered. Did this peculiar woman really think I knew whodunit? Did she seriously believe one of my staff was guilty?

Did the bizarre Mary Lou have information she wasn't sharing? Did she ask such prying questions of everyone? Had she gained knowledge that even the officers didn't possess? She seemed to be reveling in the crime.

I was reminded of a phrase my mother uses…*socially handicapped*. That's how Mom describes people who are unable to interact comfortably with others. Mary Lou certainly fit this category. She made me very uneasy. A phrase from a psychology class floated into my brain, "odd eccentric cluster of personality disorder". Perhaps apropos here, if only I could remember the definition.

I left their home with a disconcerted feeling, as if life were taking me in a direction I didn't care to go.

It was annoying, but not surprising, to see a sheriff's vehicle in the parking lot when I returned to work. It was even more annoying to find Officer Gregg standing in my office questioning Dawn while she was supposed to be setting up the dining room for dinner.

"Again? You're here again?" I tried not to sound as annoyed as I felt, but probably didn't succeed.

"Your staff are hard people to get in touch with when they're off duty," he said, shaking his head. "It makes my job much easier if I can interview people in the course of their work day. It's standard policy when a tragedy has occurred." I didn't want to interfere with his duties, but his presence created tension among the staff, which didn't lead to a relaxing atmosphere for our guests.

"I understand. But could you at least come in through the employee entrance out back," (or was that the front?) "and wait for me in the chef's office?" I laughed. "When you're in the restaurant it causes a distraction for our guests."

"I'm distracting, am I?" he gave me a slight smile, nodding. "I can see how that might be the case. I'll try to be less intrusive. Dawn, you can get back to work; I have no more questions right now.

"I won't talk with any more of your staff today; I know Friday is a busy evening here. But I have to come back tomorrow to see a few more of your employees. In the chef's office." He sighed, closed his ever-present notebook, and moved toward the door.

"Would you like to sit down for a minute? You look tired. Can I bring you some coffee?" I was, after all, in the hospitality industry. This was one small way I could help.

He plopped himself down on my desk chair, saying, "That would be great. Thanks."

"Have you eaten?"

His face took on a puzzled expression. "Probably not; I think I forgot. I've been busy."

"Stay right there."

I went into the kitchen and explained to Chef Brad that I needed some energy food. His enthusiastic reaction surprised me.

"Well, he's come to the right place. A smart guy like him should know better than to ignore nutrition. How can people not understand that? I know what he needs...let me take care of it."

Within moments I was presenting Gregg with a plate of maple-glazed salmon with grilled asparagus and apple-mango slaw.

"This combination should provide the pick-up he needs," Brad had said. "Now tell him no more slacking on foods! If he needs nutritional guidance I'm his guy. We need him functioning at peak levels."

While Gregg ate, I wondered where that caring chef had come from. It sure wasn't the Brad I knew.

"Detective Milton is conducting another search of Mark's apartment." Gregg told me as he ate. "He'll take control of any forensic evidence, and anything else that has to be dealt with via crime labs and criminal data bases. That way he can work from his office in Madison."

"I'll handle the investigation as far as local evidence and interviews go." Gregg sounded wistful as he said this. It was clear that this small town officer yearned to capture a criminal based on his own technical knowledge and clever interpretation of facts.

"Well, he might get to do the high-tech stuff, but it sounds like you're the one doing the actual investigating," I said loyally. I resented the fact that our local officers were relegated to the number two spot.

"Yeah, I guess so," he sighed.

I realized that what I had to tell him next was only going to add to the chaos at Unincorporated. It might, however, give him a chance to be the sleuth he longed to be.

"Yesterday after the memorial service Uncle Al came to the restaurant for a few minutes and looked through our old invoice files. He's pretty sure that a few knives are missing."

Gregg scowled. "A few? How many, exactly? What size?" He hurried to finish his food.

"Possibly a half dozen or more steak knives. He studied invoices and tried to figure out the maximum number we could have. Knives that get used as heavily as ours break, or just wear out. But he thinks there should be six or eight more than there are. Also, one of his personal chef's knives, the one with the longest blade, is missing. He found this picture of a similar knife in a catalog."

The grimace on his face made it evident that Gregg wasn't one bit happy to hear about missing knives. He took the catalog page I'd given him, made a few notations on it, and rose to turn slowly toward the door.

"You should have told me immediately that there are more stolen knives out there, possibly in the hands of a killer. This isn't good...not good at all...oh, and thanks for the food." He wandered out the kitchen door, got in his car, and spent quite some time on his phone.

I had to accept the unfortunate fact that Gregg and his official vehicle were going to become permanent fixtures around the restaurant. As I used the carpet sweeper to attack cracker crumbs that some child had ground into the rug, I reflected that if I couldn't get rid of Gregg and his investigation, maybe I could hurry things along by gathering information that he didn't have.

After all, locals were far more likely to share ideas and suspicions with friends than with an officer, no matter how kind he was. So it was time to get serious about listening and learning. Considering how invisible I seemed to be as I walked through the dining room, it seemed natural for me to listen in on conversations without being noticed.

What possible harm could come from some innocent eavesdropping?

CHAPTER 13

The decision to keep my ears open and aid the Sheriff's Department was easily made. The actual listening was more complicated. I'd spent the remainder of the day doing routine chores: answering phones, seating guests, packaging carryouts, smiling and greeting, refilling coffee and clearing tables. Once again we had guests sitting outdoors enjoying the beauty of Windsor Lake, but they moved indoors immediately when the sun set.

Ever since details of Mark's untimely death had been released our guests had little desire to remain on the patio after sunset. I'd personally had a constant suspicion that someone was looking over my shoulder. Apparently that feeling of vulnerability was shared by others, who no longer preferred the great outdoors in twilight. The Lounge was more crowded as a result, making the atmosphere louder and more hectic, adding a feeling of urgency to the tempo of dinner service.

Most of the staff were invigorated when Unincorporated was busy, with time passing quickly minus the errors and complaints that occurred on slower days. It always amazed me that the busier we were the more smoothly things went. Go figure.

My determination to learn by listening had initially seemed like a sound decision. Unfortunately, actual listening, while easy because conversations continued all around me, soon became so annoying that I had to tune the chatter out.

"This place has really gone downhill since the days when they had a nightly fish boil." There has never been a nightly fish boil anywhere in Windsor Grove. Those couples were thinking of a different part of Wisconsin altogether. Fish boils are common in Door County, over 150 miles away.

"...coach has to be fired, and as soon as possible!"

"Did you hear what those nincompoops on the school board want to do next?" Five people started complaining at once after that question was asked.

"...and the bait shop has the most amazing display of fishing lures I've ever seen!" *I can't believe the things men get excited about.*

"The first time I got implants one of them collapsed." I surreptitiously looked around to see who'd made that comment. A brunette in her mid-30's wearing an excessive amount of makeup sat in the Lounge with several friends. Her low-cut neckline seemed totally inappropriate in Windsor Grove; she was obviously proud of her enhancements. Her friends looked embarrassed at her over-sharing, but she continued on with details. Who talks about things like that in public, anyway?

I wouldn't admit to anyone that I was jealous of her curves.

"I don't have kids, but I've got thirty-five nieces, nephews, grandnieces and grandnephews. With every one that's born they're each getting a smaller piece of the pot!" This from an elderly man dressed like he didn't have a penny to his name.

"My grandson said the cutest thing when his mom talked to him about potty training..."

No, intentionally listening in on conversations wasn't going to be any help at all...and just might drive me to distraction. (That's another phrase that Mom uses. I don't know what it means, but it sounds appropriate).

I needed to learn to extract information from the people who surrounded me day in, day out, in casual conversation. Asking a few simple questions would seem natural for someone whose job it was to greet the public. If I could think of an ideal question that would encourage people to open up, I might learn details that Gregg didn't have. And this whole mess might be over, and life back to normal, sooner rather than later.

I'd visited the post office during the afternoon, knowing the lobby was less of a gathering space at that hour and I'd be in and out more quickly. My strategy worked, leaving me with time to stop at my cottage; a package addressed to me in familiar handwriting begged to be opened immediately.

Among the mass quantities of equipment fliers, industry magazines, and donation requests, there had been a box from Mom. She'd sent me care packages throughout college, and must have decided I needed the same attention now. Perhaps she was right.

Today's box included a scented candle, a bright pair of flip-flops, a few fashion magazines, my favorite salon shampoo, and lip gloss in a brand I'd liked when I was thirteen. At the bottom of the box, carefully wrapped in tissue paper, was Teddy Maxwell, a battered stuffed bear I'd had forever.

Missing one eye, with his torn ear and matted fur, Teddy Maxwell had helped me through a broken arm, the death of my Gramma, a failed driving test, and several early romances. Mom thought I needed Maxwell with me in Windsor Grove. Mom knows me pretty well.

"Wow! Thanks Mom!" I texted, "It made me smile."

I felt like a dear friend was alongside me now, helping to maintain my sanity.

Brad kept up an incessant diatribe about batter-fried lake perch. The famous Wisconsin Friday night fish fry was beneath his skill level, or so he claimed. He resented spending one day each week breading and frying this popular entrée, and he didn't let anyone forget it. The enticing odor of his deep-fried beer-batter breading told me he'd been hard at work, creating the masterpiece he hated. The kitchen staff had seemingly learned to ignore his ranting on the subject. I'd have to do the same.

The menu at Unincorporated displayed icons next to various entrees designating "gluten-free", "low-sodium" and "vegetarian". But that didn't stop the dietary questions; in fact it almost seemed to encourage inquiries.

"How much salt is in your haddock Creole?"

"I'm diabetic. What can I eat?" I hated that question, which was asked fairly often. Shouldn't it be their doctor who told them what they could eat, not their restaurateur?

I was learning to deal with these questions; for the most part it meant going to Brad's office to find the recipe's ingredient list. I was flummoxed that day, however, when asked, "What do you offer for vegans?" I excused myself to get information, inwardly praying that someone on my staff could bail me out.

In the kitchen I asked if anyone was vegan, and was surprised at the answer.

"I am. I've got this one," Roger, the fry cook from Milwaukee's central city who'd lied on his job application, replied. I knew I could count on detail-oriented Roger to give thoughtful informed answers to the guest's questions.

"It was something I decided to do for myself when I said goodbye to my past," he remarked. He tucked in his shirt, washed his hands, and went to the dining room to act as consultant. The guest was pleased to speak with someone who made similar nutritional choices, and didn't seem fazed by the myriad of piercings and tattoos that Roger sported.

Officer Gregg hadn't yet visited Unincorporated that day, and I foolishly thought that possibly I'd been spared, for just twenty-four hours, from any additional disturbing details. But no, that would have been too good to be true.

"That chef of yours contacted the department yesterday about something concerning," Gregg said standing in my office doorway during the dinner rush. "It seems that he cleans out his truck regularly, and yesterday morning found a knife belonging to Kellam Sharpening Services under his driver's seat. He claims it definitely wasn't there a week ago, and he's ready to blame anyone and everyone for 'defacing' his vehicle."

How, I wondered, did Brad find time to clean out his truck? Every week? I could barely get my Beetle to a car wash every month.

"For now we have to assume it was put there by the killer. Whether it happened here or at Brad's home is unknown; he doesn't have a garage, so his truck is always outdoors. We suggested that he might want to keep his vehicle locked; he didn't take kindly to the suggestion."

I could certainly believe that; he's not a man who takes direction from others willingly.

"The killer might be trying to influence the direction of our investigation. Brad's no fool; there's no way he would contact us and incriminate himself if he were guilty. We think the plan had been for us to receive an anonymous tip about the knife, but neatnik Brad found it too soon. Your knife is being held as evidence; we're just not sure what it's evidence of. Please encourage your staff to keep car doors locked. House doors too, of course. There's someone dangerous out there."

Later that day I went out to my car and searched under my seats. No knives. Thank God.

When the last diners were ordering dessert and things were winding down, I sat at my desk making notes about Mark's killer. If nothing else, writing things down meant I could clear the part of my brain that had been in turmoil trying to remember details.

I wrote *Suspects* across the top of the page, and started two columns: *Local* and *Visitors*.

I then wrote *Who Knew Mark Previously?* on the left side, and listed Todd Braun, the Village Flower Shoppe owner who'd been Mark's friend at Indiana University, in the local column. I added "Old Girlfriend", meaning the other party in Mark's recent breakup. I put her in the *Visitors* column, even though to my knowledge she'd never actually been here. That gave me one suspect in each category. Unfortunately both of them were said to have been among Mark's best friends.

Who's Met Mark Recently? was the next category. It was vast, and probably included most of Windsor Grove. I didn't put down any names; it seemed unproductive to list everyone in town.

Following that came *Enemies*, a section that remained empty.

People Who Act Suspiciously held more promise. I started the list with Mary Lou, who certainly fitted the bill. I also wrote down Brad's name, only because I'd seldom met anyone so compulsively rude. I thought about it for a few minutes, and decided to write "Man-in-Brown" in the *Visitors* column. And how about Mr. Horner? Were his idiosyncrasies enough to be considered suspicious? Come to think of it, most of Windsor Grove's residents acted oddly at one time or another, some more consistently than others. Seemingly normal, everyone in town could fit into that category on occasion.

Why Would Anyone Want To Kill Mark? remained blank. So much for the value of writing things down. I'd have to start asking questions soon, or this would occupy my mind to no avail. My mind was already overburdened and didn't need murder added to the mix.

I couldn't come up with any other potential categories. I was too tired to concentrate, and I knew that focusing on the homicide late in the evening made for uneasy sleep. I dropped the paper into the middle drawer of my desk, on top of my list of important phone numbers (repair people).

The fry cooks were mopping the kitchen; dishwashers carried out the garbage; servers were refilling salt and pepper shakers and emptying soup wells; Renata had declared "last call" in the Lounge. The day was coming to a close. I locked up my office and left the building.

Before reaching the path to my cottage, I took a few minutes to wander down toward the lake. Its tranquil water, shimmering in the moonlight, had an almost mesmerizing effect that calmed me after the hectic day. Standing and gazing at its beauty and then looking toward the stars made me feel extremely insignificant, but very in touch with nature.

I found myself contemplating life itself. The little time a person has on this earth. The waste when a life is cut short. The uncertainty of anyone's future. Violent death. Lives lost, lives changed forever, lives lived in fear; but also lives dedicated to giving and caring and sharing.

Much of our existence is beyond our control, with events around us ebbing and flowing like the waters that can give life and can take it away. People must make the most of what they are given in the fleeting amount of time they have. I hoped that I always reflected the best of things around me, as the waters reflected the moonlight.

Rejuvenated after quiet time spent by the water, I headed up to the cottage feeling good about my job, good about myself, and good about the future. Life was wonderful, well-meaning people would prevail, and the bad things were all behind us.

I should have known better.

CHAPTER 14

The beautiful weather had become monotonous; sunshine was a certainty, the long-awaited precipitation a pipedream. We were treated to another idyllic morning, sunny with a slight breeze, the scent of wildflowers filling the air. It was a gorgeous Saturday that brought a smile to everyone's face, a day meant for boating and biking and swimming and hiking.

Summer visitors were arriving in larger numbers, and I could envision families lined up at The Sundae Parlor for ice cream treats and at Confectioners Candies buying sweets by the pound. Lawn chairs were no doubt lined up around the bandstand waiting for an afternoon concert. Hopefully those families would be hungry, and would decide to enjoy a meal overlooking Windsor Lake.

The downside to this idyllic weather was the continuing drought. Area growers were increasingly concerned about the damage to this year's potato and corn crops. Even the dairy farmers were expecting huge losses; they'd have to purchase feed for their cattle which they normally grew themselves. The dry weather was a constant topic of conversation among locals, not only due to the plights of farmers but also because of the continuing threat of fire.

It wouldn't take more than one spark to start a devastating blaze; a town filled with century-old buildings could be destroyed in minutes. Park rangers reported that campers were taking this seriously, and there hadn't been any incidents. Midwesterners are responsible about the environment, and the rangers had every reason to believe our campgrounds wouldn't be harmed. We were thankful for our luck so far, and looked regularly to the skies praying for rain.

I vowed that I would greet this day with optimism, and be the kind of restaurateur who made customers come back again. I donned a short-sleeved dress in the color of spring lilacs that I always got compliments on, spent extra time in front of my wavy mirror applying make-up, and chose jewelry that would reflect the artistic character of the community.

All this was made slightly more difficult by the fact that my entire body was sore. Suzy's self-defense lesson had awoken many muscles that complained loudly; my legs felt like I'd run a marathon.

I took a few acetaminophen tablets, putting more in my purse. What would I have felt like had I actually fought off an attacker? I was in pain from punching a dummy! I wondered how the women in class who were thirty years older were feeling.

Heading over to Unincorporated earlier than usual, I was determined to stay on task, forget my stiffness, and gather information for Gregg. I'd fallen asleep wondering what question I could ask guests that would garner the information I hoped for. When I awoke I knew what that question would be: "How well did you know Mark?"

It would feel natural to drop it into casual conversation; it wouldn't sound like an interrogation. I could ask it innocuously enough, because everyone was constantly discussing Mark; in fact I'd been asked that very question numerous times. It just might encourage people to open up and share information, things they didn't feel comfortable telling the officers.

For a fleeting moment I wondered if the people who had asked me that question were creating their own list of suspects…and if I was on any of those lists. But that didn't seem possible. Definitely not possible.

I would ask the question, and I would keep detailed notes. I was determined to learn something, anything, which would help.

I'd barely reached the kitchen entrance when Brad hollered, "Ashley, there's some guy putting up a sign by our driveway. You'd better get out there and find out what the hell he thinks he's doing!"

Now what? The world was conspiring to keep me off kilter. I hurried out to our parking lot, an acre of blacktop surrounded by towering pines.

I shouldn't have been surprised at who I found: Rupert himself, pounding a huge sign into the ground alongside our driveway, VOTE RUPERT for STATE SENATE in huge red letters surrounded by blue stars. Parked nearby was a black SUV with a matching sign on the side.

"Hi, Ashley!" He beamed so broadly that I could see how artificially perfect his teeth were. "I know I can count on your vote, so I thought I'd just put this sign up. It will be great for my image to have a campaign sign in front of Unincorporated. Everyone respects your opinion," he said ingratiatingly. He huffed and puffed from the effort of wielding a mallet, and a shock of his hair stood up straight as if in protest of manual labor, but his face wore its signature grin.

"Sorry, but the answer is no," I shook my head. I remembered conversations I'd overheard. *"He's too full of himself."*

"A lot of hot air if you ask me." More than a few residents seemed to think that politically he was useless. There was no way I was going to alienate any customers by taking sides. I knew that in a small business it was important to remain politically neutral.

Rupert tried to turn on his supposedly charismatic charm. "No? But this is the best location in town. And you know I'm one of your most faithful customers." His Cheshire-Cat-grin may win the votes of elderly ladies, but it wasn't going to change my mind about a campaign sign.

"We appreciate having you as a customer and friend, and we wish you well in the election," (I can lay it on as thick as anyone). "But we have to stay out of politics, or certain guests get offended and eat elsewhere. I won't aggravate potential diners, even for you, Rupert."

I tried to say it kindly, but I was growing angry. He'd been posting his sign without asking, apparently not planning to take "No" for an answer.

"I can't believe you'd lose business if you had my campaign sign out front. People aren't like that," he argued. His face was getting red, and he seemed to be controlling himself with an effort.

"I've lost a customer because she found out I go to another town to get my hair cut," I rolled my eyes. "I'm not about to let my guests know how I feel politically, even if you are a local favorite. You've got my vote, just not our business' endorsement."

As I said that I was making a mental note to learn more about his opponent. It was one thing to tell him I'd vote for him, but was he actually the best candidate? I had no idea.

Wait. Never mind. I'm not a permanent resident here; my senate district is miles away. I couldn't vote for the guy anyway. Good. I'm off the hook.

He was putting me on the defensive, when he was the one who'd been out of line. One thing for sure, he was definitely self-absorbed. He'd probably make a good politician; all politicians seem to have huge egos.

Glancing across the driveway I was surprised to see an old-model, charcoal grey four-door sedan parked in the far corner of the lot, someone sitting perfectly still at the wheel. It wasn't unusual to have a few vacant cars in the lot before opening; vehicles were often left overnight if someone imbibed too much in the Lounge, and occasionally we were used as an informal park-and-ride lot when friends headed to Oak Landing.

It was odd, however, to see someone sitting in the driver's seat. It became even odder when Jeff, one of our young dishwashers, the one who'd been a no-call no-show days earlier, drove up in a rusted blue Chevy. Jeff exited his car, hurried to the grey vehicle, talked for a moment to the driver, hopped back in his car and drove away without looking in my direction.

The driver started his engine and took off, following Jeff down the road. When he pulled out of our lot I saw his profile and recognized that it was Man-in-Brown. I didn't give the whole episode much thought beyond the general impression of *strange activity*. I had more urgent things to think about. I did wonder, however, if Jeff needed to be added to my *Acting Suspicious* category.

I turned my attention back to Rupert and stood firm, repeating my position that, "We can't take sides on political issues." The foodservice industry is competitive enough without giving any sort of advantage to our rivals. Eventually I got my point across.

Once Rupert had reluctantly removed his sign, loaded it into the back of his vehicle, and left the parking lot, I turned to go indoors. The immediate sound of an auto entering our lot annoyed me; if Rupert had returned to plead his case he'd just lost any chance of getting my endorsement.

But it wasn't Rupert. When I saw who it was, I almost wished it were. At least I could say "No" to him.

It was a county squad car with both Officers Littner and Milton dressed in official garb, and looking serious. As they exited their car I saw the expressions on their faces and got a sinking feeling in my stomach.

"Let's go inside," Gregg said rather roughly. My morning wasn't getting off to the pleasant start I'd envisioned. At least this time the officers showed up before we started serving guests.

"Lynette and John from The Pottery Studio have left town temporarily," Detective Milton disclosed in a somber tone once we'd entered my small office. I noticed that he wasn't nearly as attractive when he wasn't smiling. He carried a hand-held digital notebook. Gregg again carried notepad and pen; I was getting really tired of seeing that tattered notepad.

"Oh?" I was puzzled. Was this important to me? I'd met Lynette and John once or twice, but we certainly weren't close. While it was unusual for a business owner to go on vacation during the busy season, it wasn't unheard of. I waited, sure that there was more to the story, and I'd be learning more than I wanted to know.

Detective Milton held out a torn piece of paper. "Does this look familiar?"

I looked down and saw writing on the paper, childishly printed in dark marker that made my heart skip a beat. YOUR NEXT, it read. It wasn't just the words that alarmed me, it was the paper itself. The words were written on a corner ripped from an Unincorporated placemat.

"Um, well, uh, yes," I stammered, ever the brilliant conversationalist. What was going on here? Whatever it was, I was pretty sure that my life and my job were going to get even more complicated. "It's our placemat, but I don't understand."

"This note was slid under the door of The Pottery Studio during the night. John found it when he went to unlock this morning. We've recommended that Lynette and John should leave town for a while, not letting anyone know where they are. No one should take chances when threats are made with a killer on the loose."

"I thought that Mark was definitely the target."

"That doesn't mean there can't be another. Lynette and John readily agreed to go. They have staff to keep their shop open, and their summer class schedule hasn't started yet, so leaving won't affect their income."

Gregg Littner nodded at Detective Milton's words, adding, "We think the note was written by someone holding a marker in their fist, the way small children do. That makes it difficult to trace the handwriting. The incorrect grammar is possibly being used to confuse the situation.

"We can't say that this was written by Mark's killer, although that's definitely a possibility. But someone who has an alibi for Mark's death may find this to be an ideal opportunity to terrorize someone. While copycat crimes are common, so are unrelated criminal activities during an investigation.

"An anonymous note is a coward's way of frightening someone without any personal risk. Just to complicate things, we can't lose sight of the fact that someone may think it's funny to add to the current atmosphere of panic by doing something seemingly harmless."

Detective Milton looked directly into my eyes, saying, "We're keeping this information quiet for now, so we'd appreciate your silence on the matter. We don't want people to panic, but there are definitely unsavory things occurring in Windsor Grove."

As concerning as all this was, my mind wandered, and I couldn't help thinking that Gregg was also far more attractive when he felt lighthearted. Relationships with officers must be very complicated. No wonder these two good-looking, intelligent, friendly guys were still single.

"What we need to learn is how long Unincorporated has been using this style of placemat," Gregg said, wrenching my brain back to reality.

Ours was a typical supper club placemat: white textured paper with scalloped edges. A sketch of our building with an unrealistically large Unincorporated road sign adorned the center, whimsically showing a hardwood forest in the background, ignoring the lake entirely. The section Gregg held had been the lower left portion, showing our web address, the Wisconsin Restaurant Association logo, and a list of after-dinner drinks.

"I'm not sure when this placemat was designed, but I can call Uncle Al and ask." I hated to bug him again, but the officers didn't look patient, and I'd have the answer more quickly by making the phone call than by digging through old invoices.

Al answered on the first ring, and sounded pleased to hear my voice. That pleasure faded, however, when I told him the reason for my call.

"I think the last redesign of placemats was about six years ago," Al said.

I put Al on hold and relayed that news to Officers Milton and Littner, who both sighed, and made notes, Gregg in that ever-present notepad, Officer Milton on his more modern hand-held device.

"I hesitate to ask, but where are these placemats stored?" Gregg asked, as if dreading my reply.

"The full cases are in the storage room out back," I answered, "but a pile of them is kept in each waitstation in the dining room, and we also have a supply behind the bar. We only use them in the dining room in the evening, but we use them all day for guests who dine in the Lounge."

"So you're telling me that even more people had access to the placemats than had access to your knives," Gregg stated with a grim look. "I know the answer, but I have to ask."

"Everyone who's been anywhere in the building could have grabbed a placemat," I nodded. "Apparently for the last six years. Please tell me you're not going to expect a list of our customers for the last six years."

"That would be foolish, of course. We might as well just assume that anyone in the entire state of Wisconsin could have one of your placemats. We could include Illinois in that too; I noticed that the number of Illinois license plates has increased over the last few days."

119

"Yes, thankfully." Then I stammered, "Not that I want your investigation to be more complicated; not at all. I'm just happy the summer visitors are finally getting here. It's better for business, that's all I meant."

"We understand," Detective Milton smiled. "Certain things have to be important to us, but other things are important to you. That's natural." No matter how annoying it was to have them around, the officers really were nice guys

I got back on the phone to spend a few minutes chatting with Al, who had numerous questions about how business was going. Most of his concerns had to do with the effect of the homicide on income, on customer count and profit. My answers allayed his worries, but I could tell he longed to be here working beside me, not sitting at home. I didn't blame him; never having been married, our guests were his family and Unincorporated was his life. He would enjoy all the fuss and commotion, and would have been energized by it.

I, on the other hand, felt overwhelmed by the restaurant, the fundraiser, the murder, missing knives and of course the constant presence and questioning of our friendly local sheriff's department. Now there was the addition of an anonymous threatening note.

I wasn't prepared to deal with all this. Seriously now, whose brilliant idea was it that I could handle this job? Definitely not mine.

"How soon can you come back to work? Will you work part-time for a while?" I yearned for an answer in the affirmative.

"Apparently my body doesn't want to get back as badly as I do," he laughed. "Things aren't healing the way they're supposed to. I have another evaluation next week, but the doctor doesn't seem optimistic. He's even talking about further surgery. Believe me, that's not what I want to hear."

It wasn't what I wanted to hear either. When would there be news that was uplifting instead of discouraging? What a mess I'd gotten myself into. The most ironic part was that I didn't have enough free time to search for jobs in the sociology field, so it didn't look like I could move on any time soon, even if Al returned.

My bank account was healthier than it had ever been. Living free-of-charge in Al's cottage and having almost no spare time were definitely good for my budget, (and the tips I made doing outdoor drink service didn't hurt either), but sooner or later I was going to need a career of my own. I wondered how "pretending to be a restaurant manager" looked on resumes. Perhaps I could add "attempting to solve a murder" to the list.

The officers had been wandering through the building, studying the waitstations, looking behind the bar, and basically getting in the way of my staff who were trying to prepare for opening. The officers finished their inspection, and when finally they hurried off I closed my eyes for a moment, vowing to myself that I'd focus my attention and be the best manager I could be.

I walked out of my office into the kitchen, and there was Brad in my face saying, "Jeff didn't show up again! Are you going to fire him this time?"

Okay. Deep sigh. A good manager deals with difficult matters efficiently, so I simply answered, "Yes," and walked right back into the office.

"Jeff, this is Ashley calling. You've failed to show up for work once too often, and I'm going to take your name off the schedule permanently," I stated to Jeff's voicemail. I can't begin to explain how relieved I was that he hadn't answered. I wasn't looking forward to the day when I'd have to verbally confront an employee.

Having seen him in our parking lot an hour earlier I was exasperated. Did he know I'd seen him? Did he care? Chances are he'd already quit in his mind, but I felt good about having dealt with the issue. If he'd been checking his caller I.D. he probably knew what the message was without listening.

"Great. Glad to hear it." Brad broke out one of his rare smiles when I reported that he would no longer have to deal with Jeff. "He's no great loss. I had to watch him constantly, or he'd throw away cutlery."

"Throw away cutlery?"

"Yeah. You know, when he scraped plates before loading them in the dishmachine, if a fork or something had been left on the plate he'd just scrape it into the garbage along with the food. I actually made him

121

dig through his garbage one night to find all of the important stuff he'd thrown out."

"It never occurred to me that anyone would do that. No wonder we're getting low on teaspoons."

"He was pretty useless, and probably cost us a lot of money," Brad lamented, shaking his head. "Now you'll have to hire someone new. Before next weekend of course."

As if there was anyone in town who was looking for work. It was tourist season, and every business in town was understaffed. Maybe our youngest employees had friends who'd like their first job…

"If Al won't trust me to run the place, at least my kitchen should be properly staffed!" he bluntly declared.

A light went on in my head. Wow! That explained a lot. Brad had expected to cover for Al while he was out, and Al had chosen me instead. Brad's attitude made some sense now; I would have resented my presence too. My inexperience had to be especially rankling to someone who valued perfection.

I committed myself to take his ranting in stride, now that I knew what was behind it. I still considered him unnecessarily and outrageously rude, but at least I knew why I was his target. I decided that hiring a replacement for Jeff needed to become a priority. For Brad's mental attitude, and my own.

A conversation I overheard that afternoon made my heart beat a bit faster.

"Wasn't that murder just too awful? Speaking of knives, I got a wonderful new knife the other day, totally by accident. Joe took his car to that full-service car wash in Oak Landing, and the car wash guy said he found it under the seat. It wasn't ours, but I guess it is now. It's amazing how sharp it is, and it's good quality, too."

I immediately texted Gregg and asked him to come back. I didn't even know the woman's name, and I hated admitting to listening in on her discussion, but I knew the officers needed to hear her story. Another knife found in a vehicle. Meant to cast suspicion in yet another direction? The sinister events in Windsor Grove had definitely not come to an end.

When Gregg arrived I explained the situation. He waited outdoors to speak with the woman, and (to my dismay) never reported back to me. If I expected to get our knife back I was in error, it was never mentioned again.

CHAPTER 15

"How well did you know Mark?"

I asked that question dozens of times that day, and began to regret my decision. Everyone had a nervous need to discuss Mark; everyone had a story to share. I learned what it was like to stand behind Mark in a checkout line. I learned that he smiled and waved when he stopped to let pedestrians cross. I learned what foods he enjoyed, what beers he drank, and even (believe it or not) what size shoes he wore.

I learned a few (very few) things that might be important. Not likely, but I could hope.

"I never actually met the man," Mr. Horner said in his surprisingly squeaky voice. "My late wife's maiden name was Fischer, spelled the same way as Mark's, so I've wondered if they were distant relatives. She was born in Green Bay, but had relatives all over the Midwest."

"We lived in various large cities; after she passed on I moved to Windsor Grove because I needed to be somewhere quiet for a while. Realized I feel at home here. Never left." (Did anyone else know that Mr. Horner had been married? The officers probably did, but this could be important information for the local gossip mill).

He fidgeted with his spoon, hesitating before he continued. "Did you know that my Abigail and I ran a restaurant at one time? It was fun, but hard work." My question was working; he was sharing information. It didn't seem particularly useful, but there were some interesting coincidences.

"I've lost touch with most of her family," Mr. Horner went on. "I wonder if I should reach out to them now, to find out if they're related to Mark. But that seems highly unlikely."

After I'd left his table he pulled a small electronic game from his pocket, and played it with the concentration of a teenager. Were his hands trembling slightly? I couldn't be sure. Probably just my imagination.

"It really is a small world," Ron Barber, the president of the Town Board, said when I asked the question of him. "I actually lived in Mark's hometown, Plainfield, for a few years, but it was so long ago that he would have been a young boy. I can't remember knowing anyone named Fischer when I was there." He hesitated, stared out the window, shook his head and said quietly, "No, no one."

Mostly I heard what a pleasant personality Mark had, how well-liked he was by everyone acquainted with him. It also became clear that many locals had never met the newcomer, and now felt guilty for not going out of their way to be welcoming.

"How well did you know Mark?" I'd asked several people sitting in Zachary's Lounge. It was a great conversation starter, but I'd almost given up on uncovering anything useful.

"It's a funny thing," Renata mentioned as she loaded the glassware washer. "Last night I heard a man at the bar say that he'd recently met Mark's ex-girlfriend. It was crowded, and I was busy. By the time I turned around I couldn't tell who'd said it. But I had the impression he'd met her somewhere here in Wisconsin." She shrugged her shoulders. "I wish I knew who said that."

So did I.

As the day progressed I added a few notes to the list in my desk drawer, mostly to convince myself I was accomplishing something. I added our ex-dishwasher Jeff to the category *People Who Act Suspiciously*, for his odd meeting with Man-in-Brown. I added Ron Barber's name followed by a question mark to the list of people who'd known Mark previously.

And I started another category, *Who Had the Opportunity to Leave the Threatening Note?* Unfortunately that list included almost everyone in town, with the entire Unincorporated staff right at the top.

I was fairly certain that the officers already knew *almost* everything, possibly *everything,* I'd been able to learn.

Perhaps it would be new information for Gregg that Mr. Horner's wife had been a Fischer, and that Ron Barber had lived in Plainfield. I was most proud of learning that someone had recently met Mark's ex-girlfriend, but it certainly would have been more helpful if I'd known who it was.

Did it matter that Mr. Horner had run a restaurant in the past? Did his nervousness indicate anything beyond a high-strung personality? He'd know where to search for professional knives...and it would be simple for him to grab a few placemats. Thinking of it, I realized that no one had torn up more placemats than him. But hundreds of other guests had the same opportunity. It probably ranked near the bottom of the importance-factor scale.

It was a remarkable coincidence that both the murder victim and the Town Board President had relocated from Plainfield Indiana to Windsor Grove, this very small town. If it had been more than pure chance, if there'd been any previous connection between the two men, I assumed that Ron Barber would have volunteered the information. He wouldn't, of course, if there was something nefarious involved, but Ron had lived here for decades; anything suspicious seemed unlikely. It was a curious factor just the same.

I'd always considered myself a good judge of character. So, which of the many suspects made me feel uneasy? Definitely Man-in-Brown, Mary Lou, and my fired employee Jeff. Mr. Horner, occasionally. I didn't know enough about Todd from the Flower Shoppe, and knew nothing at all about Mark's ex-girlfriend. I was always on edge around Chef Brad, but that was a different story altogether.

Unfortunately, Roger was probably the only person in town with a serious criminal record, and I did *not* want the guilty party to be a member of my staff. I'd have to be diligent in garnering information about Windsor Grove residents, things the officers might not be aware of.

Every guest could fill a spot on my list, it was perturbing. I found myself glancing over my shoulder, watching for unusual movements or activities. Being suspicious of every acquaintance is unsettling; it became difficult to fully relax. This whole homicide mess was definitely not good for my mental attitude.

A few hours later, when the last guests were leaving the dining room, a surge of laughter announced that we still had a good crowd in the Lounge. I wandered in to see if Renata needed help, and discovered I knew most of the bar patrons. Several couples were enjoying a nightcap. At the far end of the bar sat many of our staff, who'd come in for a drink on their night off.

Much to my surprise, at a pub table along the far wall sat Officers Littner and Milton, in casual clothing enjoying frosty mugs of beer. I knew they weren't on duty 24/7, but seeing them relaxing at a bar was a bit disconcerting.

I greeted the other guests, said a few words to the staff members, made sure Renata was caught up with drink orders, and then went to chat with the officers.

"We decided that we'd been spending so much time here, we should spend some money here too!" Gregg Littner said as I approached.

"Unincorporated is starting to feel like a second home," Detective Milton agreed, "We might as well come here to relax." With a shrug he added, "Also, every place else in town is closed already. I can't believe how early everyone around here packs it in for the night. Care to join us?"

He was right; nightlife in Windsor Grove was almost non-existent. It worked well for us. Anyone looking for a drink after dinner had few options, and Zachary's Lounge was often busier than our dining room.

With the dining room closed, and the kitchen staff finishing their cleaning, I decided it was alright to declare myself off-duty. I took the officers up on their offer, poured myself a glass of a popular California varietal, and pulled up a stool (although actually climbing onto that stool brought a painful reminder of my self-defense workout).

Gregg raised his eyebrows when he noticed my grimace.

"Yesterday's self-defense class was more intense than I'd anticipated," I explained.

"We heard that it was well-attended. That's good news; an informed populace is a safer populace."

"Detective Milton, I have a question," I said, hoping to change the subject. I didn't want to discuss the need to be prepared. I preferred to act as though there was nothing to be prepared for.

"First thing, please call me Rob," Officer Milton requested. "Especially when I'm off duty. People don't feel comfortable around detectives in social situations unless it's obvious that we're not on the clock. In small towns everyone knows who we are, so we try to have two different personas, one official, one not. Tonight is definitely *not*."

"She calls me Gregg most of the time, most of the residents do. In towns like this we're seldom referred to by title, even when on duty," Gregg explained to Milton. "It's nice to have everyone think of you as a friend. It helps when we need to gather information."

My curiosity got the best of me; I couldn't wait any longer to ask Rob the question that had been at the top of my mind and everyone else's.

"So what did you learn when you went to Mark's funeral?" Guests had been asking me this all day, and I decided this was my best chance to get an answer.

"I wondered how long it would be before someone asked," Rob laughed. "I learned exactly what I expected. Mark was well-liked by everyone who knew him. There was a huge crowd at the funeral home; again at the church. His family, friends, neighbors, school mates, and past coworkers all turned out; no one could believe that Mark had been murdered. He was apparently the same kind, quiet, dependable guy when he lived in Plainfield that he was here."

"I spent the day after the funeral talking with the people who'd known him best. The girlfriend who'd broken up with him before he moved here was devastated. She said he was the nicest guy she'd ever known. He was just too quiet for her tastes; she needed to move on. He took the breakup hard, obviously, but they parted friends according to her."

"I was talking to Renata, our bartender, earlier today," I said, "and she overheard a customer saying that he'd met Mark's ex-girlfriend recently, somewhere in Wisconsin. Has she been around here?"

"That doesn't sound likely. She has a demanding job, I don't think she gets much free time," Detective Milton mused. "Anyway, how would anyone have known it was Mark's girlfriend, unless she was announcing it? It was more likely some gal making up stories to get attention. I doubt if there's anything to it." I hoped he was right.

"I talked to some of Mark's high school teachers," he divulged, "looked at his records at Indiana U, checked the local police files, and found absolutely nothing of any help. He's a guy with a completely clean record, who seems to have been liked by everyone who ever met him. I didn't expect anything else, but we had to check," Rob said with a shake of his head.

"Mark's mother was hurt when he moved to Wisconsin, but she knew he needed a change. She didn't fully understand his choice of such a small town, but she and Mark's dad had planned to visit Windsor Grove sometime this summer." The three of us sat quietly for a moment, thinking of a life lost.

"There's another thing I've been wondering about." This was my best chance to get answers, so I continued the questioning. "Don't most killers use guns? A knife seems sort of odd."

Rob handled the answer to that. "A gun is the more common weapon; almost 70% of murders are committed with a firearm. Those are the crimes that get the most media coverage, but knives are the second most common weapon. They factor in about 12% of murders.

"Some people are uncomfortable with guns, even killers. Others just find knives more satisfying; a stabbing feels more personal, requires more emotion and anger. Also, a knife requires no skill or training, no permit, and can't be traced. Law enforcement considers knives, in certain circumstances, to be lethal force instruments, just like guns."

Okay, that answered my question, but certainly didn't do anything to make me feel any better.

"So, have any more people found knives in their cars?" I asked. That was another troubling thought that had occupied my brain; someone out there had more of our knives.

"No. So far it seems to have been just the two isolated events," was the answer. "Of course most people don't clean their vehicles thoroughly. There could be several other knives out there, and no one would know." Not really a comforting answer.

Things had quieted down in the bar while we were talking. Looking around I realized the last few couples were paying for their drinks, getting ready to leave; the staff members had gone home. I wondered if they'd left because I was there to overhear their conversations.

If so, it was okay with me. I was glad to know that our staff had formed friendships with each other, but it was obvious that many of them had no intention of becoming friends of mine. That was fine as far as I was concerned; I needed to maintain at least some semblance of authority. Not the easiest thing to do when they all had more experience than I did.

The officers moved to sit at the bar, and I let Renata leave. I ran a final load through the glassware washer, wiping down the bar surface while we talked. I told them the things I'd learned by chatting with guests; and while they listened politely I couldn't tell if I was giving them any new information. They wavered between sharing information freely and being closed-mouthed about their investigation.

I wanted to be fully in the loop about recent developments, but I could see that it wasn't going to happen. Instead the guys started a complicated discussion about baseball regulations (the Brewers were having a miserable year), followed by a mild disagreement about one model of squad car versus another. If we couldn't discuss the investigation, I wanted to talk celebrities and fashion. I needed girlfriends!

When Gregg and Rob had finished their beers and were ready to leave they offered to walk me back to the cottage. I happily accepted. As we wandered through the shadowy woods they gave me some safety tips, and then took a moment to check that my windows and doors had secure locks. After they left I felt better knowing they'd checked things out.

I climbed into bed that night hugging Teddy Maxwell tightly. I didn't want to admit to the amount of tension I'd started to feel any time I was alone.

CHAPTER 16

My night was again spent tossing and turning. I finally fell into a restless sleep with ongoing dreams of knives and strangers, torn scraps of paper and floral funeral arrangements. When my alarm went off I felt as if I hadn't slept at all.

Reluctantly admitting it was time to welcome another day, I peeled my eyes open, looked up at the ugly cracked plaster ceiling, and decided to become proactive, not reactive, at work. Four days ago I'd made the same vow, this time I intended to follow through. First and foremost it was up to me to manage Al's restaurant, and up to me to arrange for food at Windsor Day.

I would help Rob and Gregg any way I could, but I had to accept that there'd been a homicide, this wasn't a game, and it was my job to keep things at Unincorporated running as normally as possible despite it. I was anxious to have it solved and over with, but until then my first priority would be maintaining an upbeat atmosphere at work.

With little time for shopping, I was trying to make do with a few new additions to my far too casual college wardrobe. Basic skirts and slacks were in constant rotation with the workplace appropriate tops I'd purchased locally. A quick stop at Valerie's Boutique had put a dent in my wallet without adding much variety. It was clear that I was often underdressed; a stunning pair of shoes didn't do much to fill the gap.

Someday there'd be time to build a better wardrobe. The resort-wear shops in Windsor Grove had few things that were appropriate; a trip to The Mall of America would be heavenly. Or Mayfair Mall in Milwaukee. I was starting to feel like even a shopping day in Oak Landing would be helpful. Between dealing with the tourists, the officers and my staff, I didn't know how I'd ever manage to acquire more than a tee-shirt.

"I hate to whine," I'd said the last time I called Bekah, "but I'm desperate to have more clothes. Nicer clothes. Professional things."

"Whine away, that's what I'm here for. Why don't you order some fun things online? You can get tons of cute clothes, and it will be so much fun to get your mail!"

She was right about ordering clothes online. But any thought of it being fun to visit the post office was doubtful; it was clear that Bekah had never lived anywhere quite like Windsor Grove!

I made a point of dressing in bright tones that day, took a few extra minutes with makeup, put on a favorite pair of embellished flats similar to those in a recent fashion magazine, and committed myself to enjoying the day.

Practicality had finally won over fashion as far as footwear was concerned. My flat shoes were being put into constant service while my heels languished in various closets. Someday I'd be able to resume my relationship with favorite footwear, but I was currently resigned to choosing comfort and safety above style. Mom would have been proud; Bekah, horrified.

While walking to the restaurant I took a moment to listen to the sounds surrounding me: the gentle splash of water on the shore, the roaring sound of a jet ski, children's shrieking laughter, a single-engine plane overhead, all the things that could easily become background noise, but when brought to the forefront could alter a person's perception of reality.

Reality was not murder in the woods, reality was a resort community filled with vacationing families. Or so I told myself. Constant worry would do me no good, and wouldn't lead to anything constructive at Unincorporated either.

The shining surface of the lake reflected a shimmering image of blue sky and lush greenery. A mallard couple, gliding sedately by, seemed to have the right idea; enjoy the moment, relax, go with the flow. A wise bit of advice.

"Great outfit, Ashley! I love that color combination."

"Thanks, Renata. These colors make me feel good." I started the day off with a smile.

If I had to focus on the concept that life was continuing on as usual, then focus I would.

That sounded like a wise plan, but I was too keyed up to fully relax as if everything was normal. I caught myself jumping at sudden noises, and obsessing over any phone call that was a "wrong number."

During one afternoon lull I tried to unwind at my cottage, to decompress from recent restlessness. But rather than relaxing I found myself pacing in circles. I had too much nervous energy to stay still so I decided to use another tactic I'd always found calming, a good brisk walk. I changed into athletic walking shoes (which looked ridiculous with my outfit), and headed into the forest hoping no one would see me.

Various paths and clearings made for an interesting trek; I found myself reliving the days when my cousins and I spent hours imagining ourselves adventurers in the wilderness. We'd played Robin Hood, Lewis and Clark, and African Safari. I had many great memories from times in this forest. As I walked I felt a renewed connection to the wooded area.

When I neared the dusty narrow fire lane I realized that I had unintentionally wandered toward the site of Mark's untimely death. At least I hoped it had been unintentional; I've known my subconscious to play stranger tricks on me.

Heaps of accumulated debris told me I'd reached the secluded clearing where local teens hung out. It was bad enough that they had illegal drinking parties in the woods, couldn't they at least clean up after themselves? *I was starting to sound like my mother...*

Gregg had said that the murder had taken place very near this clearing, and my curiosity led me over to the road, as if there might be something dramatic to view. There wasn't, of course, it appeared to be the same peaceful road it had always been. Any sense of something amiss would exist only in a person's mind.

As I surveyed the scenery, a jogger came trotting along the road. As he neared I realized it was Ron Barber, town board president. He stopped to chat, running in place for a moment.

"Hi, Ashley. It's nice to know that you get some time away from work. That's a tough job you've got." He never focused on my face, looking off into the woods instead. "I think everyone in town is being drawn to this site. I can't count the number of people I've met along this road during the last few weeks." He paused, wiping the sweat off his face with the hem of his shirt. *Gross!*

"I wanted a relaxing walk, but somehow this is where I ended up," I shook my head. "I should have gone in another direction. This isn't very calming."

"In the past I've always enjoyed running along this fire lane. Ever since I moved here these woods have been my favorite place to find solitude, it's been the perfect mid-point in my workout. Now that I'm constantly meeting people who want to talk, I'll have to find a different lonely road." He'd been staring at a spot on the road, then again gazed into the woods.

"Maybe someday soon people will stop coming out here as if it's a tourist attraction." He followed that comment with a deep-throated hearty laugh that sounded forced. His mouth twisted into a smile that didn't reach his eyes.

"If you'll excuse me, I have to get going," he was suddenly speaking hurriedly, "there's a zoning meeting tonight that I can't miss. Thanks for understanding."

Ron jogged quickly away, leaving me contrite for interfering with his workout routine, and giving serious consideration to the route I'd chosen that day. Was I so fixated on Mark's death that my mind had led my legs directly to the one place guaranteed *not* to make me feel calm and relaxed?

It seemed ironic that I'd wandered to this area intending to be alone with my thoughts, only to encounter someone who'd lived in Mark's hometown. Ron had seemed ill-at-ease; what was up with his constant staring into the woods or at the ground? He'd never looked directly at my face; that seemed out of character for this gregarious man. Should I read anything into it? Probably not.

This section of the forest seemed so peaceful, and was such an ideal place to commune with nature, that it was hard to conceive of brutality being part of this scene. If anyone concluded that it felt *different* here since the tragedy, as several guests had told me, it was purely a function of an overactive imagination.

I moved slowly back into the woods, turned toward the road, and stood there trying to envision what happened on that fateful day. What kind of person could deliberately contrive to kill another human being? In this idyllic setting it seemed impossible, but it was fact, not fiction.

The only way I could make any sense of the murder was to conjure up a person who had psychologically lost touch with reality. I had to imagine someone who was emotionally unstable, who had developed brutal, almost animal, instincts. It wasn't a pleasant thought.

My plan for afternoon relaxation had only added to the unease I'd been feeling; I would have been better off surrounded by the diners and staff. How could the beauty of nature compete with the horror of homicide? It didn't seem fair somehow. It was as if the world had to stop spinning on its axis in order for such a horrendous crime to have been committed in this lovely setting.

Windsor Grove had once been my happy place, my refuge. What had happened to that tranquil town? The air itself now seemed filled with fear and anger and apprehension. I missed the old Windsor Grove. I wanted my carefree community back.

Increased determination was building inside me. Whoever was responsible would live to regret it; someone had to pay for the assault on our content lifestyle; murderous actions couldn't be allowed to go unpunished. I felt offended on Mark's behalf, but also on behalf of our picturesque forest and our trusting community, on behalf of myself and everyone else whose world was in upheaval over this senseless crime.

Windsor Grove residents are normally easy-going, but we have our limits, and those limits were stretched to the breaking point. The crime would be a constant thorn in everyone's side until there was closure. Even though I was new in town, I'd spent vacations here since I was young and felt the community pride as strongly as anyone. The crime wouldn't be allowed to grow cold; the guilty party would be hunted until caught. The community was demanding vengeance, and vengeance it would get.

So much for my walk being calming; I now felt enough anger and tension for the whole community, for every area native, and for anyone who'd ever called Windsor Grove home.

Over the past week, when I listened to music I found myself selecting loud angry tunes that reflected my mood. It wasn't my normal choice of genre, but currently it felt right. I was becoming a different person, a vindictive person. A person I didn't really like.

In daylight I was constantly aware of the killer on the loose, of my own vulnerability and the potential threat to everyone in Windsor Grove. My stress level was at a previously unimaginable height. I couldn't shut down the threatening pictures in my brain.

My nights, however, were the worst. I'd never before had trouble falling into a deep sleep; I would crawl into bed and immediately doze off. Suddenly I restlessly slumbered only after my exhausted brain rehashed all the ongoing horror.

"It's ironic that my restaurant dreams aren't about dropping things anymore," Carrie commented as she rushed past me carrying a tray laden with sizzling steak plates. "Now they're about guests getting stabbed in the dining room!"

"You too?" asked another server nearby. "I'm glad I'm not the only one. But those aren't dreams, they're nightmares!" They laughed at the shared experience, and continued on with their duties as if this was a normal part of the restaurant world.

Smack in the middle of that evening's hectic dinner hour, when I was wishing I'd scheduled another server, and had a few choice thoughts about the busser who'd called in sick at the last minute, I noticed a guest waving frantically to me from across the room.

"It says here we can have a tour of the kitchen," an artificially blond woman wearing too much perfume and a gaudy flowered blouse announced as I approached. "We want one as soon as we're done eating."

Her three tablemates nodded, but remained silent, as if accustomed to her taking charge.

"Of course. I'll be happy to do that for you. If I'm not nearby just ask your server to get me. My name's Ashley."

"Okay, Ashley. We'll tell you when we're ready."

I headed to the kitchen to inform Brad. I knew next to nothing about the kitchen procedures and equipment, so he would have to take the lead.

"You're kidding me! Now? Why now?" He turned to glare at me. "This is the worst possible time!" My thoughts exactly. The clattering of dishes, the sizzling of the grills, orders being called from one frazzled fry cook to another, told me that no one had a moment to spare.

"Why can't anyone ever ask for a tour when it's slow? I love showing people my kitchen, but Jesus Christ, you'd think they'd use some common sense! Can't they see how many tickets are hanging on the wheel? Our customers are freaking idiots!" He did, however, grudgingly agree to conduct the tour.

Shortly after, when I took the two couples into the kitchen, Brad was effusive and welcoming. He explained how the Alto-Shaam cook-and-hold oven produces exceptionally tender prime rib; he showed them the inside of the walk-in coolers and freezers; he demonstrated the use of a trunion kettle. He answered the men's mechanical questions, and was charming to the ladies. I didn't recognize this Brad; it certainly wasn't the chef I usually dealt with.

He looked toward me and rolled his eyes when the woman complained, "I can't believe how hot it is in here! You should crank up the air conditioner."

She then made a huge show of using her hand like a little fan, as if to prove her point. No matter that she was standing in a room filled with ovens, fryers, grills, and compressors. Commercial kitchens get hot for a reason, and mandated ventilation systems move cool air out along with warm. Her comments did nothing to endear her to Brad. Or to anyone else working in the kitchen.

"If you'll excuse me, I have to get back to work," Brad said immediately after that. Inhaling deeply, then exhaling slowly, he looked to the ceiling, turned away and went to assist the fry cooks. I was left to finish with the guests.

As soon as he was out of hearing range, I was bombarded with questions.

"So where did you keep the knife that killed that young man? Did you get to see it afterward? Was there still blood on it? Was it totally gruesome?" the perfumed lady demanded impertinently. Her dining companions looked a bit shocked, and tried to pretend they hadn't heard her.

"Is it true that more knives were taken? I really want to see where you store your knives! Do you have a duplicate of the murder weapon?" *Word travels way too fast in this town*, I thought, *and everyone thinks they have a right to know everything.*

I don't remember how I responded, but I know that somehow I managed to usher them out of the kitchen. As they headed back to their table I heard Perfume Lady say, "You know, we never did see their knife storage! How disappointing! And wouldn't you expect the manager to dress more professionally?" *If Uncle Al doesn't get back to work soon my brain might explode.*

"Thanks for helping me out. I appreciate it," I said later to Brad.

"This place is turning into some kind of sideshow, or maybe the whole damn three-ring circus!" he grouched. I stifled a laugh, and was surprised when Brad smiled in return.

He was right about the circus. Our well ordered and efficient restaurant had become a curiosity-seekers destination. And there was no end in sight.

CHAPTER 17

There's something wonderful about waking to the scent of a forest. It's effective aromatherapy, calming yet energizing. The absorption of nature and the environment…an ideal way to start a week…a reminder that good things and honest people can prevail.

On Monday mornings my sales reps drop in to pick up their weekly orders. That Monday, when I brought up the topic of Windsor Day, they were all immediately on board. I was elated; it wasn't going to be the nightmare I'd imagined.

"I'll talk to my boss about donations. There's an account for things like that," the rep from our major food supplier offered when I broached the subject. He proceeded to pull up figures on his laptop showing how much food other area communities had used during similar fundraisers. "We can give you a fairly accurate idea how much you'll need for this type of event."

"We have portable freezer bins for ice cream products. I'll get you the details. You can use them free of charge as long as you get the frozen treats from us," our dairy deliveryman offered.

The new driver from Wholesale Wholegrains called Bob Winchester right away to ask about discount pricing for bread products.

Our equipment provider started making lists of things we'd need, things I hadn't thought of like napkin dispensers and extension cords, suggesting area businesses we might borrow them from. I made a note to find out who was getting the hundreds of pounds of charcoal we'd need. I assumed there was much useless duplication here; The Marys were probably way ahead of me on many things. But it would be better to have duplication than to fall short.

Everyone's helpfulness and enthusiasm amazed me. Each vendor I talked to had suggestions, along with equipment available on loan, and special pricing providing they could get publicity at the event. It was all in a day's work for them, and it added variety to their jobs. Several even offered to be present on Windsor Day to make sure things ran smoothly and we wouldn't run out of product. It became apparent that Uncle Al had been right. It wasn't going to be an ordeal after all. Still, I kept my fingers crossed.

With that task underway, I left work and drove my Beetle across the county to the Wholesale Wholegrains production facility. I thought it would be courteous to deliver the invoice for Mark's memorial desserts in person. Truthfully, I have to admit, I was curious about his workplace and coworkers.

As I exited my car a woman on the sidewalk, camera in hand, yelled, "Do you work here? Do you have any new information about the murder investigation?" *Another intrusive reporter. They had become fixtures in the area.* I kept walking, feeling sorry for the employees who dealt with this every time they came to work.

Rose was at the reception desk when I walked in. We chatted for a minute, then I handed her the statement.

"Is that all?" she asked when she saw the total. "For all those scrumptious desserts? We expected the total to be much higher than that. The trays were being refilled for a couple of hours! Are you sure you included everything?"

"Actually, a dessert buffet is one of the least expensive things you can do," I explained. "That's because nothing on the table was full-sized. The bars were cut in thirds, pies and tortes were cut in tens, we had mini-éclairs, tasting portions, and so on."

"If someone orders a carryout dessert tray that's how we size things," I was probably telling her more than she wanted to know. "That way each guest can enjoy several smaller portions. And you were all enjoying our bottomless cup of coffee, which also kept the cost down. The total does include tax and tip, so it's a complete number, nothing needs to be added."

"Well, the total is certainly reasonable. It was a great buffet, we appreciated it. I think everyone needed sweets after such a sad afternoon." She hesitated, and then made the offer I'd been hoping for, "Have you been to Wholesale Wholegrains before? Would you like a tour of the plant?"

"Yes, I sure would, if it's no trouble." I was enthusiastic about her offer. I'd never been in a commercial bakery, and I'd been hoping for the opportunity to look behind the scenes.

Rose picked up her phone, paging the shift supervisor to explain her request.

The man who joined us at the desk a few moments later handed me a lab coat, hair covering, and shoe covers. "Leave your handbag with Rose; it will be safe here," he instructed. He then led me to an access room where I donned the provided attire, which matched his own, while he explained that the coverings were a required part of creating a sterile environment for food preparation.

"We only do tours for people on a need-to-know basis. As a customer of Wholesale Wholegrains you and your staff can request a visit, but you'll never see us give a tour to a scout troop or service organization. Please don't touch anything once we're beyond this door." He proceeded to lead me through the vast work areas.

I was shown proofing cabinets, a huge dough mixer, banks of commercial ovens and convection ovens, the packaging equipment, the loading dock, and a massive silo filled with flour. Everyone was hard at work, paying no attention to me as I watched the commercial baking process. Most memorable was the permeating aroma; I love the scent of bread baking in an oven, and I was salivating after my time in that factory.

After the fascinating tour, I thanked the shift supervisor profusely, and went out front to say goodbye to Rose.

"The state crime lab has released Mark's delivery van," she said, "but no one wants to drive it. It's had a thorough sanitizing, but everyone knows what happened. We don't know if we'll ever use it again. We all feel numb about…the incident, and we still refer to 'Mark's Route' and 'Mark's Locker'. Even though most of the workers didn't have much contact with him, it's going to be hard to put behind us." She looked down at her desk, slowly shaking her head.

Having a better understanding of the baking industry, and a clearer picture of Mark's job, I thanked Rose for arranging my tour, and left to return to work. As I drove, I wondered about the Wholegrains workers. Could any of the employees, working so diligently, have disliked Mark? Did any of them belong on my *suspects* list?

I realized for the first time just how many acquaintances Mark had whom I didn't even know. Any thoughts I had about helping solve the crime suddenly seemed totally unrealistic.

During lunch that day I made a point of chatting with guests at every table, and complimenting each staff member for something they did well. It was more difficult in the kitchen, where I felt overwhelmed and uninformed. But I found reason to praise every employee, and lunch service seemed to flow smoothly.

I took a phone call in the early afternoon and heard Bekah's voice. "Ashley, it's such a beautiful day I just had to call you!" Talking to Bekah always cheered me; it seemed appropriate that she should call on a day when I was determined to remain upbeat.

"Can I come visit tomorrow, and stay a few days? I have to get away from this whole job search thing. Sunning on a beach and checking out trendy shops and boutiques is just what I need." Always impetuous, spur-of-the-moment plans were exactly what I expected from Bekah.

We discussed details for her visit. She'd stay with me in Al's cottage; I'd take extra time away from Unincorporated to spend with her. I had gained confidence in my staff's ability to function without supervision; long-time staff could carry the load, seasonal staff had become dependable followers. When I did have to be at work Bekah could easily occupy herself visiting art galleries and souvenir shops. We'd catch up on each other's lives when I could be away from work.

"I miss our long chats," she said. "You'll have to tell me absolutely everything about your job, especially about that murder. I saw it on the news…they're calling it 'Heartland Homicide'." I crossed my fingers and assured her that of course I'd tell her everything. The details that I'd been told in confidence I'd remain mum about. She'd never know the difference.

The officers had asked me not to mention the message on the placemat scrap; amazingly it seemed to have remained a secret. Our guests, who couldn't keep quiet about anything, hadn't mentioned it, so I assumed that word hadn't gotten out. I hadn't heard any conversation about a threatening note or a torn scrap of paper; everyone was taking Lynette and John's sudden absence for granted.

The two knives that had been planted in vehicles had also not been mentioned. It was curious, given the way word spreads in Windsor Grove, that those things could remain off the radar.

With Mark's death several days removed, the locals' main topic of conversation had reverted back to Rupert's campaign. I was glad I'd refused to display his sign on restaurant property; he was becoming more controversial as time went on. He was running unopposed in his own party, but the competing party was busy trying to make him seem ineffectual (successfully, as far as I could tell). I really wasn't interested in local politics, but I was fascinated by the average citizen's sudden opinionated positions.

"He's definitely the kind of guy who runs for office…thinks his opinion is more important than anyone else's," a particularly verbal guest in the Lounge announced. "We were together in college, and he was always in the middle of whatever had people riled up."

"I heard he got in some trouble back then," another man remarked.

"It never amounted to much. He had to pay a few fines. Leading protests; handing out inflammatory pamphlets; making speeches. Everyone knew he was mainly interested in getting attention; a collegiate version of a professional protester."

The word *narcissist* popped into my head, a memory from a psychology lecture, something to do with an inflated self-image, and a demand for admiration. At the time I'd thought it applied aptly to Dr. Rogerson, the professor giving the lecture. Fantasies of success and power…an accomplished person who exaggerates achievements and abilities…it still sounded more like the dictator who ran my psych lab, but it could easily describe someone in politics, too.

"If there's attention being handed out, he's there to grab his share," criticized a man nearby, nodding. "He still tries to create divisive issues. Did you hear him prattling on about wanting a debate on increasing the military budget? If he's supposed to be so smart, how come he hasn't figured out that the Wisconsin State Senate doesn't control the military? I think he's got a few screws loose!"

"Oh, but he shows up at every church event, and all the fundraisers. He really does help our community," the man's wife argued. "And he's so friendly whenever I see him," she remembered with a wistful smile.

Another woman at the bar piped up, "He has a personality that makes a person feel good when he talks to you."

Her husband grumbled, "I'd rather elect someone who can actually accomplish something than someone who smiles pretty at the ladies." The men laughed at that comment, but the women all shot dirty looks in his direction.

I was happy to see Renata quickly change the subject. It was never good business to have disagreements get out of hand. I had visions of calling Gregg to break up a political argument in the Lounge. I never wanted that picture to become reality.

After closing, when I headed out the back door, I was startled to see several off-duty employees hanging around the wooded area beyond the dumpsters along with some young people I didn't recognize.

The odor of beer mingled with that of tobacco and other smoked substances as the group laughed at a story that Roger, the fry cook who'd lied on his job application, was telling.

"Um…hi Ashley," several of them mumbled rather insolently, indicating I was unexpected and unwelcome, even though I was the only one who belonged there at that hour.

I realized that one of the group was Jeff, who I'd removed permanently from the schedule the day before. I didn't mention this in front of his former coworkers; it didn't seem right. It might even have been illegal; labor law and confidentiality was a field that I knew little about. However there were things I could say, and I didn't hesitate.

"You shouldn't be smoking this close to the woods during drought conditions…or ever! You're all smart enough to know that the woods are like tinder right now. Grow up! Don't let your bad habits risk other people's lives. Go out front to the parking lot if you're smoking. There's better lighting out there anyway. Move! *Now!*"

I knew that better lighting was the last thing they wanted, but I really didn't care.

Being young and foolish is no excuse for being careless too. I was angry, and I knew it showed. I'd never spoken to the staff that sternly, and they seemed shocked. I might not have been accomplished at my job, but I certainly knew that I had to protect Al's property.

"Put your ashes in the sand urns by the door. And don't leave cigarette butts lying around!"

They grumbled goodbyes, put out their cigarettes, and headed toward their cars. It may have been my imagination, but I thought I heard "bitch" muttered under someone's breath. Well, I'd done what had to be done. *Live with it, Ashley.*

Tires squealed as cars sped out of the parking lot. I wondered what they'd been laughing about. Actually I wondered why they'd been out back at all. It seemed like an odd place to gather, whatever the reason. Now my relationship with the staff would be more tenuous than ever.

Heading along the path to the cottage, I stopped for a moment to look through the trees and down toward the water. I was suddenly aware of the darkness, and remembered that I wasn't supposed to walk alone into the woods at night. There was a fair amount of moonlight; with the additional reflection off the water I could clearly see my way to the cottage. But dark waving shadows surrounded the area, creating mysterious shapes that made the back of my neck tingle.

What was that sound? An animal, no doubt, rustling along the ground. And that movement in the trees? Nothing to be concerned about. *Stop worrying.*

"Help!" An ear-piercing scream echoed through the trees. A familiar voice again shouted, "Help!" from the direction of the parking lot.

145

"Help! Ashley! Help, somebody, please!" The shrill frantic plea ended in an eerie whimper.

Alarmed, I ran back toward the restaurant to find Carrie O'Brien, the new server, leaning against her car, shivering and sobbing and looking terrified. Renata had reached Carrie before I did, and was trying to comfort her. In the artificial light of the parking lot Renata's dark hair and height made Carrie seem even more pale and petite.

"What's wrong? What happened?" I reached out to give Carrie a hug, but her tense body didn't respond.

Through the darkness I could tell that her usually calm demeanor had given way to panic. Her lips trembled as she tried to explain, teary streaks of mascara running down her cheeks.

"I found...I found...in my car..." Carrie gulped back sobs, and reached out her hand.

She was holding a note, written on a torn corner of a placemat that said YOU TOO in a large childish scribble. In a quavering voice she explained that she'd found the note on the seat of her car, with a knife slashed through the paper and into the upholstery. I'm sure I don't have to tell you that the knife appeared to be one of ours.

"What does it mean? Who would do that to my car?" Carrie didn't know about the note at The Pottery Studio; she was panicked about the brutality of the knife piercing her car seat. The horror of the recent stabbing was never far off anyone's radar; the note itself meant nothing to her. I'd leave it to the Sheriff's Department to decide how much to divulge. It wasn't my information to share.

I pulled my phone out of my tote bag and called Gregg, who thankfully answered immediately.

"You'd better get over here right away. Our server, Carrie, just found one of those placemat notes in her car, and she's frantic," I demanded.

Renata and I tried to sooth Carrie and keep her calm, but our good intentions weren't accomplishing much. Within minutes I heard the sound of a siren approaching. Swift response speed is one of the benefits of a sparsely populated area.

My tension level relaxed a bit when Gregg arrived to take charge. By then Carrie was hyperventilating, breathing in uneven gasping spurts, and the Sheriff's officers had all undergone EMT training. Gregg helped Carrie slowly into the building, and spent a few minutes coaching her on deep, deliberate, slow breaths. Renata kept one arm around Carrie's shoulders, and talked to her in a quiet, soothing voice.

Detective Milton arrived shortly after Gregg; I quickly explained the situation. Once Carrie's breathing was controlled, her heart rate had slowed and she'd calmed down, the two officers shifted into investigation mode.

"Has anyone seen anything suspicious?" they questioned.

"When I was leaving work there was a group of young people hanging around behind the building. Teens. Some college kids. Most of them were employees, but not all. They were laughing and smoking; I told them not to smoke near the woods, to go out to the parking lot. They headed out front and left almost immediately, right before Carrie went to her car," I reported. I provided names and numbers, even though the last thing I wanted to do was direct suspicion to my staff.

The officers wasted no time in calling those staffers and demanding that they, and their friends, get back to Unincorporated pronto.

It wasn't unusual that Carrie had left her car unlocked; everyone did. This led to an unwelcome lecture from Detective Milton about basic security procedures. Again I heard from Gregg about not walking alone into the woods after dark. This was just not a pleasant evening in any sense of the word.

When the young employees and their friends started arriving back at Unincorporated two or three at a time I was surprised at their apologetic and embarrassed demeanor. After much questioning, they hemmed and hawed, finally admitting what they'd been doing.

"Well, you see, we'd been, um...in the woods," one of our dishwashers started, in a faltering voice. "We had a few drinks, smoked some weed; we didn't do nothing really wrong."

"Then we heard some sounds, like someone was watching us from behind the trees. It was really dark, and kind of scary," continued a girl who was a stranger to me.

One of my fry cooks picked up the narrative. "It sounded like someone moving around, trying to be quiet, but we heard cracking sounds, like someone stepping on twigs and stuff." His voice became stronger as he went on. "We thought it might be you guys, sheriff's guys, watching us, so we high-tailed it out of there, back to the restaurant. But we were just drinking, not doing anything really bad. We'll go right home."

"I'm not supposed to go into the woods at night, ever. Please don't tell my parents," a thin, dark-haired girl begged in a trembling voice. "They'd be more angry about the woods than about the drinking."

Many heads nodded in agreement.

"You all knew that your drinking party was illegal, or you wouldn't have cared if someone from the sheriff's department saw you! And you're smart enough to understand how dangerous it is to smoke in the woods, especially during a drought!

"And then to top it all off," Gregg continued, his voice getting continually louder, "you get in your cars and drive away after you've been drinking! And you have the nerve to ask us not to tell your parents?"

He paused and seemed to gather his emotions, then said more calmly, "Now, what can you tell me about this note?"

"Note?"

"The note that was left in Carrie's car."

Shoulders shrugged among the group, and puzzled expressions indicated that no one knew what he was talking about.

Detective Milton and Gregg explained about the note, informing the group that it had definitely *not* been an officer listening in the woods.

"What else did you see or hear, other than cracking twigs? It sounds as if there really was someone watching you, and listening. Whoever it was, was possibly the person or persons who left this note. If you know anything that might help we want to hear it. Now!"

No one in the group had anything to add. They'd been mostly concerned about how much trouble they were in. It was finally sinking in that they had been in real danger; somber faces attested to their developing fear. They seemed to notice for the first time that Carrie was upset, and a few of the girls went over to hug her, concerned expressions on their faces.

"Is there anyone here who didn't drink?" Detective Milton asked. A few heads nodded. "You drive everyone else home. They can come back for their cars tomorrow," he said. He took everyone's name, then dismissed the group.

The officers shook their heads disgustedly as the group left. "Foolish kids," Gregg said. "They think they're invincible."

"Are you going to call their parents?" I asked.

"Not this time. They realize now that there was a serious threat, that they were taking a great risk with their *party*. They've learned enough of a lesson. It's never a good idea to have groups of young kids feeling like officers are the enemy. But I am going to file an official report. In case anything comes of this, we need the details on record."

The process of dusting Carrie's car for fingerprints, searching the grounds for evidence, interviewing witnesses and taking statements began again. This was becoming annoying for everyone involved. (Well, not necessarily *everyone*...mainly me. The officers were just doing their job, and Carrie and Renata hadn't been continually subjected to questioning. I felt like I...me...Ashley...had just about had it).

When you live in a normally crime-free resort community you aren't supposed to be familiar with police investigation procedures. But it was becoming a part of daily life, all in a day's work. Literally. It was almost making me yearn for term papers and exam week!

Why was all of this drama centered on Unincorporated? And why did it have to happen during the summer I was here? To say I found it disturbing would be an understatement. Words like aggravating, and even terrifying, would have been more appropriate.

When I heard Gregg tell Carrie that it would be advisable to take time off from work and visit friends in another town, I mentally reworked the server schedule for the rest of the month.

"Yes, yes, of course I'll go...I want to get away from this...I want this all to end," Carrie said. "I haven't been sleeping well, and this will make it worse." There was a tremor in her voice, and tears still ran down her cheeks.

I understood the urgency of her leaving, but I was annoyed by the constant turmoil. At least I didn't have to lie about where Carrie had gone. Unlike when Lynette and John from The Pottery Studio had left town without explanation, my entire staff would know the details about Carrie's departure.

"We learned something today that you need to be aware of," Gregg informed me once Renata had given Carrie a ride home. "You know that officers regularly check the doors of businesses to make sure they're locked after hours?"

I nodded, even though I'd known no such thing.

"Well, several months ago, before you came to town, the main entrance of Unincorporated was found unlocked several times. It was put down to Al's health challenges, thinking he was either not feeling well or was distracted worrying about his upcoming surgery. The officer checked the premises, locked the door, and left it at that.

"Now we realize there could be another explanation. Any customer could have stayed in the building, maybe hiding in a restroom, leaving the front door unlocked when leaving. With knives and placemats missing, we wonder if there was any unexplained vandalism shortly before you arrived here. Or anything else suspicious?"

"Nothing that I've heard about," I shook my head. It was shocking to think that someone might have deliberately remained in the building after closing. I didn't know if I'd ever again feel comfortable in the building after hours.

"Next time we talk I'll ask Al if anything was damaged or missing." But how could I bring it up without it sounding accusatory, like people thought he hadn't been diligent about securing the building?

"Thanks. Let us know if you learn anything from him."

"There's one more piece of information that you should be aware of," he added.

Now what? More information about the ongoing horror was not likely to put my mind at rest.

"We've tested the note that Lynette and John received for fingerprints. We found John's prints, and no others. Whoever left that note took pains to avoid touching it; our suspect apparently knows that we can occasionally get prints from paper. It's something many people learn from TV detective shows and mystery novels. But it's also common knowledge among hard-core offenders."

Detective Rob nodded, "We'll test this new note for fingerprints, of course, but if it was left by the same perpetrator chances are we won't find any. It's not as easy to get prints off of paper in reality as it is on TV. But still, it seems like the person who left the first note was definitely taking precautions. Please remember to be careful; we don't know who we're dealing with, but it could be a career criminal."

Shaking his head he continued, "I don't suppose you could convince your uncle to get a security system that actually works?"

"I doubt it. He's a stubborn man who knows his own mind. But he can be stubborn in a foolish way."

"You might want to remind him that dead cameras are useless in an investigation."

I nodded. I'd feel better with a functioning system myself, but it wasn't my decision to make.

The tension I felt was growing exponentially. I breathed a sigh of relief that when we finally said goodnight the officers were there to walk me home.

I let myself in with my key, relocking the door immediately. I checked that every window was secured, blinds were pulled, draperies drawn. I had a glass of wine, and did some deep breathing exercises that were supposed to be calming, listening to cheerful classical pieces that my Gramma had always enjoyed.

I will never admit it to anyone, but for the first time since I was little Teddy Maxwell and I went to sleep with a light on.

CHAPTER 18

Bekah rushed in the front door of Unincorporated around 11:00 a.m. the next day and engulfed me in a bear hug, downloading all the while about her tedious drive and the terrible drivers.

"Ashley, I'm so glad I finally got here! You look terrific, by the way. I love your hair pulled back like that! What a morning; I never saw so many people that don't understand what a center line is for! They were swerving all over the place, and driving 10 miles per hour under the speed limit. I couldn't pass anyone, and was afraid to get too close behind. It was like Senior Citizen's Day on the highways!"

This was immediately followed by, "I'm starving. Can you leave work now?"

With glossy blonde hair lying in gentle waves on her shoulders, ivory skin, eyes like blue sapphires, a brilliant smile, and long shapely legs, she'd always been an attention getter. Her oval face with its clear complexion, high cheekbones, thin nose and dainty chin, could have been designed by the editors of a fashion magazine.

Now, personality bubbling over, wearing a shocking pink shirt, white slacks and sandals embellished with rhinestones, Bekah was gathering admiring looks from staff and guests alike. I was proud to have her for a friend, although I'd always known that when she was around I seemed bland by comparison.

"Look at those toned arms. You must have been working out; you look really buff," I said enviously. In college I'd spent hours each week at the campus fitness center; since coming to Windsor Grove I'd been slacking on my workout routine.

"Well, when you don't have a job there's lots of time for the gym. I feel really healthy, but I'd rather feel *employed*," she laughed.

After another quick hug I gave Bekah a set of keys to the cottage so she could drop off her luggage. I know how she travels, and I assumed that she'd brought enough clothes for several vacations.

"You know your way around from when we've come up together, you can choose either of the smaller rooms" (yes, there were bedrooms even smaller than mine). "Go over and unpack. I have a few things to finish here; as soon as I'm caught up we'll go for lunch," I told her. "We've got so much to talk about!"

I'd adjusted schedules so that the head server, Dawn, would be on duty throughout most of Bekah's visit, Renata would be behind the bar, and as usual Brad would have the kitchen under control. I felt confident that with my strongest staffers on duty our guests would get great service even if I wasn't around. I badly needed to get away from work and have some girlfriend time.

"Call my cell phone if you need me," I instructed the staff. I headed to the cottage and changed into a pastel flowered sundress with designer flip-flops, listening to Bekah's chatter all the while. Apparently Duncan, last week's Mr. Wonderful, hadn't been so wonderful after all and was no longer in the picture. Recent job interviews hadn't garnered any offers. And Bekah was not thrilled to be living with her Mom and Dad.

"You're so lucky to have an exciting job; if I don't find something soon I'll go crazy," she smiled, "and so will my parents!"

"Anyplace in particular you want to eat?" I asked, changing the subject. I wasn't so sure that my job was exciting; at least not in the way she meant it.

"Somewhere that we can eat outdoors. It's such a thrill when it's nice enough to eat outside in Wisconsin. A table with a view of the lake would be perfect; someplace where we won't be rushed. Is there any place new?"

It was indeed a great day for outdoor dining. In the mid 80's, sunny with a light breeze, there was no reason to stay indoors if it wasn't necessary. We were all spoiled by the extended period of picture-perfect weather. The drought continued, disappointing campers who still couldn't have campfires, but on days like this Windsor Grove was a summertime paradise, even without s'mores.

We headed to The King's Tavern. A longtime gathering spot, it was a popular downtown pub that had foodservice on a deck overlooking the lake. Known for huge burgers and an extensive deep-fried appetizer menu this isn't a place anyone would ever go for healthy dining. But the view from their multi-level deck is spectacular, and they have a sizeable crowd all summer long.

We were shown to a patio table with a breathtaking view and comfortable cushioned chairs, covered by a huge umbrella advertising the newest flavored vodka. The soft blue sky was dotted with puffy clouds, looking like a painted backdrop on a stage. I sat back, inhaling the fresh summer air, ready for some casual conversation.

"Now, tell me everything about that murder. Did you know the guy? I heard he wasn't much older than us...was he a hunk? Do they know who did it yet?" Bekah said excitedly. Perhaps the conversation wasn't going to be all that casual.

"Remember when I told you that one of our delivery people had died? Well, that was him."

"No!"

"It's true. And it's been a huge annoyance."

Once we'd placed our orders I filled her in on the details, which took quite some time. I started with the missing bread delivery, ending with anonymous notes on scraps of placemats. Unusually, she listened without interrupting. When I'd finished, I wasn't a bit surprised at her questions.

"Are the officers good-looking? Are they married?" Typical Bekah.

Hearing my affirmative answer to the first question, and the negative answer to the second, Bekah grinned and asked if she'd be able to meet them. My comments about the officers' busy schedules didn't seem to have any effect on her enthusiasm.

"I'll just watch the parking lot at Unincorporated and come over to visit any time I see a squad car."

Just what I needed. It was aggravating enough to have Gregg and Rob dropping in on a regular basis. Now I'd have Bekah showing up at inconvenient times too. As much as I would love having her around, there was no denying that she might quickly become an unwelcome distraction. Not for the first time I thought that this investigation couldn't end soon enough to suit me. My actual job was too often taking a back seat to other events going on around me.

As we enjoyed overpriced frozen fruit drinks the conversation flowed. It felt like old times when we would spend an entire day together and not run out of things to say. After a long leisurely lunch we decided to spend the afternoon relaxing in the sunshine. We headed back to the cottage, donned swimwear, gathered beach chairs, towels and bottled water, and then made the short drive to the public beach at the other side of the lake.

"How can you survive with those tiny closets?" Bekah questioned as we drove. "I'd never be able to find anything. And do you know you need a better mirror? That one's impossible!" She acted like I was roughing it in the cottage; I just laughed. She pretended to be quite the princess, but she was actually tougher than she let on.

"I do love how you've enhanced the 'décor' of the living room with your handbag display," she giggled.

The beach was crowded with sunbathers, picnickers, and kids building sandcastles. A smaller number of people waded in the water, which hadn't yet warmed to its summer temperature. Numerous fishing boats could be seen on the lake, as well as several jet skis, a few pontoon boats and one water skier.

We selected a sunny spot with a great view, kicked off our sandals to dig toes into smooth soft sand, covered ourselves with sunscreen, reclined our chairs, and laid back to unwind. I tried to relax my muscles from head to toe, and could feel the worries of the last few weeks fall away from my shoulders. It had been cathartic to share my thoughts with Bekah; I'd missed having a friendly ear to vent to. My rejuvenated feeling, however, was short lived.

"Bang!" a high-pitched voice shrieked nearby, "You're dead!"

"I'm not dead. I killed you first!" hollered a second voice. My eyes flew open, and I saw two boys in brightly colored swim trunks, six or seven years old, run past us along the beach, pretending to shoot each other.

"I'm gonna stab you in the woods!" I heard the taller one yell as they ran off.

"Nah-ah you won't! You can't get in my truck while I'm driving. So there!" was the other boy's response.

I winced. It made me uncomfortable to watch Mark's brutal death being turned into a game. Not only was it completely inappropriate (where were these boys' parents, anyway?), but with a killer still on the loose it could be dangerous.

I tuned in to the conversations around me, and was shocked at what I heard. Parents chatted about the murder in front of their kids, as if it were a part of the area entertainment. Kids took their parents lead, laughing about it as if it were the newest video game.

Why was everyone else able to be so cavalier about the dangers, as if the threat couldn't possibly affect them? Why did all of the drama seem to center around Unincorporated? Andy why did I feel as though I was trapped in this relentless horror? This was supposed to be my day to relax; I felt as if I were being led into a permanent state of anxiety.

A group of older boys, around sixteen years old, bragged to a bikini-clad group of girls about a party they'd had in the woods near the deserted road where Mark was killed. They said the murder took place the very next day, and they'd gone back to search for clues. The girls acted horrified, but were blushing and giggling all the same.

I wondered if the officers knew that the homicide had turned into a kids' game on the beach. Since he came from a larger community I didn't expect Rob to be in tune with the local chatter, but small town officers often know everything that goes on. I made a mental note to mention it the next time I saw Gregg. As far as I knew no high school kids had come forward mentioning anything about being in the woods the night before the murder; I hoped that those bragging boys were all talk and weren't actually holding back vital facts.

"What kind of a name is Zachary's Unincorporated, anyway?" Bekah wondered. At first I thought it was a weird conversational twist, even for her, but then I realized that she had no idea what I'd been thinking about. Her eyes were closed, and she'd apparently not paid any attention to the boys' game.

"The man who founded the restaurant about 80 years ago named it Zachary's Supper Club, after his grandfather, and the name Zachary's stayed through several owners," I explained. "About 20 years ago a windstorm blew down the huge sign in the parking lot, and the only way anyone could explain the location was to tell tourists that it was near the road sign that said WINDSOR GROVE, UNINCORPORATED."

I sat up and turned to face Bekah, continuing the complicated explanation. "Friends of the owner laughed and started calling it 'The Unincorporated Restaurant'. Months later, when the insurance company finally agreed to pay for a new sign, the locals were all calling it 'Unincorporated'; so the owner decided to change the name permanently. They kept Zachary's as the name of the lounge, and it's still called Zachary's Lounge today."

I shook my head. "Some old-timers still call the restaurant *Zachary's*, most locals call it *Unincorporated*, and many use both names together. Frankly I think it's confusing. Uncle Al actually has it listed under both names in visitor's guides and online, because otherwise there's always someone who complains that it's not listed."

"So who do you think committed the murder?" Bekah's mind really did bounce from topic to topic like a kid on a trampoline.

I sighed. "It could be almost anyone, I suppose. I'm keeping my fingers crossed that it's nobody I know, definitely not someone who works for me. I hope the officers figure it out soon, so I can forget about it and get back to just running a restaurant."

"Wouldn't it be exciting if they arrest someone while I'm here? It would feel like important things were going on all around me. I wonder if you've met the killer. I hope you don't get a threatening note, I just want to relax while I'm here."

I didn't comment on that, and she didn't seem to notice. I'd made a huge mistake when I told Bekah the reason that Lynette and John had left town. I'd forgotten that I was supposed to keep it quiet. Now I had to hope that she wouldn't blab it all over, to everyone she met. *Good one, Ashley.*

"You have to keep that quiet, okay? No one's supposed to know about the first note."

"Don't worry about me. It's exciting to have secret information. I won't tell a soul!"

I hoped that I could believe her. She'd never divulge anything intentionally, but who knows what she'd blurt out in conversation? When she becomes excited her thoughts just come tumbling out.

We spent the next hour enjoying the sunshine, gathering up our things when ice cream cravings hit. We approached my car, arms loaded with belongings, shaking sand from our sandals.

Out of the corner of my eye I noticed movement in a dusty dark grey sedan a few cars away from mine, with the hot sun beating down on the roof. Someone was sitting in the driver's seat, scowling under dark sunglasses. Trying to be inconspicuous, I glanced over to get a better look. Sure enough, it was Man-in-Brown, looking out of place in his surroundings, wearing a button-down shirt in an earthy tone.

He may have been scrutinizing someone or something on the beach, or perhaps he was just casually observing. This guy was really odd, and certainly didn't fit in this friendly community; he wasn't a local but didn't act like a tourist. Who goes to a beach in a button-down shirt? I added Man-in-Brown to my mental list of people to question Gregg and Rob about. There seemed to be a pattern of him sitting quietly in his parked car. His presence made me increasingly uneasy.

Once we had our cones, mine plain chocolate, Bekah's a coffee mocha topped with sprinkles, we wandered past quaint little shops, gazing at window displays, dreaming of spending money we didn't have. I was enthusiastic about the sweaters in the window at The Peacock; Bekah was drawn to the elegant jewelry at Silversmith's.

We quickly passed The Scentsory Shop with its candles and lotions, or the temptations would have been too hard to resist. We speculated that this had to be the premiere place in the state for gift shopping, with everything from Teddy Bear Corner to Confectioner's Candies.

The best part of Main Street is the buildings themselves. Not a new structure among them, each shop has its own history. Valerie's Boutique occupies a building that originally housed a general store, then served as a medical office in the early 1900's; The Forest Café still serves the comfort food that was available when it was the Windsor Diner in 1910; Rick's Tap occupies the original blacksmith shop and is decorated with mementos of its previous life. Each current shop has a story to tell, and local residents are justifiably proud of their preservation of history.

In front of Twisted Threads, an eccentric little weaving studio that had once been a barbershop (and still displays the requisite barber pole), we saw Mary Lou, the most peculiar of The Marys. She gazed in the window, murmuring unintelligibly.

At first glance she appeared to be carrying a baby, tenderly covered by a pastel quilted blanket. But no, a second glance revealed it to be a doll, probably an antique, with a lovely porcelain face and a lacey cap. She cradled that doll softly and lovingly, the ultimate in protective care.

When she saw us her haunted eyes opened wide, she shook her head, uttered, "You're the one with the knife, very interesting. And concerning. You must be terrified," then winked at me, again that conspiratorial wink as if we shared a special secret. She then wandered away, speaking softly to the doll in her arms.

Where were her sisters? I'd been told that The Marys were seldom seen alone. It was out of character for just one Mary to be out in public. Especially *this* Mary. It was almost as if she'd momentarily escaped and was roaming free. Watching her shuffling along talking to herself, I noticed several pedestrians pick up the pace and look away as she drew near. I wasn't the only one who felt uneasy in the presence.

"Who was that?" whispered Bekah.

"I'll tell you later," I murmured. "It's a long story. She's from a wealthy local family; I'm not sure I understand her myself." I mentally added her to my list of questions that needed to be asked. I had the unfortunate feeling that if I had more time to get out and observe life in Windsor Grove I'd eventually have most of its residents in my *acting suspiciously* category.

I decided that even though I really wanted to relax and enjoy my guest for a few days, I couldn't wait any longer to contact the officers about my concerns. I knew Bekah wouldn't mind; she'd asked to meet the officers. As a good hostess it was my obligation to provide the opportunity!

Back at Unincorporated things were functioning in the usual way, a form of controlled chaos. Brad announced that the salmon steaks for the next evening's herb-buttered entree were the wrong size, and said it in a way that insinuated it was my fault, even though he was the one who placed seafood orders. One of our evening servers who'd been trying to get someone to trade shifts with her, had called at the last minute unable to work due to some sudden unnamed illness. And the sodas on the carbonation system had gone flat.

On the plus side, the Lounge was full and we had numerous reservations for the evening. Just another day in the restaurant industry.

Bekah stood off to the side taking it all in, becoming aware for the first time that I was actually responsible for something besides my latest hair color.

I did what I could to straighten out the restaurant's difficulties (call a repairman, adjust start and end times for servers, console Brad about his salmon), then headed into my office to call Gregg. *Might as well get it over with.*

Gregg and Rob arrived together almost instantly after I called, impressing Bekah no end. For once, they used the kitchen entrance, which for some reason felt gratifying, and waited for me in Brad's office. That didn't necessarily make Brad happy, so I moved the discussion into my own crowded office; I knew this one might take a while.

"Gregg and Rob, this is Bekah, a good friend who's visiting. Bekah, Officer Gregg and Detective Rob."

"It's nice to meet you. I always like to know who's looking after Ashley." Her flirty smile made me cringe. "Ashley's important to me, you know."

There I was, trying to act like a serious adult, and she made it sound like I needed a nanny. How humiliating.

Bekah then perched herself on the edge of my desk, legs crossed at the ankles, eyes open wide, ready to take part in our discussion. I wasn't surprised that Gregg took her presence for granted; he was a small town officer after all, and was accustomed to having the public involved in discussions. However it did seem a bit unusual that Rob also assumed she'd remain.

I expected it had something to do with her glowing praise of the State Department of Justice, along with her look of awe when he gave his full name and title. As if she'd ever before cared what the department of justice did! Her eyes had that glistening shimmer they get when there's a handsome guy around, and she smiled brightly each time she looked at Rob. I had to give her credit for attempting to remain at least a little businesslike; being serious is not part of her nature.

"Let me explain why I called," I began. I talked about murder games on the beach, teens bragging about hunting for clues, and the general perception that this was merely an entertaining diversion.

When the officers heard about the children's murder games they grew somber, immediately understanding my concern about a potentially dangerous scenario.

"We've been tossing around the idea of a community awareness program. This could be the catalyst we need to get it going," Rob said. "It's a struggle to convey a sense of urgency in an area where everyone is so laid back. People who live in communities that are virtually crime-free take their security for granted."

"Awareness programs can be difficult when most residents are seasonal and don't receive mail here, but this gives us a reason to contact everyone, even visitors in the cabins, cottages, and rental condos." He was entering things in his laptop as he spoke; I was gratified he'd taken my observations seriously.

I brought up another topic that had been bothering me, "How is your investigation into area residents, especially the people on my list, coming along?"

"You know we can't give out certain information when an investigation is ongoing," Gregg shook his head, smiling. "But if you have any knowledge you think we should have, we are more than willing to listen."

I proceeded to give him my thoughts, whether or not he really wanted to hear them. I mentioned Roger, the fry cook who admitted to lying on his job application. I expressed curiosity about Jeff, who was a no-show for work but hung around outside the restaurant smoking with staff.

Then I tried to deflect the investigation away from Unincorporated by asking if they'd explored the background between Mark and Todd, his friend at The Village Flower Shoppe. I brought up local characters like Mary Lou, and Mr. Horner. Then I got to the person that really had my curiosity on alert, Man-in-Brown.

Gregg had been writing in his notebook while I talked. He grinned, asking, "You do realize that we're looking into everyone's background, don't you? You're not bringing up anyone we're not aware of. It's time-consuming, but we'll get it figured out in the end.

"We've eliminated everyone who has an alibi for early that Thursday, now we're analyzing the backgrounds of everyone else." He almost laughed, which I found embarrassing. "We're happy to hear your thoughts, but please don't think for a minute that we're neglecting anything.

"We are in a unique position. On a local level our officers have small-town personal knowledge about all the residents; there is a grapevine here that can't be rivaled. On top of that, the State Department of Criminal Investigation adds the technology and resources we normally lack. It's an ideal situation that works on several levels. Yes, we're going to get this solved," he declared, rather hesitantly I thought.

"There are a few more things I can divulge about the investigation," Gregg's voice became more confident. "An autopsy, of course, is performed in all non-natural deaths, and the coroner has released the autopsy report. It's no surprise that the official cause of death will be listed as 'foul play'.

"There are related tests which then give us further evidence in traumatic injury cases."

Gregg continued his explanation, "We learned that, of the fifteen stab wounds, at least one of them penetrated the heart, the right ventricle, and would have caused almost instantaneous death. If Mark suffered at all, it wasn't for long."

I took several deep breaths trying to calm my queasy stomach. How could one human being abuse another to that extent?

"The severity of the attack caused considerable hemorrhage. I'm not clear on the science involved, but the final report said," Gregg checked a page in his notebook, "the 'left anterior descending coronary artery' was severed. Death was due to a combination of 'hemothorax, external blood loss, and hemopericardium', if that tells you anything."

He closed the notebook and continued, "The Medical Examiner made a notation that most stabbings don't result in death. Our perpetrator was either very fortunate, or had done extensive research regarding the exact entry points required to fatally damage the heart."

"We also learned that Mark's toxicology report showed no drugs or alcohol in his system when he died, as we expected."

I felt relieved at that last item. I didn't want Mark to have any black marks against his character.

"Microscopic examinations showed no evidence of the perpetrator's DNA on Mark's body or clothing, or on Mark's vehicle. No stray hair follicles, no flakes of dry skin, no fingerprints. The killer possibly wore gloves, definitely took precautions."

"The angle of the stab wounds indicates a right-handed person using a back-handed motion while reaching through the window. That only eliminates about ten percent of the population; it's not much, but it gives us a little more guidance."

Hearing details from the autopsy report made me feel uncomfortable and squeamish. There were parts of the investigation I didn't care to think about. The expression of distaste on Bekah's face told me she felt the same.

"So you know about Man-in-Brown?" I changed the subject back to a topic I found less troubling.

"We know about your Man-in-Brown. But we appreciate you alerting us to some of his activities," was his reply.

"Can I assume that you're in touch with Lynette and John?" I'd been concerned about the owners of the Pottery Studio after they'd had to leave town so abruptly. I wondered if they had enough funds to be comfortable wherever they were, and if someone was checking on them regularly.

"And with Carrie?"

"Trust us," was Gregg's answer, indicating that I wouldn't be getting the details I wanted.

Then, the question I just had to ask, "So what's up with The Marys? I've been asking people, and everyone knows who they are, but no one knows their story."

The officers laughed. The question obviously had nothing to do with the investigation; I'm sure I sounded like a Nosy Nellie. This was my best opportunity so far to learn about the local residents, and I wasn't going to pass up my chance.

"Not regarding the crime, just in general," I hurried to explain. "I've ended up on one of their committees, and I can't quite figure those ladies out."

"Mary Rose, the most personable and outgoing one, was married to Clyde Brinkley," Gregg explained, "who inherited a fortune from one of the early lumber barons in the area. He was much older, and she's been a wealthy widow for years. That extravagant home The Marys live in belongs to her.

"She owns acres of property all over the county; the Brinkley Art Studio belongs to her; her husband donated the land for Veteran's Park; and her sisters live very well on Brinkley money. She calls the shots for the sisters, and decides what charities they'll work for, what organizations they'll join, and apparently she even decides what and when they'll eat.

"MaryBeth, the studious sister, was married to a college professor out east. The marriage didn't work out, but no one around here knows any details. There's never been mention of a husband; all we know is that she moved in with her sister about 20 years ago and helps run

Mary Rose's charities and functions. She has a businesslike analytical personality.

"Mary Lou, the youngest one, is another character altogether. She's never been married, and possibly has never even held a job. She was already living with Mary Rose and Clyde before he passed away. It seems that her sister has always looked after her. "We can't quite get a handle on Mary Lou, she's scatterbrained and quite a busybody. Most people think she's a few planets short of a solar system, but she actually has a normal intellect. She's just socially inept and people feel uncomfortable around her. You never know what she's going to blurt out, or who she's going to offend."

"Is that the one we saw downtown?" Bekah looked at me.

When I nodded, she said, "Oh, so she's the Scary Mary."

I laughed at that. Now I'll always think of Mary Lou as *The Scary Mary*. It's inappropriate, I know. But once I got it into my mind, it stuck.

This explained the dynamics controlling The Marys' relationships. While ostensibly they were three sisters sharing in the adventures of life, in reality two of them were financially reliant on the third for their upscale lifestyle. So when Mary Rose chose an activity, or a cause, or a hobby, all three took part as if it were a joint decision. On the surface they were comrades, but it was a situation that could lead to a lot of resentment.

"I suppose you know that this fundraising event you're working on is going to pose quite a security problem. It's our job to keep everyone safe, but in this case we don't know who we're protecting people from. Or why. Everyone here is so accustomed to assuming they're perfectly safe that no one is taking any precautions, even though they know there's been a homicide."

I glanced over at Bekah, and noticed that she had a shocked expression on her face. It occurred to me that even Bekah had considered the murder mostly a horrifying but exciting event; she hadn't thought of it as anything that might affect her, or me, until that moment.

"I thought you were convinced that Mark was the intended victim and everyone else was reasonably safe," I said. Gregg nodded.

"At first that seemed like the obvious answer. The longer the investigation goes on without a solution, the more questions we have. The anonymous notes are introducing another element of concern; we're less certain of anything right now."

"Well, I'm only purchasing the food for the festival; I'm not doing any of the actual planning for Windsor Day. But if there's anything I can do to make things safer let me know." *Oh no, I didn't really say that, did I?* The last thing I wanted was to be responsible for anything more.

Thankfully both officers shook their heads, cutting me off.

"No, the safety of the community is our job", Rob said. "We have to be diligent and thorough. The Marys are keeping us informed about all the details, so we're doing our best to be prepared for every eventuality." *Whew. Off the hook.*

Bekah, with a serious and concerned expression on her face, spoke for the first time since this conversation had begun. "But how sure are you, really, that you can keep everyone safe?"

"We know we can do it. On the state level we've planned security for events far larger than this, in the aftermath of much more gruesome crimes. Don't worry, we know what we're doing," Rob said comfortingly. "We'll bring in help from other towns to have complete coverage."

Bekah sighed as if a great weight had been lifted from her shoulders. The look she gave Detective Rob said that she thought he was a wonderful, dedicated, selfless person. He may actually have been all those things, but her adoring look was a bit much.

Rob seemed to take her attitude for granted, as if gorgeous women were always fawning over handsome officers. When the officers were about to leave Unincorporated, he slowed his pace at the door, turned back to Bekah, and asked if she was busy later that evening. I'd watched her easy relationships with guys forever, and this didn't surprise me. But on her first night here? Really?

"Do you mind, Ashley?" She looked at me expectantly.

"Of course not," I lied. "I really should be here to keep an eye on the dining room tonight anyway."

"Great!" she smiled, and she and Rob spent a few minutes planning their evening.

Yes, I lied. I totally resented Bekah going out with Rob on her first night in town. For weeks I'd looked forward to having someone to talk to and relax with. I was in town to do a time-consuming job, and hadn't had an opportunity to make friends. I had innumerable acquaintances, but real friends? No. Now my guest who'd just arrived already had a social commitment. Just great.

My comment about keeping an eye on the dining room didn't have basis in reality. The evening never developed, and the main thing I did was send staff home as soon as they weren't needed. As had been the case since Mark's murder, two main topics of conversation flowed through the dining room; the murder and the election; the election and the murder.

"Can't these people talk about anything else?" I complained to Renata. I was in a bad mood with Bekah out on her date, and my patience was nonexistent.

"What else is there to talk about around here?" was her response.

"Art shows…local sports…environmental issues…the Windsor Day fundraiser coming up. It would be great if we could get the locals as enthused about the children's playground as they are about the murder investigation. I suppose a murder has more of a glamour factor, if you can call it that."

Renata thought my comment was hilarious, but I was serious. The fundraiser hadn't attracted much attention so far, and wouldn't be a success without the support of the community.

I took advantage of the slow evening, and asked more people my constant question, "How well did you know Mark?"

I was reminded how many locals had never actually met the man they'd been mourning, and how many had known him only enough to nod and say, "Hi". But one silver-haired elderly woman with a tight perm and rouged red cheeks had an enlightening comment.

"He tried to pretend he loved my little Lizzie. But you know, Lady Elizabeth is a very good judge of character, and she didn't like him at all. Lizzie has such severe anxiety issues, when we'd meet him on the street she'd tremble and try to go the other direction. If my Lizzie didn't like him, then he wasn't a good man!"

It took me a few seconds to realize we were talking about a dog. Mark continually asked people about their pets, but that didn't mean that Mark actually liked pets, just their owners. I'd heard that dogs instinctively dislike people who dislike them. Was Mark a bad person, or was he a good person who didn't get along with dogs? If so, why pretend? Because it was a good conversation starter?

Should this detail be added to my list of motives? Nah. I couldn't imagine anyone being killed for lying about loving dogs. Even dogs with anxiety issues. This woman had decided that Mark wasn't a good person, based totally on Lady Elizabeth's reaction. Others could have formed opinions for reasons just as frivolous.

Turning away from that table, I heard a local man at the next table mutter under his breath, "She acts like her dumb dog is smarter than anyone in town. The dog might be smarter than *her*, but that's because she's a nut case!" It was difficult to ignore his comment as I walked by. But I managed not to smile, I think.

No, *being a dog lover* wasn't going to make it to my list of possible motives. But I had to remember that obscure things can seem vitally important to some people while seeming inconsequential to everyone else. This could make finding the motive almost impossible...

Once we'd closed the kitchen, I wandered to the patio to visit with the few guests who were out there enjoying a nightcap. For once it was an overcast night, without the canopy of stars that usually decorated the sky.

"Maybe this time we'll finally get some rain," someone commented, but rain had been predicted so often that no one took him seriously. It was a calm night, darker than most, but with just enough light from surrounding buildings that we could see the serene surface of water surrounded by tall trees that had existed for generations.

Leaving the patio, I crossed the lawn to start up the path to the cottage, when I stopped, alarmed. There was a light shining behind the drawn draperies, and I knew I never left lights on when I was away. Well, once or twice I had, but I was quite certain I hadn't done so that day. I'd reminded Bekah to take her key, and I'd locked the door myself after she'd gone.

Was that someone's shadow moving in the woods? Officer Gregg's warnings about not walking home alone after dark echoed through my brain. An intruder may have been in Unincorporated several times over past months, according to him. Could the same intruder be inside my cottage?

Slivers of moonlight flickered through the trees, creating eerie shadows and curious shapes that moved haphazardly through the dense woods, concealing more than they revealed.

I rushed back to the kitchen, to ask someone to accompany me.

"Please walk to the cottage with me, and wait until I'm sure things are safe," I asked Brad, feeling humble. I reminded him of the officers' warning; he shrugged and followed me. As we walked up the dark path he made comments under his breath about the foolishness of living in the woods. I had no idea where he lived himself, I'd never been curious about his private life. I doubted if he lived in any secluded location, he seemed far too methodical.

After the short walk through the darkness we climbed the stairs to cross the porch. Hesitantly inserting my key I realized the door wasn't locked. Positive I'd locked up, I tensed, standing stock-still and panic-stricken when Brad pushed past me, opened the door, and barged inside. My heart skipped a beat or two, and I did a quick pivot, ready to bolt.

CHAPTER 19

An ear-piercing shriek greeted us, its shrillness spine-tingling. "Christ Almighty!" Brad hollered. He jumped backward, but immediately straightened up and struck a stance as if ready for attack.

The scream had been followed by a screeching, breathless, "Who are you and what are you doing here?" I'd almost taken flight, when I recognized that voice.

Bekah. I sighed. It never occurred to me that she would be home from her date already. Her dates traditionally went on late into the night.

"It's alright," I mumbled to Brad, "She's a friend." I tried to stop my voice from trembling, but I'd been more panicked than I cared to admit. My nerves were shot; I couldn't take many more surprises. And once again Brad had been witness to my insecurities.

The withering look he gave me was deserved. He turned and stomped off down the path without a word. I didn't want to know what he thought of me at that moment. I was sure I'd hear about it the next day.

"What happened to your date?" I demanded, turning to Bekah. I knew I sounded blunt, but I wasn't in a frame of mind to react calmly.

"First, who was that guy? He scared me half to death, walking in here like that!" She'd been curled up in a chair, phone in hand. Now stood, staring at the door.

"He's my chef, Brad Galenburg. He was trying to protect me from whoever was in my cottage! What are you doing back so soon?" I tried not to yell at her, but I was still seriously tense. I imagine I sounded like an accusatory schoolmarm whose regulations had been violated.

"Well, we went to a place in Oak Landing called Antonio's, and decided to start with an appetizer at the bar," Bekah explained rather defensively. "We talked for a while, but it turns out he isn't at all interested in the boutiques in The Third Ward, or the new pubs in Walker's Point. Once I got done telling him how fascinating law enforcement is, it turned out that new developments in forensic science really don't interest me." She didn't seem to see the irony in that statement at all.

"We didn't have much to talk about. He's a nice guy, very polite and all. And waaay cute! But I was bored, and I think he was too. I felt really young when I was with him; our lives have nothing in common."

This had to be a switch for Bekah. She was used to being the center of attention, the life of the party. Still a collegiate free spirit at heart, she apparently couldn't relate to a serious professional who put in long hard hours on detail work. This may have been her first taste of adult reality; it would probably do her a lot of good. Unfortunately she scared a few years off my life in the process!

"You gave me a key; I let myself in. I didn't want to bother you while you were working," she justified. "I hope that's alright."

"Sure it is." I counted to ten, trying to calm myself.

"I just never expected to see you back here so soon. Maybe you'll need to let me know any time your dates don't go well," I teased as I kicked my shoes off and reached into the fridge for a soda. "Thirsty?"

"Hungry too. We nibbled on some snack mix, and shared an order of coconut shrimp, but never had a meal. It's been a long time since I went out with a guy who lost interest so fast. Must be losing my touch!" Her infectious laugh made me smile. I settled down, ready to talk the night away, enjoying the company of my long-time friend.

After pulling a pizza out of the freezer, I preheated the oven and headed into the bedroom to change. Once we were both in PJ's I lit a fire in the fireplace, even though the night was really too warm for that. I put the pizza in the oven, poured us each a large glass of soda, and collapsed into an inviting chair.

I'd always thought of this vast main room as the perfect vacation site. My oldest memories were of family gatherings spent at Windsor Lake, biking and hiking, swimming, doing jigsaw puzzles, and roasting marshmallows. The blanket chest still held toy trucks and building blocks that had entertained myself and my cousins on many a rainy day. Barbie dolls resided in the bottom drawer of an old oak desk. The bookshelves were filled with board games and unfinished craft projects along with well-read books.

Brightly colored mismatched area rugs defined various seating, dining, and games areas, and covered a weathered wooden floor that spoke of years of family vacations. Sleeping bags and inflatable mattresses were stored in huge chests, ready for overflow occupancy.

Lofty exposed timber beams supported rustic metal chandeliers that cast warm light throughout the room. This enormous space would never be featured in any elegant design magazines, but if there were a magazine for soothing relaxation sites it should make the cover.

A few delicate raindrops began decorating the picture windows; everyone in the county would rejoice at each drop of moisture. It was a great time for the gab-fest I'd been looking forward to.

Over the next several hours we finished the pizza, open a pack of cookies, talked about everything and nothing, and graduated from soda to beer. When it was well past midnight we headed off to bed listening to the soothing sounds of gentle rain on the roof. In my mind this was a classic evening at the lake. I fell asleep feeling more relaxed and content than I'd been in weeks.

It was dark when my alarm went off, and after some bleary-eyed confusion on my part I realized that rain continued to fall, with skies the darkest I'd ever seen in the morning hours. The air in the cottage felt thick with humidity, and there was a dank musty smell from the forest.

No longer a gentle shower, it appeared that we were getting the long-awaited cloudburst we'd been praying for. I hurriedly closed windows and turned on the noisy seldom-used window air conditioner.

I felt sluggish and apathetic as I dressed, wondering what business would be like on such a dismal day. The weather must have affected my clothing choices; I was wearing earth tones that could be seen as calming or gloomy depending on your frame of mind. I left jewelry off completely; it didn't feel like a day for accessories.

The path to the restaurant had turned muddy and slippery during the night, I was glad I'd chosen dark brown slacks that wouldn't show every mud-splatter. My Monet-print umbrella protected my hair and my silky beige shirt from the rain, but I was regretting the shoes I'd chosen. Wouldn't you think I'd have been smart enough to wear old running shoes for the rainy walk, then change into better shoes once I'd arrived? But no, now I'd be in soggy shoes all day.

Unusually, the kitchen was vacant when I arrived. A retired construction worker came in most mornings to meet delivery trucks; by the time he left Brad was normally there getting things ready for lunch. If they didn't manage to overlap, the kitchen door was left unlocked for any late deliveries, assuming employees would be arriving soon.

There was no reason Brad had to arrive so early other than his own desire to be a complete hands-on chef. The temporary Wholesale Wholegrains deliveryman was becoming more accurate in his estimates; I hoped he'd be kept on as our permanent contact, letting Brad off the hook for bread inventory.

Brad's absence shouldn't have alarmed me; I knew he'd have everything prepared on time. Recent events, however, were making me suspicious of anything out of the ordinary. I'd become so accustomed to hearing rude comments directed at me when I entered the building that the silence seemed out of place and oddly uncomfortable.

I turned on a few lights in the kitchen, moving to the dining room, then the bar, checking that things had been properly cleaned and organized after closing the previous night.

As staff started to arrive they updated me on developing weather conditions.

"The ground is so hard that the rain isn't soaking in, it's running off and heading downhill toward the lake," was a common observation.

"North of town the farm fields are flooding. That could be a disaster for the crops," someone said. Everyone knew that a slow steady shower would be far more helpful than a downpour.

"Rain is good for business," Dawn enthused, coming in with an energetic bounce, planning for a hectic day. "No one has anything else to do, they can't go to the beach or cook out, or wander through downtown, so they all come in to eat." Dawn usually knew what she was talking about, so I had the staff prepare for a full house at lunchtime.

The weather became increasingly threatening; wind gusts increased in intensity causing sheets of water to assault the windowpanes as thunder boomed. The angry sky remained eerily dark, an ominous purplish-grey, but now the darkness was interspersed with bright flashes of lightening.

The kitchen staff began arriving, dripping, soaked like drowned rats. Thankfully the front of the house staff was more concerned with appearance, and arrived appropriately dry thanks to ponchos and umbrellas that left puddles all over the staff break room.

Brad barged through the door like a white tornado, barking orders to everyone, and apologizing at the same time for being tardy. "There are trees down on my street from the storm, and I couldn't get my car out!" At least I think that was an apology.

"I've got to get moving. This weather is a pain. I'll be behind all day now!" I assured him I was confident that with his skills he could handle everything. He grumbled under his breath and turned away.

I decided to leave him alone; I knew he could set things right, it wasn't going to be any better with me standing there. The kitchen staff had begun to hustle as soon as he arrived, and things would be just fine.

Through the dining room windows I could see nature's fury. The normally calm lake was whipped into dark waves that pounded the rocks with such force that geysers erupted onto the shore. At nearby lakefront homes boats bounced in the water and crashed into the piers where they were moored. I don't know anything about watercraft, but I hoped that the owners had some kind of padding along the piers to protect those expensive boats.

Just then a huge log was tossed from the tumultuous lake onto our shore. I stopped worrying about other people's watercraft and became concerned about whether Unincorporated's outdoor furniture could be flung about in the gusting wind.

No sooner had that thought occurred to me than I saw several kitchen staffers rush outdoors to move chairs, benches, and tables into our storage building. Our patio furniture was good quality with heavy weight, unlikely to budge in the wind, but I was happy to know any possibility had been removed.

"Thanks for sending your staff out into the weather," I said, looking into the kitchen. "Only you would think of outdoor furniture being a liability in a storm." I'd thought of it myself, of course, but flattery can be a useful tool.

For my thanks I got a grunt, followed by, "That's what I'm here for."

The drenched staffers were coming back into the building and I made a point of thanking them. They ignored my thanks; it was obvious that they saw Brad as their authority figure, not me.

In one way that hurt, but in another it was fine. As cantankerous as Brad could be, I knew he wouldn't do anything to hurt our reputation. The food served at Unincorporated was his top priority. As long as the kitchen staff followed his lead we'd serve amazing delectable entrees from an immaculate kitchen. It couldn't get much better than that. A little respect for the acting manager might improve the atmosphere, but not the food.

A loud crack of thunder convinced me to unlock the front door ahead of schedule. Better to have guests inside before we were ready to serve than to have them wet and unhappy outdoors. A few people who had been sitting in their cars rushed toward the entry when they saw me unlock the door and turn on the lights.

Shared experiences create instant friendships, so conversations were in full force among people waiting to be seated.

"Isn't this wonderful? We've needed this rain so badly," a retired gentleman said to a female friend.

"But why today, of all days? I just had my hair done." The retired gentleman didn't seem to care.

"We'd planned a 20-mile bike ride for today. The kids are *so* disappointed," a young mother said. Her kids, busy with electronic games, looked at her with raised eyebrows.

"I could be imagining it, but I think my azaleas are already perking up." This observation came from a regular guest whose eyesight was failing badly.

Not all the conversations were comforting. "The road out by the Higby farm is completely under water," a woman told her friends.

Not to be outdone, a companion offered, "A branch from their hundred-year oak tree snapped, broke a window, and landed in John and Jackie's bedroom. They weren't hurt, but are really shook up."

I hadn't realized just how vicious the storm had become, and found the details alarming. New people came rushing in with weather stories, and I heard the phrase "flood warning" being used.

Flood warning? Didn't water around here just run down to the lake? Maybe the warning was meant for individual properties that were on level land…surely there couldn't be danger of having too much rain water in the middle of a drought.

Customers continued to pour in the door (sorry, I just had to say that) faster than our lunchtime crew could serve them, but the guests didn't seem to mind. They were taking shelter from the elements at Unincorporated; eating would be the icing on the cake, but wasn't the reason they'd come. I saw faces that usually only came in the evening, and locals who I'd never seen at Unincorporated at all.

Our guests nervously chatted about roof shingles tearing loose in blustery winds, water damage to historic homes, downed trees, and power outages at the other end of town. Homeowners anxiously watched the weather, while visitors varied in attitude from excited to frightened.

We seldom lit the fireplace in summer, never at noon, but this day called for a roaring fire that would warm shivering bodies and calm anxious minds. Kneeling in front of our fireplace I arranged tinder, kindling and logs in the huge stone opening, reached inside to open the flue, and lit a match under a few purchased fire-starters (this was considered cheating by any woodsman, but I was never adept at one-match fires).

Dawn had been right about inclement weather bringing good business. Several shopkeepers hadn't opened that day, no power meaning no lights and no cash registers; we had a good group of Chamber of Commerce members sitting together at a large table. The Marys, perfectly quaffed and in proper resort wear were sitting by the windows; the Winchesters who owned Wholesale Wholegrains were in a corner by the kitchen; Rupert sat at the bar. Even Man-in-Brown was there, alone at a table staring at the wall.

Our building held a veritable Who's Who of Windsor Grove that day; it was nice to know that everyone chose Unincorporated as the place to turn when they felt the need to gather. Of course, several other possible gathering places had no power, but it was gratifying nonetheless.

Also gratifying, in a personal way, was the unruly state of many women's hair. I always looked for affirmation that I wasn't alone in having out-of-control hair in humid weather. Despite having a million other things on my mind, I smiled inside each time a frizzled head walked in.

A tiny paper airplane sailing through the air told me that Mr. Horner was dining with us that day. Perhaps storms brought out his inner child even more than usual. I tossed the airplane in with recycling, and kept moving. Now was not the time to discuss dining room etiquette.

"Say Missy," said one elderly lady who looked vaguely familiar, "How's your Uncle doing?"

"He's recovering, but not as quickly as he'd like," I answered. That name again; I'll never get used to being called *Missy*, but it's better than *Hey You*, so I answer to it. Actually, I also answer to *Hey You*.

"I hope he gets back to work soon. It's not the same with you here." I had to agree, but I thought it rude of her to say it. I moved on to the next table as soon as I could.

Several local resorts and inns had power outages, and their guests sat at our tables discussing their options: should they check out and head for home, or wait out the storm hoping power would be restored? I suddenly wondered what I was supposed to do if power went out at Unincorporated.

A quick conference with Dawn gave me the answer; put candles on all the tables, and switch to a salad-and-cold-sandwich menu. An auxiliary lighting system would provide minimal light in the kitchen and restrooms for several hours, and there was an emergency button on the cash register so we could open the drawer to accept cash and checks.

I decided to be proactive, moving the votive candles and holders from the stockroom. It made sense to have them on a convenient shelf below the main waitstation.

The large number of staff in the kitchen, which had been vacant not long ago, was surprising. There were far more people than would have been scheduled for a Wednesday morning. I soon received the answer to my unspoken question.

"We came to see if you need help with…uh…anything. Like… um…you know, in case we have any flooding or stuff like that. Let us know what we can do to help, okay, Ashley?" one of the young dishwashers requested eagerly. He seemed excited by the thought of flooding, and I was reminded that several of the staff were local teens who had little adventure in their lives during summer break.

I was taken aback by the idea that these young staffers had gravitated to Unincorporated at the threat of disaster. I hoped it indicated a protective feeling toward their work environment. Sure, I knew it was more likely that they wanted to get away from storm-related chores at home, but it made me feel good nonetheless. I promised to keep an eye out for something useful they could do.

"Get all these people the hell out of my kitchen!" Brad was obviously not enjoying the company of his unscheduled staff. So what else is new?

The staff moved to the back entryway, rolling their eyes, but knowing they truly were in the way. I continued to be amazed at how faithfully the kitchen staff idolized the chef, considering how gruffly he treated them. His leadership skills must be palpable when you work around him; I'd never spent enough time in the kitchen to know.

Guests were still crowding through the door, water flowing off their raincoats and umbrellas. And yes, though it made me cringe, a few older women wore those little plastic rain bonnets they always seemed to have in their purses. The soggy people coming in the door made me realize what the young members of our crew who weren't on the schedule could do to help.

"Bring your umbrellas and raincoats to the front lobby," I told them. But I was reminded that kids are too *cool* to carry umbrellas or wear raincoats. Luckily we had quite the umbrella collection in our lost and found cupboard, and I distributed them among the crew.

"Watch for guests to arrive, then run out to their cars to escort them to the front door," I instructed my young staffers. They seemed to appreciate the opportunity, and started competing to see who could best keep their charges dry. The guests were thrilled to have umbrella escorts, and it created a party-like atmosphere.

A bit later, once a few diners were ready to leave, some of the staff offered to run to their cars and drive them up to our canopy. I agreed to this unexpected service, although I wasn't at all certain it was legal, or covered by insurance. I rationalized that exceptional circumstances made some rules superfluous.

The treacherous weather seemed to bring out the best in everyone, and much laughter accompanied the kids rushing around under umbrellas, escorting friends and strangers alike to our front entrance. I saw several cash tips change hands, bringing pleasure to kitchen staffers who are normally not tipped employees. Several comments were made about how wonderful it was that we provided this service. I wondered how Uncle Al would feel when he saw the additional wages that were adding up.

All the while, there was constant motion in the dining room. Everyone wanted a view of the turbulent lake; if they weren't at a table convenient to the windows they made continual excuses to wander over....saying "Hi" to a friend...taking a detour on the way to the restroom...until eventually people just came right out and said they wanted to watch the breakers crash against the shore.

One of Wisconsin's 15,000 lakes, Windsor Lake covers less than 500 acres, in many parts of the country not large enough to be called a lake at all, but a lake by Wisconsin standards. Fed by streams and tributaries it has no major outlets, so the water level varies with the seasons and the weather.

In the recent drought our sandy beaches had become larger, with several piers no longer reaching water's edge. But it only takes a little rain, running down the surrounding topography, to raise the water level quickly. (I learned all this at the local visitor's center; they sell brightly colored posters filled with "Fun Facts" about our town and our lake. Visitors had constant questions that I tried to answer, and those posters were amazingly helpful).

The fascination with watching our angry, churning body of water was understandable. The lake level appeared to be rising quickly, although it was hard to tell between the dark skies, the constant downpour, and the rough surface of the water in the blustery wind. Whitecaps rushing across our normally smooth lake made a statement about the storm's fury.

One of our regular guests, a self-appointed expert on everything, was lecturing in a supercilious tone, "When unseasonably dry conditions, as we've experienced during this current atmospheric pattern, create a soil as severely parched as it is in this interval, a continuing downpour is more likely to run off our sandy loam soil than to be absorbed. Meteorologically speaking, this drought phenomenon won't be alleviated by today's precipitation."

He was right, of course, but he was acting like he'd just made some amazing scientific breakthrough. I saw more than a few guests walk the other way when they saw him coming.

The ferocity of the storm increased as the afternoon wore on. Dark heavy storm clouds released torrents of rain. Thunder became a constant rumble, occasional deafening cracks reminding everyone that nature knows no mercy. The sky fluctuated from brilliant flashes of light to stormy obscurity.

Dangerously powerful winds pounded relentlessly on our little community, and created a stressful environment for the towering trees in the forest. Our lights flickered a few times, warning that we just might need those candles.

In the kitchen Brad was in his glory, shouting orders to an energized staff, and turning out plates of food so fast that our servers had trouble keeping up. A cacophony of sound told me his staff was hustling to stay on task.

I went to the front entrance and called one of the unscheduled staffers over and asked him to help in the lounge. "If you're over eighteen you can serve alcohol, if not wash glasses, clean the counter, and ask what else you can do to help."

"I turned eighteen last December, so I can help with everything," he grinned as he rushed to the back room. "I'll wash my hands and be right back!"

He was the dishwasher who had so eagerly volunteered to help anywhere he could. I wondered where this enthusiastic kid had come from. He'd never given the impression of caring much about his job or anything related to it. His lackluster hours at the dish machine hadn't led me to expect that he had much energy, but I was seeing a different side of him. Now I had to figure out what his name was...

"Renata, I'm sending you a helper. He'll need a lot of guidance!"

I'd barely gotten the words out when the dishwasher bounded into the bar with a huge grin on his face. He'd combed his hair, tucked his shirt in, and seemed transformed. "Tell me where to start!"

"Hi Mike!" Renata said, answering one of my questions. "The men down at the end are waiting for refills. Domestic beers are in the far cooler." Mike quickly got to work, chatting with the guests while he filled their orders. I could see Renata's shoulders relax even while she continued mixing cocktails.

Create a new position for Mike got added to the list in my head; if he could be cross-trained he could be invaluable. I'd find out from Brad if he was dependably on time, and whether he followed directions. It wouldn't be the first time a staffer with tons of ability wasn't able to conform, but I could hope. Only time would tell.

I'd been wondering how Bekah was occupying her time; this definitely wasn't the casual sun-filled day she'd looked forward to. I took an opportunity to duck into my office and send a text. "What's up? It's crazy busy here. Come over if you want. No idea when I'll get free."

There was no immediate reply, but at least I'd reached out. She may have decided it was a day to hibernate; if I hadn't been working that's what I would have done. Bekah was a big girl; she could take care of herself, I wasn't going to worry about her.

Hurrying back to the entry to greet more guests I was dismayed to see our constant visitor, Officer Gregg. He was the last person I wanted to deal with at the moment, especially entering through the front door. I hoped that he hadn't used a young staffer as an umbrella escort.

"Hi Ashley," he said in what I'd come to recognize as his bad news voice. "We're visiting all the lakefront businesses to warn them about the weather."

His words seemed totally unnecessary. Did he think I hadn't noticed the weather?

"Flood warnings have been posted for the entire lake area. The streams are already over their banks, several roads are flooded, and water is rushing down land at a dangerous rate. The DNR thinks that the lake will overflow its banks within the next two hours, even if it stops raining. We're warning everyone with lakefront property to be prepared to vacate."

Vacate? Was he kidding?

"I have a dining room and bar full of customers. Paying customers. This could turn out to be a great business day. What am I supposed to do, tell them to leave?" I'm sure he could tell I was annoyed by his suggestion. I'd never been testy with him before, but I felt like I'd reached my limit.

"Well, they don't have to leave immediately. But keep an eye on the lake, and get your customers out of here as soon as the lake overflows, which could be quite soon. Once that happens it won't be long until the water reaches your building; at that point you *must* have everyone out of here! When they leave tell them to head to higher ground and not remain anywhere near the water." His voice, filled with authority, left no room for debate.

"That goes for you too," he advised. "Don't stay in your cottage if the water's getting close. That's not a suggestion, it's an order. Rushing water can be treacherous; no one should ever take chances, because when you're up against nature you lose. Thanks for your help. Gotta go." And with that he turned and left the building.

Now what? This was out of my comfort zone, if I had a comfort zone at all. I glanced around to see if anyone had overheard Gregg's words, but he'd been discreet and no one seemed to be any the wiser. I was considering turning off our OPEN sign and locking the doors, when an exceptionally loud clap of thunder and a blinding explosion of lightening occurred simultaneously, immediately followed by a darkness unusual in daytime. Our lights flickered, and died.

There was a moment of silence in the dining room while everyone expectantly waited for our lights to reawaken. This was followed by a huge groan as everyone realized that we, too, had no power. The gloomy half-light made my decision easy, and I locked the doors for the day.

The kitchen staff plated up the hot food they'd already prepared, and with Brad barking orders, started creating salads and sandwiches for guests who still waited to order. Everyone was good natured about the diminished menu; I was happy to see that no one left without eating. Lounge sales were also good, as several visitors had said they had nothing else to do, they might as well have a drink.

"Hi, is this Ashley?" said a male voice when I answered the phone. "This is TJ, Renata's fiancé. I want to warn her about bad roads." I remembered that he worked for the highway department. "There's so much water that cars are hydroplaning. I know she's probably busy; can you give her my message? And you might want to warn everyone else, too."

I thanked him for calling, repeated his warning to Renata, and then made a point of cautioning every departing guest. I was starting to feel responsible for their safety. For the first time I realized that many of these people had become important to me.

I did manage to get everyone out of Unincorporated, fed and happy, before the banks overflowed, but only by a short while. The rain continued to pour down from the skies, and water created gullies in our yard as it rushed toward the lake.

I shooed the staff out the door with an admonishment about staying high, dry and safe, and proceeded to lock up. There didn't seem to be much point in doing any cleaning. Dirty dishes wouldn't go anywhere; I preferred to follow Gregg's orders and stay secure. I thought about calling Bekah with a warning about the rising wataer, but decided against it; I'd be at the cottage myself in a few minutes.

While completing a few closing duties, I glanced into the kitchen, noticed a large box sitting on the chef's counter, and went to investigate. I was glad I'd looked; it was a frozen case of tuna steaks needed for the next day's sesame encrusted appetizer. Brad must have forgotten about it when the power went out. Even with my limited knowledge of foodservice, I knew that foods should never be thawed at room temperature. Risk of food borne illness, especially with seafood, was too high.

The tuna hadn't begun to thaw, so I hurried to return it to the walk-in freezer. I was anxious to get out of the restaurant and head home, if only to decide what my options were. Was the cottage unsafe in these conditions? It was an uncomfortable situation; I felt flustered and vulnerable.

The wind whistled through the kitchen's duct work and the thunder increased in volume, vibrating through the rattling delivery door.

I carried the bulky case into the freezer, careful not to fully close the heavy stainless steel door behind me, and peered into the darkness searching for an open shelf. The floor was slippery where water had dripped and turned to ice.

Struggling to keep my footing and carry the box, I noticed a change in the air flow pattern that I couldn't readily define. There was a subtle difference in the sounds vibrating through the kitchen, making me wonder if the roof had developed a leak, or if perhaps a door hadn't been properly secured.

Turning to look over my shoulder, I saw the thick freezer door slowly moving into the closed position. At first I thought I was imagining it in the shadowy gloom of the partially-lit kitchen. But it quickly became apparent that the massive door was inexplicably closing, smoothly and steadily. With me inside.

CHAPTER 20

Whoomph! My ears popped from the pressure as the door latched, the no-nonsense effect of an oversized airtight freezer door closing firmly, trapping cold inside, and warmth and freedom out. A perfect seal created after years of study, to completely deny transference of air until something breaks the suction.

I tried to navigate toward the door to shove it open, but slipped, losing my balance. The tuna dropped to the icy floor, and I stumbled over it, flailing my arms, unable to right myself, and slamming my butt down onto the unyielding cold surface. The walk-in was kept at well-below-freezing temperatures; the darkness was complete.

My discomfort level was compounded by the fact that I'd landed on a frozen patch of ice. I wasn't scared, exactly; I knew the freezer had a safety release to prevent anyone being locked in, but I'd never actually looked at it, and certainly didn't know what to feel for, or how it worked. In my slightly panicked state I'd sadly lost track of precisely where the door was.

I stood up, using shelving units for leverage. I'd never realized that the entire floor could be like a skating rink (it didn't help that my shoes were still damp from my walk to work that morning). Once on my feet I tried to remember what direction I'd been facing when I fell, and where the door was in conjunction with my position.

I moved slowly in the direction I expected to find the door, immediately tripping over that stupid box of tuna. Alright, I knew there wouldn't be anything else on the floor; once I got around that carton I should be able to locate the door.

But finding the door wasn't as easy as it sounded, I wasn't familiar enough with the various shelves. Unlike a home freezer, the walk-in was about the same square footage as my current bedroom, with shelving units arranged in aisles. As you'd expect given Brad's organizational skills, the frozen products were precisely placed, but in the complete darkness I couldn't recall any details about the layout.

I kept feeling blindly for a doorway, and would end up grabbing a tray of food waiting for the next stage in its preparation. Move a few feet further, and reach out to a solid case of who-knows-what. I knew that becoming disoriented could be fatal; a person in distress who keeps their wits about them is more likely to survive. Hundreds of people have perished in survivable circumstances when they failed to concentrate. But concentrating in a desperate situation can tax the fortitude of even the strongest person.

I put my hand out, touched something soft and slimy, and almost screamed. *Okay, take it easy* I told myself. *Breathe deeply and slowly, and concentrate.* I remembered seeing Brad putting raw chicken breasts on a tray with sauce over them, and laying a sheet of plastic wrap over the top. Even though they'd looked disgusting at the time I was happy to recognize that the squishy substance in the freezer was being precisely held for the next stage in preparation. Should it be covered with more than plastic wrap? Surely there was a health code about covering stored food. It's funny what goes through your mind during a crisis. Why worry about plastic wrap now?

Getting colder by the minute my wet shoes were stinging my chilled feet. Shivering, I finally found the door, and gratefully felt for any kind of handle. I thought I'd located the safety release, but it wouldn't budge. Was there a second latch? My fingers were numb, and it didn't help that I'd never paid any attention to the door mechanism.

Pushing, pulling, lifting, pounding and shaking didn't have any effect on the latch, and I began to panic. I knew the building was vacant, I'd sent everyone home. With the storm raging and the power off there was no chance of anyone wandering in to make a delivery, or do a cleaning project, or turn on ovens for baking.

What if I couldn't get out? I didn't know how long people could survive in a freezer, but it definitely wasn't overnight. I was no expert, but I knew that hypothermia could be fatal. *Keep moving, keep your extremities warm, and find a way out!*

In a frenzy I pounded on the door with closed fists, and then stopped. It wasn't going to help, and I was getting winded. I had to conserve energy and formulate a plan, so shivering from cold and trembling with fear, I started to grope along the shelves for anything that might help.

Beside the door I located a pair of gloves, probably used during freezer inventory. Having gloves for my hands was so exciting I could feel myself smiling, which was a substantial overreaction under the circumstances. They gave me some hope, but I found nothing else that seemed useful.

I tried to think of a way to escape, but my brain kept reverting back to the genesis of my dilemma. In the forefront was a vision of the freezer door, standing open a few inches, perfectly balanced in the position it normally held when staffers made a quick trip to the interior.

There hadn't been a breeze in the kitchen, despite the sound of whipping wind; there was no reason the door would have closed itself. I'd heard unusual creaking before the door moved, and my confused mind could think of no explanation unless someone had been in the building. In the kitchen. Closing the door.

But it wasn't possible that anyone would have deliberately trapped me. Was it? A horrifying thought. I couldn't focus on anything else; I could only envision the door slowly moving to create my current prison. Who could have done it? Just about anyone, actually. Almost the entire Unincorporated staff had been there, along with huge numbers of guests.

In the chaotic atmospheric conditions, with the staff gone, and diminished visibility, it didn't even have to be someone who'd been in the building while we served. Anyone insidious enough could have entered the kitchen through the unlocked staff entrance.

My teeth chattered, my nose was running, and the frigid cold chilled my back making my neck tense, my shoulders hunched and painful. I had a headache between my eyes, and seriously regretted the lightweight fabric of my summer shirt. Every part of my body suffered. Even my brain seemed to hurt.

What could I do? Why didn't I have my cell phone with me? If I could make a phone call everything would be fine. My staff weren't allowed to carry phones while on duty, but I was the boss wasn't I? I could have a phone if I wanted to. No one could complain about that.

That was it…I'd carry a phone…my predicament would be over… my problems solved. I was proud of my solution; pleased at the thought of how organized I'd be. I saw myself multitasking…accomplishing overwhelming things. I closed my eyes, imagining myself the envy of every other restaurateur…what a wonderful plan…I congratulated myself on this perfect solution…I could rest now…

With a start I realized I'd been dreaming…hallucinating… fantasizing. *No!* I couldn't lose concentration. Clear thinking was difficult while shivering and miserable, but clear thinking was vital. *Pay attention, Ashley!*

I felt exhausted. I wanted to sit down and sleep for days. *Why am I here? Oh, I remember. Tuna.*

I had to devise a solution for my predicament, and soon. Unfortunately, frantically pounding on the freezer door was the only thought I had. So I pounded…and pounded…stopping to fight for a deep breath, inhaling frigid air, then pounding some more. Relentlessly, hopelessly. Losing track of time…struggling for each breath… shivering…gasping and pummeling…*inhale…exhale…pound on the door…don't lose focus Ashley.* How long had I been in there? It seemed like forever. How long until someone else would come by? That also seemed like forever. And forever is a long time…

Suddenly I thought I felt vibrations through the door, like a weird phantom tremor, and I feared I was again losing touch with reality. Terror added to my building anxiety. *Keep breathing, keep breathing.*

Without warning the freezer door flung open and I lost my balance, wobbling forward into the kitchen, falling clumsily against Brad's muscular chest. He stood there staring down at me as if I were some exotic, unknown and unwelcome creature. After a few moments he stepped back, letting me move past him.

"What do you think you're doing in there? You've got no damn business meddling in my kitchen. Explain this!" he demanded in his most accusatory tone. Shivering, I tried to stammer some explanation, but nothing that came out sounded like English.

"I come back here to finish putting things away," he grumbled, "and I find you creating a commotion in my freezer. Do you want to tell me what's going on?"

I managed to get out the words "...put food away..." and that made him angrier than ever.

"Well that was stupid, didn't you know I'd come back to finish up? I left to make sure everyone else got home safe, especially those young kids. I wasn't done cleaning up. What kind of a chef do you think I am that I'd leave food out to spoil?" he thundered. "Go on home. I'll take care of things, like I always do. Do I have to walk you home, too?"

"No, no," was all I could get out. Still trembling I careened unsteadily to the office, grabbed my shoulder bag, and started to stumble out the door.

"Hey Ashley, that safety latch in the freezer is broken. You should get that fixed!" were his parting words. A fact that possibly should have been mentioned sooner.

"Some storm, huh? Crazy weather." Arriving back at the cottage I found Bekah primping in front of the mirror. She'd slept in, and then spent the stormy day hanging out in the cottage. After I relaxed in a warm shower, and began to calm down, I told her about my freezer ordeal.

My thoughts came out in disorganized fashion, accompanied by the clamor of rain on the roof, wind screaming through the treetops, and lightning bolts like electric shocks.

She listened politely as I wondered aloud if someone had deliberately closed me in. Who could have done it? Brad was there, or at least nearby.

If he hadn't done it, wouldn't he have seen whoever did? Not really, not with the downpour and the darkness and his leaving with the staff.

Come to think of it, it really was great of him to go out into the elements to ensure the staff was safe. I'd have to thank him for it, and also thank him for rescuing me…and apologize for not being confident that he'd be back to finish organizing his kitchen. It was a humbling situation, with Brad coming off as the hero, and me as a bumbling bystander. So what else was new?

I was becoming embarrassed about the whole incident. The door probably did just close on its own with the day's weird air flow patterns. My imagination was far too active lately; I blamed that on Officer Gregg and his constant admonishments.

Once I'd decompressed enough to stop talking, Bekah took a deep breath and looked at me with eyes full of excitement.

"Guess what?" she grinned bouncing with pleasure. "I got a phone call about an hour ago…maybe not that long…no, about an hour. Anyway, I have a job interview tomorrow! I'm already packed, and Mom wants me to leave right away before the roads get any worse."

I must have been more shaken than I'd admitted, because I hadn't even noticed her packed bags by the door. The short-sleeved lilac shirt and lilac twill shorts she wore should have given me a clue. Her choice of sunny attire on this gloomy day told me she was ecstatic; it finally sunk in. Had she listened to my rant at all?

I sat stunned. Here I was, in the middle of a crisis, totally overwhelmed with dangers and problems and responsibilities, with a murder investigation going on around me, and my best friend was leaving and was happy to go. What was wrong with this picture? On her first night in town she went on a date; the next day she leaves. Some friend!

I tried to be supportive, but couldn't bring myself to share her enthusiasm. I needed Bekah's company now more than ever. What an awful time to have a job interview. But I helped her carry her things through the howling gale to her car, getting drenched while I hugged her goodbye.

"If the roads are flooded turn around and come back," I warned. "Good luck with your interview. Let me know how it goes. Thanks for visiting. Next time I hope you can stay longer." I tried to sound upbeat, but doubt if I succeeded. It didn't matter; Bekah wasn't paying attention.

Looking past my shoulder with a puzzled expression she asked, "What's that sticking to your door?"

Whatever it was, it hadn't been there when I'd come home a short time earlier. It looked like paper trash blown by the wind, and I said, "I'm sure it's nothing. Lots of debris is flying around today." So as I stood getting wetter by the minute, we said quick goodbyes and she drove off, waving and excited.

Rushing through the howling, raging storm back to the cottage, I thought about how comforting it had been to have company. Wrapped up in my thoughts, I almost ignored the paper on my screen door, until with a sinking feeling I realized it wasn't stuck there by wind and rain. The paper was a corner torn from one of our placemats, and anchoring the paper, driven deeply into the wooden door frame, was one of Unincorporated's missing knives.

I ripped the soggy paper from the door, without touching the knife, and my heart skipped a beat when I read the words childishly scribbled on it.

Trembling and unable to catch my breath, I stood staring at the sinister scrap of placemat.

CHAPTER 21

STOP HELPING THE COPS it screamed.

Helping the cops? Is that what I was doing? No, I was trying to learn the truth. And someone didn't like it. The notes to Lynette and John, and to Carrie, had been reasonably generic, but this one was specific, and felt threatening.

My brain went through several stages of panic, and I felt my heart pounding. My mouth was suddenly dry, my hands trembling. When I could finally think clearly I knew I had to call Gregg. Immediately.

I ran into the cottage and reached for the phone, then realized it had been years since an old rotary phone sat on that corner of the desk. Phone…where was a phone? Oh, right. In my purse. An hour ago I'd decided that a phone was the answer to all my problems. Now I'd forgotten where it was.

Digging the device out of my vast shoulder bag, I struggled to keep my hands steady. It was difficult to punch those few numbers… nine-one-one. My call was answered quickly with, "Emergency Services. How can I help you?"

Unsure of how much to divulge, I answered in a weak quivering voice, "I need to talk to Officer Gregg. Or Detective Milton. Right now."

"Is it an emergency? We are in the middle of a significant storm event."

"Yes, it's an emergency. Sort of. I think. Yes…it is. An emergency."

"I'll have an officer return your call as soon as possible."

So I waited. I toweled water from my face and arms, shivering though it was a warm day. Alone with my thoughts, my tensions and fears all rose to the surface. I sat trembling, tears running down my cheeks, hugging Teddy Maxwell, wanting to be anywhere but Windsor Grove.

When my phone vibrated in my hand I jumped, and stared at it for a moment before answering.

"Hello," I stammered.

"Ashley, what's up?" Gregg's voice said in my ear.

Trying to compose myself, I squeaked, "I think someone tried to kill me today!"

"I'll be right over. Stay right where you are. Oh...where are you?"

I laughed at that, and told him I'd stay in the cottage. In fact I didn't move an inch until I heard his knock. I peered through the daytime darkness at my visitor before I opened the door.

A dripping fluorescent yellow official sheriff's department hooded poncho moved forward into the cottage, and once the cumbersome raingear had been removed Gregg was revealed underneath.

Stamping his feet on the doormat he quietly repeated his initial question.

"What's up? I take it you called about that knife so prominently displayed on your door." He gave me a slight smile. "Can I assume this is a recent development?"

The concerned tone of his voice and the caring look on his face was more than I could take. I started sobbing, couldn't catch my breath, and felt like a fool.

Gregg pulled out his phone, pressed a few digits, and began speaking intently at low volume. When he'd finished he turned back to me, putting an arm around my shoulders and leading me to the couch. He offered to bring me a glass of water, and when he returned he'd also brought a box of tissues. He sat down next to me, talking slowly and quietly about some of the ongoing problems from the storm: flooded roads, downed trees, residents being evacuated. His soothing voice was calming, and soon I was less hysterical, breathing more normally. When eventually I could speak coherently I told him about finding the note.

His eyes widened when I showed him the soggy torn scrap of placemat. He pulled his notebook from his pocket and began writing.

"You're telling me it wasn't there just a short time earlier?"

"Right. I'm positive it wasn't."

"How long were you inside?"

"Probably less than a half hour."

"So in that half hour someone stuck a knife in your doorframe. Did you see anyone nearby?"

I shook my head.

"How about Bekah? Is she still here? Did she see anyone?"

I shook my head again. "No, and she just left."

"Did you hear anything unusual? Any pounding?"

"All the racket from the storm. A lot of thunder and rumbling. Branches hitting the cottage. Boats crashing against piers. I didn't notice anything specific..."

He stopped making notes and looked quizzical; he could tell that I hadn't divulged everything yet.

"There's...there's more...," I stammered. My voice trembled as I started to describe being locked in the freezer. I was still unsure whether that was a fluke or a deliberate attempt to scare me; but I knew the episode had to be reported in detail. And detail is what Gregg got.

As I talked I regained some composure, and my words rushed out, thoughts and ideas sometimes coming faster than I could articulate them. Partway through my download, I rubbed a tissue under my eyes, and realized I had mascara running down my cheeks. I must have been a real treat to look at, but Gregg didn't seem to notice.

"I'm going to give you the same advice I gave to Lynnette and John after they got their note and to Carrie when she got hers: get out of town! Go away and don't let anyone but me know where you are."

"That's not possible...I can't. I'm the only person in the family who is free to run Unincorporated. I can't leave now, it just won't work." This sounded lame, even to me. He knew as well as I did that I had little or no knowledge about the restaurant industry, and that Unincorporated would function almost as well without me. But he tactfully pretended to understand my reluctance.

"We can't force you to go, but it would be for your own safety. I can't stress that enough. I'm sure your family will understand. Please think about it. And if you don't leave, do *not* go anywhere alone, not the grocery store, not to the beach, not to church, not *anywhere!*" His stern expression left no doubt about how seriously he meant this advice.

"Is there someone who can come and stay with you? I want to know you're safe. Try to find someone, okay?" he said it kindly, but it was clearly an order, not a request.

"Maybe Bekah, if she doesn't get her job," I agreed. I really didn't want a full-time roommate. And Bekah would be useless as a protector. But she was someone I trusted completely, and lately I wasn't sure who else I could trust.

His next words would stay with me for a long time. "We don't know what's going on here, but you have to consider yourself to be in constant danger as long as you're in Windsor Grove. Whoever put the note on your door felt fearless, undefeatable, bold enough to come right onto your porch. If our killer feels that invincible you may not be safe anywhere.

"I'd like to find out how many people knew the safety release inside the freezer was broken. Also we have to consider that most people probably don't know the safety release exists at all. *If* you were deliberately trapped in the freezer, the only people above suspicion would be those who knew about the release but thought it was working."

That was complicated, but he was right. Anyone who thought the freezer had a working safety release would have no motivation to use it as an instrument of torture. Or execution.

In denial, hoping that being closed in the freezer was a freak accident, I didn't want to talk about it. Denial was more comforting than acknowledging ever-present danger.

"Whether or not you're willing to leave town, and I sure wish you would, you have to come to the station to file a report," he continued. "Actually two reports; one on the note stuck to your door, one on the freezer incident. There's a mighty good chance that the two incidents are connected. It would be an amazing coincidence if they're not. I'll drive you to the station; the weather is making navigation difficult."

"Do I have to come? Today? I just want to lock the doors and crawl into bed."

"Yes, you have to. And yes, you have to do it right now while the details are fresh in your mind." I was surprised at how firmly he delivered this statement. It was apparent that when he wanted to, Gregg could manifest undeniable authority.

"Can I at least spend a few minutes making myself look better?"

"You look fine," he shrugged. But he pulled out his phone and checked messages while I tried to make myself appear human again. Between my damp stringy ringlets of hair, my smeared make-up, and an unnaturally pale complexion, I was mortified when I looked in the mirror. I looked like the victim in a horror film.

I had to give credit to any guy who could say, "You look fine," with a straight face. Maybe he hadn't really looked at me, but for an officer who was supposed to be observant that didn't sound very likely.

Once I was a little more presentable we headed to the Sheriff's Office. The sky wasn't as dark as it had been, the thunder had died down, but the rain continued to fall in torrents.

As we rode through town I could see obvious destruction. Branches and limbs lay on the ground with an occasional uprooted tree for emphasis. Brilliant flowers that had been saluting the sky all summer were flattened to the ground as if trampled by elephants. When I'd get a glimpse of the lake I saw areas where new erosion was evident. More disturbing was the obvious danger from power lines on the ground.

Despite the continuing deluge, there were people everywhere. The large amount of traffic on the roads was surprising, but more fascinating were the number of citizens who were already pitching in to help where they could. Wisconsin Energy technicians corralled downed power lines; families pulled large tree limbs from the road; and drenched strangers standing ankle-deep in water directed traffic around flooded intersections. This was humanity at its best…neighbors helping neighbors. It seemed impossible that anyone from this wonderful community had left the note on my door.

"I'm going to leave you here," Gregg explained after we'd entered the Sheriff's Office. "We were having a hectic day already, and now we're learning about the people who couldn't be bothered to follow orders, and are now calling us for help." His facial expression made it clear how disgusted he was.

"Apparently some teenagers decided to ride out the storm in their summer home, and are surprised to be surrounded by rushing water. We're going out to rescue them in a motorboat. Foolish kids!

"I'll arrange for someone to get you home," he said as he left the room. "Take care of yourself; keep your doors locked; don't go anywhere alone; call me if you have any other problems. I want to know that you're safe."

I was surprised at how comforted I felt at his concern. And how alone I felt when he'd left.

My statements were recorded, then transcribed for my signature. Despite the fact that no one was paying much attention to me, I felt like I was on display in a cage. I wanted to get out of that office; the process seemed to take forever. I wanted to see what was going on outside, but mostly I just wanted to be anywhere but there.

Eventually I was allowed to leave, and as good as his word, Gregg had a county employee waiting to drive me home. The storm had lessened in intensity, leaving devastation and destruction behind. Dark, heavy clouds continued to roll across the sky, depositing their contents on Windsor Grove.

"The lake overflowed its banks; the water level was almost two feet higher than normal. That, combined with the wind and waves, caused up to a foot of water to flow inside some waterfront buildings. With so much danger of injury and electrocution all local emergency personnel have been called into service. The volunteer firefighters have been pressed into action, along with all our sheriff's officers," said the staffer, who asked me to call her Lisa.

"We put out a mutual-aid call, but nearby towns are overwhelmed too, and can't help. That's the way it goes in a storm, every department is stretched to the max. We've identified a way to get vehicles through town, even with all the closed roads," Lisa continued as she drove a circuitous route.

Looking around, I was reminded of a *what's wrong with this picture?* puzzle. Homes had obvious damage, tourists' cars sat in water above the floorboards, and an amazing conglomeration of unidentifiable debris floated in soggy yards.

"Someone said that a huge oak tree fell on that new bed-and-breakfast north of town," Lisa commented, "and a big branch flew through the window at Bonnie's Bakery. The officers are estimating that some wind gusts may have reached 60 miles per hour." She was younger than I, maybe eighteen, and seemed to be enjoying the disaster.

During our ride I noticed that dozens of roofing shingles had blown off the Brady Museum, and several local businesses sported broken windows and damaged signs. Rupert's yard-signs littered several properties, adding a touch of brightness to the general gloom. I suddenly realized I should be concerned about Unincorporated, and began to stress out about what I'd find.

As we neared the property I grew apprehensive. I'd been so wrapped up in my own troubles that potential damage to the property had fallen entirely off my radar. My stomach clenched in trepidation of what I might find.

The restaurant...the cottage...my car...what was I returning to? From what I could see there weren't any areas in the community that remained unaffected.

Lisa stopped her car before we entered Unincorporated's parking lot so we could move a few tree limbs out of our way. Nearby, a large oak tree lay on the ground, partially blocking the highway. I was dismayed to see the level of the lake, with waves lapping increasingly closer to the building. If the rain continued to fall at this pace the historic restaurant would be one more flooded building.

Other than a plethora of branches, twigs, and leaves covering the blacktop, there wasn't any damage visible from the back. It would have been ironic if either our road sign or the sign on the building had sustained damage. Considering how, and why, the name had evolved, the business name could end up being Zachary's Unincorporated Fallen Tree by the time we had new signage.

"Thanks for the ride. I really appreciate it."

"I'm happy to do it. Good luck getting things cleaned up." Lisa drove away through the downpour, looking fascinated by the uncharacteristic bedlam. Shouldn't she have waited until I entered the cottage? Oh well, she was following her orders. Apparently they hadn't included waiting for me to get indoors.

I stood, becoming drenched, realizing just how upset I must have been to have thoughtlessly travelled without an umbrella. Well, I was wet. So what?

My faithful dented red Beetle sat sedately near the back of the parking lot. Numerous small branches and twigs decorated the roof and hood, but if there were new scratches in the paint I couldn't tell. I felt myself relax; the VW had been part of my life since its purchase as a used vehicle after high school graduation, and felt like an old friend. Buildings could be repaired without emotional implications. Knowing that the Beetle was okay, I felt more capable of dealing with bricks and mortar.

Moving toward the lake to survey the front of the property, I felt a sense of relief. Things could have been a lot worse. A small window near the staff entrance had been hit by flying debris of some sort. Made of safety glass, it was now fully crackled, but still in one piece within its frame. There was no other obvious damage, and I breathed easier. The flowers, both those potted and those in the ground, were as flat as the ones near Town Hall. But flowers are replaceable, and are certainly not vital to the running of a business.

The lawn would need lots of TLC, whenever the water subsided. My guess was that no guests would be asking to sit outdoors anytime soon, not on the sodden area we'd be left with.

I had no desire to inspect the building's interior; the freezer episode had left me uncomfortable. So I started along the trail toward my cottage. What had been slightly muddy early in the day was now a mucky, slippery slope, and I was not in the right frame of mind for a wilderness adventure. Hoping I could make it to my front door without falling into the sloppy mess, I almost ignored my phone when it started to ring.

Seeing Uncle Al's number on the screen I quickly answered, and rushed back to the restaurant, trying to take refuge under the canopy.

He was understandably worried about his property, and had numerous questions, some I could answer, some not.

Had he been worried about *me* at all? If so he didn't mention it. I was starting to feel more like his business manager than his niece, and wasn't sure I liked it.

"Document any restaurant damage caused by the storm," he instructed me, "no matter how insignificant. Keep an extensive list, and call McClaine Insurance Agency tomorrow to find out what's covered. The same goes for the cottage, and the grounds. It's all on the same policy.

"And ask about business-interruption coverage. I'm not clear on the details, but we might be covered for the amount of income we've lost. Oh, and with the power off, you'll also need to document any food we have to throw out. I've been paying for the policy for years; might as well try to get some of my money back," he laughed.

It's easy for him to laugh, he's indoors where it's dry. It was one of the few times I've ever been annoyed by Al's easygoing manner

Howling winds pelted the persistent rain around the building and around me; there was no escaping it. By the time we said goodbye I was even more drenched and miserable than before. Normally I could see the cottage from the parking lot a few hundred feet away. Darkness had fallen early on this stormy moonless night, and I couldn't see 10 feet ahead on the trail.

Shivering, I struggled up the path, only sliding backwards a few times. Once inside I got out of my clothes as fast as I could, throwing my destroyed shoes away in the process, and took my third shower of the day.

It was some time before I felt warm, but when I finally did I stepped out of the shower, toweled myself off, and put on my warmest most comfy PJ's. I texted my parents that I was safe, then laid down on one of the huge sofas, took a deep breath, and started to cry. Not a deep sobbing cry of devastation, but the silent tears of sadness. How had I gotten myself into this mess? And how soon could I get out?

A voice that I recognized as my own whimpered, "I want to go home. I want to go *home!*" Teddy Maxwell was the only one listening. I'd never felt so alone.

I considered my options. *Maybe I should leave. Everyone else did after getting an anonymous note. Why am I even here? I'm not enjoying it one bit. The staff certainly wouldn't miss me. It might be better all the way around. I'd definitely be safer. I've never been one to run from trouble...well, not too often...but trouble has never been quite like this. What about Uncle Al, though? He needs someone he trusts, here, keeping an eye on things. I have to stay...for Al. What a mess!*

I gradually calmed down and began to assess my reaction. I was being weak when I should be strong. I was a capable person; I had to learn to accept whatever life threw at me without holding a pity-party. Many people were worse off than I. I was a competent person; it was time to get my act together. *You're an adult, Ashley, time to start acting like one.*

After lighting a fire in the fireplace, I faced its bright glow, practiced some calming yoga poses and, not for the first time, resolved to make the most of the situation, letting recent challenges strengthen me as a person. How often, I wondered, would I vow to become stronger before it actually happened? Would it ever happen? I believed that it would. No two-bit criminal was going to control *my* life!

The rain finally stopped. I went to bed and slept more soundly than I had in days. In my dreams I floated on water, surrounded by the sound of voices singing "Stop helping, stop helping!" I was joined by a tall faceless man with dark hair. We fell through a hole in the water to a dining room filled with beautiful floral arrangements, with well-sharpened knives being the only dinnerware.

Somehow, despite my disturbing dream, I awoke from a deep sleep feeling rejuvenated. Determined. Committed.

CHAPTER 22

Clearing my head after that sound sleep, I lay staring at the ceiling, trying to process the previous day's events. First and foremost, I had to deal with the storm aftermath. A major cleanup detail should be at the top of my to-do list, but I had no enthusiasm for the project, and no concept of where or how to begin. A phone call to Uncle Al might be a potential starting point. I certainly wasn't providing him with a calm convalescence.

It was beyond ridiculous that Wednesday had provided events even more dramatic than the horrendous storm. The debacle in the freezer resembled a bad movie, and I tried to convince myself that it had been a freak accident. *No one would deliberately close me in the freezer*, I decided; *that's impossible.*

But what about the threatening note? I didn't imagine that, it had been very real. Still, it was hard to process. Sighing, I decided I'd better get my body out of bed and get over to Unincorporated. Somehow storm cleanup sounded almost calming when my option was to dwell on other unimaginable things.

Even with the curtains drawn I could tell it was a bright sunny day. The birds were singing so enthusiastically that I could hear them through the closed window. I hopped out of bed and opened windows to let fresh air in. My first deep breath, however, was not what I expected. The humid air smelled of wet leaves, damp moss, and mud. The rain may have ended, but conditions had not returned to normal.

When I flicked the light switch in the bathroom nothing happened, and I remembered that power wouldn't be restored until crews repaired downed lines and could guarantee safety. My first question had been answered; there wouldn't be pressure to reopen Unincorporated quickly. It was a relief to know I'd have time to decompress, not having to deal with staff and guests.

The breeze carried the sound of truck traffic, chainsaws, and various other noises related to a concentrated cleanup effort. I hurriedly threw on some clothes, pulling on a pair of ripped jeans I hadn't worn since arriving in Windsor Grove, along with a beat-up tee-shirt that said *UW-Platteville* on the front. An old boyfriend had gone to college in Platteville, and somehow thought I needed an oversized tee announcing the fact. It seemed perfect for storm cleanup.

I made quick work of an energy drink and a granola bar, then decided there was no time like the present for inspecting the grounds. Exiting the cottage I came immediately upon a sheriff's deputy I didn't recognize, middle-aged with a big frame, a slight paunch and thinning hair, wandering around, surveying the sloppy ground.

After introducing himself as Officer Collins he asked, "Do you build bonfires out back very often?"

"No, never." I shook my head. It seemed like an odd question. "Down by the lake occasionally, other years, but not this year with the drought. Why?"

"The wood arranged up against your cottage concerns me. You're familiar with it I assume? It looks like someone is planning a substantial fire. Right there."

I must have looked puzzled, because he quickly explained. "There's a good size array of firewood and branches, tinder and kindling piled up against your home. Somebody was laying a fire, methodically constructed, with your home a part of it.

"Given the previously parched state of the forest, that fire would have posed a danger not just to you, but to the entire community. It's too soaked right now to be of any concern, but I'd recommend moving that wood away as soon as possible."

Numbly nodding, I stood stunned. Firewood definitely hadn't been there a few weeks ago, but I hadn't been behind the cottage lately. I was certainly aware that during a drought it was unsafe to have piles of wood close to any structure. Especially *my* structure. I felt violated.

Had someone been trying to frighten me? To destroy Al's property? To start a forest fire? All horrifying thoughts.

"Back to why I'm actually here," Officer Collins continued. "It will probably be a waste of time, but I was sent to search for footprints or other evidence regarding the trespasser who vandalized your building. I can see that someone slid in the mud heading up the path. Was there anyone here yesterday besides yourself?"

"My friend Bekah Greene was visiting. No one else. Oh, Officer Gregg was here, too."

Officer Collins asked about Bekah's shoe size and style, and mine. My answers seemed to verify what he'd expected.

"The only prints that are even a bit clear are probably yours and Gregg's. Usually ground that's damp from rain can give us clear footprints, but yesterday's rain was just too violent; the ground became so soggy that everything's been obliterated. I'm not learning anything," he said, shaking his head. "It's frustrating."

I thanked him for trying, said goodbye, and headed along the path which, as he'd said, was a soaked sloppy mess. My brain was having trouble processing the firewood. It made no sense.

Approaching the restaurant I could hear metallic scraping sounds accompanied by shouting and laughter. As I neared the parking lot I saw the source: Brad and several of our staff were busy with rakes and shovels, clearing debris from Unincorporated's driveway and parking lot. An impressively huge pile of branches, twigs, and leaves was collected alongside the highway. A few tree limbs had been chopped into firewood.

Steam rose from puddles on the blacktop as moisture evaporated in the warm sunshine. Smiling faces, casual clothing, and a break in routine gave the clean-up detail a party atmosphere. It was apparent that someone had put much thought into exactly what needed to be done, and who could best accomplish it.

"Hi, Ashley!" Brad yelled as I approached, "We've got extra rakes if you want to help. If we get everything cleaned up we can reopen as soon as power is back on."

He seemed happier and more at ease than I'd ever seen him. Wearing worn jeans and a torn shirt that announced *Life is Short... Eat Dessert First* he was less intimidating than usual, and seemed more approachable. A streak of mud adorned his unshaven cheek, the blond hair on his arms was caked with dust, and the sweat on his shirt attested to how hard he'd been working. No one could accuse this man of slacking when there was work to be done.

He'd obviously put together this crew with little or no notice, and had been more thorough in planning for storm recovery than I would ever be.

"Thanks for all the organizing you've done. I can't believe how much you've accomplished already," I said, reaching for the rake he offered.

"It's fun. We're having a good time. I called around last night to ask for help, and everyone I talked to agreed to come. Others are coming later, if the water level goes down, to try to get the lawn back in shape. We already dragged the large limbs out to the road, so some gentle raking will make a huge difference."

He gestured toward the front yard, "We can get the furniture onto the patio in minutes, but those huge planters stayed outside during the storm, and the flowers are a disaster." Ceramic planters filled with pink and white geraniums, speckled burgundy coleus, and purple and yellow pansies had added a bright colorful touch to the patio.

"Todd from the Village Flower Shoppe was so thankful for our dessert buffet after Mark's funeral that he offered to come over with new flowering plants to replace what we lost," he continued. "Everyone wants to help. This really is a great community!"

"Well, I'm grateful that you're on top of the situation. I obviously haven't held up my end of the clean-up detail so far." I moved to start raking.

"It's not the kind of thing a gal would think about," he said. He didn't say it rudely, but it certainly wasn't a flattering comment.

"I've been around here longer than you, no one expected you to know what had to be done. I figured you wouldn't even know where to find the rakes. If the work was gonna get done, I knew it had to be me that planned it."

Yep. I should have known better than to think that this was a new Brad; his abrasive personality was still there, although under a layer of friendship. But, once again, he was on point. I hadn't thought about putting together a clean-up crew. I had no business being offended by his comment when he was, unfortunately, correct.

The staff was making quick work of the cleanup, so I pitched in, using muscles that hadn't been put to use lately. I knew I'd be in touch with those muscles later in the day.

Brad had said the cleanup was fun, and he was right, mostly because of the cooperation of our staff. The feeling of camaraderie that had formed among my employees was palpable. They were a hard-working group of all ages, thrown together at random, and bonded over a shared desire to give good service to guests. What could be better than that? On that particular morning I felt like I was surrounded by friends, not employees. It was a satisfying sensation.

I asked a few of the workers to help me clear "some debris" away from my cottage. Expecting remnants of the storm, they were surprised to see the burning materials so expertly arranged against the back wall.

I made no explanation, just saying, "I want this wood to be far away from the cottage. Let's add it to the piles of brush from the storm." That earned me some odd looks. Who knows what they were thinking? I did notice a few of them off to the side talking with Brad later. It could have been my imagination, but Brad seemed very thoughtful after that.

My own thoughts were simple. *Farewell firewood, hello one more concern.*

Occasionally a driver would turn a car into our lot, asking, "Are you going to open tonight?" or, "When will you be serving again?" The community might be in shambles, but those tourists who hadn't left town were still hungry and wanted quality food. We reassured people that we'd open as soon as possible, but had no definite timetable.

Other staff members arrived, sharing information about how local residents were coping. We learned that everyone living, or staying, in a home near water level had been relocated to motels or inns on higher ground. We learned that power crews and road crews had worked all night trying to get everything up and running again. We learned that The Marys were preparing box lunches for workers and volunteers, and distributing them at the old firehouse.

"As long as the walk-in cooler stays closed the inside temperature should remain constant," Brad theorized as he and I piled up branches, "but even so, we've got some things in there that shouldn't be kept any longer. We might as well donate anything to The Marys that we can't safely use a few days from now. There are sliced meats and cheeses, and some breads that will be exactly what they need."

"Great idea. There's no point in letting food go to waste. Can you gather together the things that should be used soon? We'll get someone to take it over to The Marys, and they can decide how to use it."

"You've got it," he replied, turning and heading quickly into the building. I felt confused. It was as if there were two Brads; the Good Brad who cared about his work and his kitchen and felt responsibility for his staff, and his Evil Twin Brad who had sarcastic and rude comments available for every circumstance. The man was a conundrum.

Eventually I was the one who took cases of food over to the firehouse. Once again The Marys had come through in a big way. An assembly line of residents prepared, packed, and distributed meals, all volunteer help that The Marys had seemingly put together with no effort. I wondered if every small town had people like these sisters, always there to organize things at a moment's notice. Windsor Grove was certainly better off for having them.

The old firehouse had been decommissioned years ago, replaced by a modern facility at the north end of town that is the envy of many a larger community. The late 1800's building currently houses historic firefighting memorabilia, and due to its location along the main road is used by various community groups who need a small meeting space.

A sturdy stone structure set into the side of a hill, it was designed to shelter horse-drawn pumpers, and the horses to pull them. The word FIREHOUSE is carved in bold letters into a sandstone plaque inset above weathered wooden doors. Adding another touch of quaint charm to this waterfront community, it is often photographed, and has become a favorite subject for area artists.

With doors open wide and vintage fire engines moved outdoors, no one could ignore the activity going on inside. It called to the residents, saying *Help yourself, or if you are able, come on in and get to work.*

Mr. Horner was staked out at the back of the open area, (in a corner, of course) feverishly and methodically creating attractive sandwiches from donated foods, slicing them, wrapping them, arranging them on trays by ingredient, ready for packaging. His speed and accuracy reminded me that he and his late wife had owned a restaurant. He'd apparently been no stranger to kitchen duties; his familiarity with quantity food preparation was evident.

Mary Rose walked among the many volunteers praising their efforts and building their confidence, while MaryBeth checked that no box lunch went out without plastic cutlery, napkins, and beverage.

Mary Lou (a.k.a. Scary Mary) however was harder to decipher than ever, slyly coming up to me with wide eyes, saying breathlessly, "Did anyone get hurt? Were there any injuries at all? It would be a shame if there were any injuries! I was listening for sirens, but didn't hear any. Were any homes completely destroyed? How awful if someone has to rebuild." She winked at me, then moved on to ask the same meddling questions of another visitor.

I felt even more uncomfortable than I normally did around Mary Lou, and was relieved to see her sisters keeping an eye on her.

As the day progressed, the storm water slowly subsided and roads became passable again. The previous dryness of the terrain was proving to be advantageous, as the ground helpfully began to absorb the standing water.

An upbeat atmosphere filled the town as residents and visitors alike congregated to help wherever they could. Piles of soggy belongings from lakefront homes appeared along the roadways; owners of vacation homes who hadn't been in town during the storm arrived to check on their property; total strangers dug in and got dirty helping with the cleanup; floating storm debris created intriguing patterns on the lake.

Members of the town board visited every home and business, documenting damage, verifying that there were indeed no injuries, and keeping everyone updated regarding power restoration. Volunteers drove through town delivering The Marys' box lunches, and as can be the case when normal routine is thrown out the window, there was a festive mood with everyone happily lending a hand. Adversity truly does bring out the best in people.

By early evening power had been restored to most homes and businesses, including Unincorporated. It was too late to consider opening, but it allowed me to verify that everything was functioning correctly. It was reassuring to know that the refrigeration equipment was again cooling, although a brief glance into the walk-in freezer made my heart beat faster.

I hurriedly left the kitchen to check on the building's public areas. I found no indication of interior damage from the weather; if you didn't look out the windows you'd never know there'd been a storm. I assumed the pilot lights needed to be relit, but that was something I could leave for the kitchen staff to do in the morning (mostly because I didn't know how). Thankfully the battery back-up for the time clock seemed to be working, and I knew Brad would know what timers needed to be reset.

Straightening a few things that really didn't need it, I verified our ability to re-open the next day, and went back to the cottage. It was a relief to know we wouldn't be closed on a Friday, traditionally the busiest day of our week. I made some phone calls to staff, so they'd know we would definitely be back in business the next day, showered, put on loose comfy clothes, and picked up a magazine Bekah had left behind.

Glancing at my phone I realized that sometime during the day Bekah had sent a text. "Had fun!! Sorry to leave so soon. What a great town you live in! Interview went well (I think). Wish me luck!!"

"Good luck. Was nice having you here. Exhausted from storm cleanup," was my reply. I didn't feel very enthusiastic, and I'm sure it came through. I'd leave all the exclamation points to Bekah.

I made a quick call to Margaret Hunter, my elderly friend who'd been unable to sleep soundly after Mark's murder, to check on how she'd come through the storm.

"Well aren't you kind! I'm just fine, sweetie. You could say I weathered the weather! It's so nice of you to ask." Her voice sounded strong and healthy. "Wasn't it exciting? I love storms!" Apparently the previous day's conditions hadn't bothered her a bit. Good for her! We chatted a few minutes about the damage, then said goodbye.

When my phone rang a few minutes later my first thought was that my parents were probably calling to check on me. But caller ID told me that it was Officer Gregg. Groaning inwardly I was tempted to ignore the call. I wanted some quiet time, and he was the last person I wanted to talk to.

Against my better judgment I answered glumly, "Hello."

"Hi, Ashley. I called to find out how you're doing. Are you alright?" This wasn't what I'd been expecting to hear. Again I realized that this was a thoughtful man, who just happened to annoy me when he did his job too thoroughly.

"I guess. I've been too busy to think about it," I replied, wondering what the real purpose of his call was.

"Have you decided to leave town?"

"Um…no."

"No you haven't decided? Or no, you're not going to leave?"

"Not going to leave. I think. Probably."

"Have you eaten yet?"

"Huh?" I wasn't exactly being a scintillating conversationalist.

"I'm finally off duty and was going to go up to Oak Landing to get some food and try to relax. I thought you might want to come along. If you're not busy, that is."

I couldn't think of a response. I'd just settled down and it felt good. Since coming to Windsor Grove I'd spent most of my waking hours at Unincorporated; I barely remembered what it was like to have someone invite me to go anywhere. The days of spending time hanging out with friends seemed years ago.

"Um…sure…okay." *Yikes… I had just agreed to spend an evening with Gregg; possibly not the smartest decision I've ever made. Take a deep breath, Ashley, and try not to sound like you've never been asked out before.*

"It's so nice of you to ask. I just need a few minutes to get put together." *So much for a quiet evening.*

Well, why not? If it was a miserable evening, I'd know better next time. It was ironic that the first person in Windsor Grove to make any effort toward actual friendship was someone whose presence I usually dreaded.

"I'll pick you up in about 20 minutes," he said, and he was gone.

With little time to decide what to wear, I threw on the first outfit I grabbed. Dress is casual in the area, so as long as your attire is clean you're good to go everywhere from ice cream parlors to steak houses. My beige textured skirt with a pale peach gauze shirt over a matching tank would be appropriate, no matter where we went. I added some chunky coral jewelry, and realized that no matter how tired I was, it still felt good to dress for an evening out. I added brown ankle-strap pumps to my ensemble; I may have given up on wearing heels to work, but I wasn't going to abandon them entirely.

The few extra minutes I had were spent on hair and makeup; I'd worn my hair pulled back so often that it felt liberating to let the waves loose onto my shoulders. Then I stood in front of my wavy mirror to apply mascara, powder and lip gloss; it was like a reminder of my college days when I'd had an actual social life.

When I heard a knock I peered into the darkness and recognized Gregg's silhouette before unlocking the door; I didn't want him trumpeting that I hadn't been cautious.

"You look great!" he said, handing me a bunch of flowers. Scraggly flowers with bent stems, but flowers nonetheless. "Obviously I didn't buy them, they were knocked down in my front yard, and I didn't want them to be wasted," he laughed. "I thought they should go to a lovely lady instead of into the garbage." He really was a nice guy, if a person could ignore the constant feeling of being interrogated when he was around.

I put the flowers in a pretty ceramic pitcher filled with water, certain they weren't going to perk up, but willing to make an effort.

Once again the difference in Gregg's appearance when he wasn't on duty came as a surprise. In a plaid pastel button-down shirt with khaki shorts he was dressed like any relaxed summer traveler visiting for the weekend. Even his mannerisms seemed different when he wasn't in his official capacity. I wondered if that was the mark of a true professional, the ability to change personality when necessary.

"Let's set some guidelines for the evening," Gregg announced.

"Oh? Such as?"

"No talk of anything related to Mark or to the weather. I've been dealing with disaster and tragedy 24/7 and I need a break. Deal?"

"Sounds good to me. I've had enough of both topics myself, and I'm nowhere near as involved as you are. It will be refreshing to talk of anything else!"

Before we left the cottage he checked that the windows were latched and that the door had locked completely, and then laughingly apologized.

"I can't help it. That's my life. I'm sure you know that an overhead light on your porch would be a good idea."

I nodded. Of course he was right.

Somehow I'd expected Gregg to arrive in his squad car (riding in it would have been really embarrassing), but he led me to a late model Toyota, black and shiny. He gallantly held the door for me, as I tried to avoid getting mud on his spotless floor mat.

Once we were on the road we started getting to know each other. We talked about small town life, big city colleges, music, movies, hopes and dreams. We'd been together so often lately that it seemed we'd known each other forever, and the conversation just flowed.

We decided to visit a seafood restaurant that had a good reputation but neither of us had been to. The food lived up to the reputation, the atmosphere was comforting and cozy, and by the time we'd shared a Triple Chocolate dessert I felt as if I was with an old and dear friend.

Gregg was an attentive listener, making me realize how I'd yearned for someone to hang out with. His comments were witty and sensitive, and his conversation was entertaining.

I hadn't felt so calm in weeks; I'd really needed a night out, a night without responsibilities. It made me feel like singing and doing a happy dance, which I knew would be a bad idea. Acting foolish was fine with old friends, but I thought I should behave with a little more decorum around Gregg. Embarrassing a man in public doesn't normally lead to a lasting friendship! And I did want us to become friends.

Gregg apparently felt the same, because he was talking about places we could go "next time". With various theatrical productions and art festivals scheduled throughout the summer, and several pubs offering outdoor entertainment on weekend afternoons, we would have many choices available. We learned that we both preferred comedy over drama and classic rock over easy listening.

We laughingly recounted our respective skills at bowling (non-existent) and miniature golf (slightly better), making those activities sound like enjoyable options. Social possibilities seemed endless, as long as you had someone to enjoy them with. It felt good to think that I finally had a friend in town.

When we eventually drove back to Windsor Grove we walked from the Unincorporated parking lot across the slippery, muddy lawn to look at the lake. I carried my shoes in hand; once again I'd found myself in totally inappropriate footwear. Bare feet, in this case, worked just fine.

The lake was unbelievably calm; the brilliant reflection of the moon giving it a silvery mirror-like quality. We stood silently looking across the water, so peaceful it was like a mirage. Property damage that would have been obvious in daytime was invisible in the moonlight.

"Nature really is incredible!" Gregg exclaimed. "It has the power to do so much damage, but then it rights itself and has the most enthralling, alluring enchantment. I wish I were an artistic person, there would be so much inspiration to be gained just from observing everything surrounding me."

"What an intriguing idea." I understood his enthusiasm. "I feel calmer when I'm by this lake than anywhere else I've ever been. Nature seems so much closer here; it makes me want to stay in Windsor Grove forever."

"That would be nice," he replied quietly.

Once we'd turned to wander up to my cottage I realized we'd been holding hands. Maybe it happened when he'd helped me up the slope, but I didn't really know.

Gregg unlocked my cottage door, gave me a quick hug, said, "Thanks for a fun evening," and left.

As he walked away he turned back and hollered, "Be sure you lock up!" I had to laugh. It was so typical of him.

I slept soundly. Apparently an evening out with a friend was exactly what I'd needed. It helped me forget all the horrors that had taken up residence in my brain.

CHAPTER 23

woke early Friday, spent extra time dressing and fixing my hair, and felt almost giddy as I headed to Unincorporated. It was going to be fun to reopen, interesting to talk with the locals about aftereffects of flooding, and enjoyable in some gruesome way to describe the storm to newly-arrived travelers. Best of all, I would have reason to concentrate on things other than the locked freezer, scraps of placemats, and firewood against my cottage.

The breeze carried with it the sound of chainsaws still operating in the distance, and the lake was greener and more cloudy than usual. No one could deny the storm, but it was time to look forward to a fine day.

Heading to Unincorporated I heard a shout, "Do you feel any responsibility for the murder? Could your staff have prevented it by safeguarding your cutlery?' I hurried on. Would these reporters never go away? *Alright, just ignore them, it's going to be a good day; don't let them ruin your mood. They're just doing their job, no matter how annoying that may be.*

Being the first to arrive at work except for the stockman, I had plenty of time to verify that everything was ready for a hectic weekend. The local visitor's center was predicting almost 100% occupancy in local resorts and inns, which meant that vast numbers of people would be seeking a good place to eat.

I'd recently hired several additional employees, many of them college kids who'd worked here in the past. We were ready for the tourist season, which thankfully was finally here. Even the weather was expected to cooperate. The sun was shining, the lake was down to a near-normal level, and there certainly wasn't an elevated fire risk.

As other staffers arrived it seemed that everyone shared my enthusiasm for expected crowds. Dawn had called in extra servers, and asked others to arrive earlier than scheduled. Brad had put on an extra fry cook, and had extended the number of hours the prep workers would be there. Our pastry chef, Amanda, had increased the number of desserts she'd prepared. And Renata had come in early, anticipating a lunchtime rush in the Lounge.

As soon as we unlocked the door it became clear that everyone's instincts were correct. Guests began arriving immediately, and came in a steady stream throughout the day. Spirits were mostly high, except for a few local residents who were impossible to satisfy: the woman who was upset because our flowerbeds weren't up to her expectations; the man who complained loudly that we didn't have a salad bar any more (we'd never had one); a few children who were overdue for naptime.

The spirit of fellowship among guests and staff was permeable, and it was a pleasure to be working. I smiled inwardly when I overheard snippets of conversation as I moved among the constantly filled tables.

"...should have known better than to have bought a cottage right on the water..." This was said with a smile and a shake of the head that said *I'd do it again in a minute.*

"When things go wrong, that's when you find out who your friends are."

"And to think we were all praying for rain..."

"I stopped at Windsor Farm Market this morning, and the owners are ecstatic about the rain."

"My brother's knowledge about disaster procedures was invaluable. It's not always what you've done that matters, it's what you know. Do you get what I mean? Even if you don't realize how much you know." The others at the table all nodded, as if that actually made sense. Maybe it did.

"All those tiny cottages south of town...those dilapidated rentals that are such an eyesore...they're in worse shape now than ever. Hopefully the owner will finally have to spend some money fixing them up." That comment met with universal approval.

"Did anyone hear how many inches of rain we actually got? Our rain gauge overflowed."

"I'm going over to the museum this afternoon to see how I can help. There was a lot of damage…"

"Bob and Doris are in Europe, and their classic Ford Mustang sat in water above the floorboards. Their insurance company might have to total it." Everyone at the table tried to look sympathetic, but there was a bit of serves-them-right evident in a few faces.

And then I heard the whispered words, "…it's all over facebook… Betty told me about her, the new manager…she used to date the bread man…followed him here from Indiana…you think she killed him?" I glanced toward the source of that information, and sure enough, the elderly women at that table were looking at *me*. I wondered how anyone had missed the fact that I was Al's niece from Milwaukee. And who was putting this stuff on facebook?

My first inclination was to set them straight. But then I saw the gleeful expressions on the faces at that table.

Let them think what they want, I decided. They'd learn the truth soon enough. Windsor Grove women love knowing some juicy piece of gossip, and get almost euphoric when they can get a shocked reaction by sharing it.

I was still smiling to myself over their "revelations", when Brad came to tell me Gregg was out back asking to see me. I headed into the kitchen, realizing that it was probably the first time I'd ever looked forward to talking with Gregg.

"Fancy meeting you here," was my first comment. "Nice of you to come in the back entrance for once!"

"Hi Ashley," he laughed. "I hope you managed to get a good night's sleep after all the food we ate."

I assured him that I had. "And you?"

"Slept like a baby. Most relaxed I've been in days." I suggested that we get out of Brad's way, and we headed to my office. Gregg casually perched himself on the corner of my desk; I crossed my fingers hoping that he wouldn't knock over the mountain of paper that was growing by the day.

"I had a good time last night; we need to do something like that again real soon." His gentle smile softened the lines of his face.

"I'll be happy to, if we can ever get away from work at the same time," I laughed. "Without another disaster, that is. As fun as it was, it wouldn't be worth another flood!"

He nodded. "It's a shame work gets in the way. Between your schedule and mine, we'll be lucky if we can ever do more than chat in this office."

Then he continued, in a more somber tone, "Speaking of work getting in the way, the reason I'm actually here..."

Oh no, here it comes, I thought. I should have known he hadn't dropped in for a pleasant chat.

"...need a list of everyone who was in Unincorporated the afternoon you got locked in the freezer," he was saying. "Also, if you have any insight about who had knowledge about the safety release, I need that too."

I sighed. I couldn't get away from it. Every time I managed to push aside all thoughts of homicide and knives and threats, something happened to return them to the forefront.

"You don't want to think about it, I know. But we have to consider that perhaps someone was intentionally trying to harm you, certainly to scare you. There was the threatening note, too, you know. And we're not ignoring the firewood piled against your building; if you didn't put it there someone else did. The department is strapped for resources right now, but we do have to investigate every incident, and all suspicious activity."

I thought back to Wednesday morning. The restaurant had been packed with locals who had no power, with travelers coming off the highway to escape the storm, and with tourists who had nothing else to do. Guests had been coming and going continually until we finally locked the door. Almost my entire staff had shown up to see if they could help, and doubtless there were numerous people I'd never even noticed.

Once we'd closed for the day Brad had left to make sure all the staff got home safely. The back door had been unlocked while he'd been away, and with the power out and diminished visibility from the storm almost anyone could have wandered into the kitchen unnoticed.

As I explained all this, and started listing the guests I could remember, Gregg shook his head. "My job would be a whole lot easier if Unincorporated wasn't such an iconic place."

Was he serious? No, it was ludicrous to think anything about the investigation would be simplified if Unincorporated were less successful. Sure, there'd be fewer people involved next time tragedy struck, but Gregg couldn't mean that.

Anyway, tragedy would never strike again, not at Unincorporated. We'd already surpassed our tragedy-probability statistics for a lifetime. I was certain of that.

"You understand," Gregg grinned, as he realized how his comment sounded "I feel like I'm continually getting lists from you that include everyone who's ever been in Windsor Grove. We can't investigate the entire state of Wisconsin! I hope this is over soon, and I won't need any further lists.

"I don't want to worry about you any longer." It made me feel good to hear him say that; it was nice to know someone was worrying about me. If only there had been nothing to worry about.

"And speaking of worrying…why did I have to read about firewood behind your cottage from the overnight notes at the department? You couldn't tell me about this? We were together all evening."

"You set the ground rules last night. You said no talk of Mark or of weather. I had the impression you didn't want to discuss police business at all."

"I did say that. But when someone's in danger, social etiquette goes out the window. And there was definitely significant danger involved."

"The wood was soaked by the time I knew about it. Soaked wood equals no danger."

"After this, you let *me* decide if there's danger, okay? Protecting people is my job.

"Seriously, you have to let me take care of you," he said firmly, looking into my eyes. "There are too many odd things occurring. I need to know that my friends are safe.

"One other thing," he lowered his voice, "Your uncle trusts his chef completely?"

"He seems to. Brad has keys to almost everything in the restaurant. Everything except this office. Oh, and he doesn't know the combination to the safe, but he has access to everything else."

"We were just curious; it's unusual to see someone with such an obnoxious attitude having so much authority," he mused.

"I have to admit I've wondered about that myself."

"How about the rest of the staff…is anyone holding a grudge? Are there any disgruntled ex-employees? Has anyone been fired recently?"

"There was Jeff, one of our dishwashers," I began, "No one else since I've been here." I pulled Jeff's folder from the filing cabinet and gave Gregg the date of his dismissal. "Jeff was fired a week before the first note arrived. There's a chance he's trying to get revenge, I suppose.

"You've met Jeff; he was one of the kids smoking in the woods the night Carrie found the note in her car."

"That's right." He pulled out his notebook and pen. "Skinny kid with shaggy hair? Acts bored?"

I nodded. "He didn't seem like an angry kind of guy. He was a fairly useless employee, but not a mean one." Of course then I had to remind Gregg about seeing Jeff with Man-in-Brown. I didn't want to get Unincorporated any more involved in the investigation than it already was, but facts are facts.

Gregg looked puzzled; talking with guests was a totally acceptable activity, even if someone has since been fired. I had to admit that a conversation near a car didn't sound the least bit threatening when I verbalized it. My imagination had been projecting intrigue onto everything; I was obsessing again.

"Well, I have to get moving, duty calls. I always appreciate your help." He reached out and squeezed my shoulder reassuringly. "Stay safe. I'll be in touch." For once I was happy to hear him say that, instead of annoyed. He left through the kitchen, walking slowly with a quizzical expression on his face.

"One of the tables near the window is complaining about the room being too cold," I was told by a server. "They've all put on sweaters and are grumbling."

"I'll adjust the temp by a degree or two," I offered, and did just that.

Predictably, a short while later a different server approached me. "Table nine is asking if we can crank up the air conditioning. They're really warm."

"I'll adjust the temp by a degree or two." You couldn't make this stuff up. How had Al managed to keep his sanity after so many years? He must have the patience of a saint.

Gregg's question about Brad had given me another thing to wonder about. Al's complete trust of Brad was indeed puzzling. Was there more behind Al's choice of me to manage in his absence than just Brad's poor people skills?

Al was no fool; certain employees are only useful in the back of the house. But could there be more to it than that? I wondered if it would be bad form to come right out and ask. Al may not have even known that Brad wanted to manage the restaurant.

My decision to gather information might require that I ask more questions of my favorite uncle.

The increasing sound level from the dining room demanded that I get back out there to keep things moving along.

"Ashley, what have you heard about the investigation?" asked the woman at the podium, a regular guest who wore too much makeup and had hair the color and texture of straw. "Is there any news?"

"I haven't heard anything. Table for two?"

"Oh, we're already on the list. We're waiting in Zachary's. I just thought you might have some new information."

"What's the word from the Sheriff's Department?" asked a large bald man standing nearby.

"Really, I don't have any more details than anyone else. Excuse me, I have to go seat a table."

"Are you sure there's nothing new? Didn't I just see Gregg leaving?" Those questions came from a complete stranger.

And so it went. Question after question. Couldn't these people tell I was working?

"Officer Gregg spends a lot of time here; you must know something you could share. I'm sure you do." A middle-aged woman who looked vaguely familiar actually followed me around as I cleared and reset a table, somehow determined that if she pestered me enough I'd come through with some juicy detail. I tried to be kind, but it was all a little much.

By the end of the evening I couldn't wait to leave. I had the kitchen put up an order of Tempura Shrimp to go, and left before anyone else could start asking questions.

The citizens of Windsor Grove could change from being friendly and effusive to critical and bitchy in a heartbeat. On the surface they appear laid-back and welcoming, but I've learned that it comes with an underlying impatience demanding that their desires be immediately dealt with. There are times when I love these people, and times when I find them on the far side of aggravating.

Is that what it's like in every small town, with everyone overly involved in their neighbors' lives, with opinionated long-standing rivalries? If I stayed in town long enough would I become like them? Now that was a disturbing thought.

Bekah called that evening to say "Thanks" for her short but enjoyable visit, and spent most of an hour speculating on whether or not she'd get the job she'd interviewed for. Still feeling miffed about how little I'd actually seen of her, I mentioned how hard it was not having a good friend nearby to talk to.

"Why don't you just go get a mani-pedi any time you feel lonely? That always makes me feel better," was her solution.

"That sounds like a good idea, but it's nearly impossible around here. You've seen this town; Edith's Cut'n Curl is the only salon. The stylists there are all old enough to be my grandmother!" We both laughed at the idea of going to Edith's to get rejuvenated, and decided the Cut 'n Curl probably wouldn't provide the emotional therapy I was hoping for.

"There's a popular salon in Oak Landing that many locals use, but their spa services book up weeks in advance. I'm never sure that I can get away..."

We continued chatting, switching from one topic to another and back again. I didn't mention the threatening note on my door, or the firewood out back. Sometimes Bekah's version of empathy was just too dramatic for my taste, and would only increase my tension. Much as I appreciated her friendship, I preferred to deal with some things internally.

When we said goodbye and I'd invited her to visit again, she replied, "I'll come back soon and spend more time with you and your Gregg."

When I said, "He's not *my Gregg!*" she just laughed. I hadn't mentioned his name once, and didn't understand where she'd gotten any ideas about Gregg and me.

"Did you see the way he looked at you? Of course he's your Gregg," she responded. "Are you telling me you've never gone out together?"

"Well, sort of..."

"See? I knew it! I'll call again soon."

She hung up, and I sat staring into space. No, Gregg and I were just friends. Nothing more.

CHAPTER 24

I was nine years old. My ballet class had become more intense that year; we were suddenly expected to take our talents very seriously. Madame Isabella accepted no nonsense. "First position…second position…Ashley, keep your chin up…Third position…Ashley, where do your hands belong?…Fourth position… Ashley, don't lean forward…"

And on it went. Madame, with her perfect posture and her background in theatre, had no patience, no tolerance for anything less than perfection.

No one else was corrected nearly as often as I. I left class in tears. I begged Mom to let me quit, and after seeing my anguish she agreed. To this day I had nightmares of, "You're a talented girl; you just don't concentrate, you have to work harder. You can do anything if you really want to. Just try, try, try, and you'll get it right!"

I awoke in a sweat, with Madame's words in my head. "Concentrate… try harder…you can do anything…try, try, try."

Amazingly, this time her words seemed surprisingly apropos. This many years later, her words finally hit home. I was not going to quit! Someone had to figure out what was going on. It might as well be me. I really could do anything if I tried!

Over the next few weeks the activity level heightened to the hectic resort-community experience we'd been anticipating. Remnants of the storm had been quickly cleared away. Evident property damage was not good for tourism, and residents had hurried to restore Windsor Grove to the idyllic destination visitors expected.

Oppressive humidity had settled over the area, and the air was redolent of damp forest, but the sun shone brightly and a welcoming spirit pervaded. With the resilience of nature, flowers beaten down by the storm had recovered their brilliance as though the storm had never happened.

On weekends our resorts and inns were filled to capacity with tourists. Midweek the condos and cottages played home to guests spending extended periods with us. Days flew by quickly. I learned to have my staff prepared for everything and anything, never knowing what each day would bring.

Business was booming; Unincorporated kept me busier than I'd ever imagined. My parents kept telling me how wonderful it was that I was enjoying so much time at the lake, as if I were on an extended vacation with no responsibilities. They planned to come to town so we could visit Mom's favorite shops and enjoy a few relaxing meals, and didn't seem to understand that during the height of summer I was too busy to kick back and relax.

My threatening note seemed like a thing of the distant past, and even Mark's murder had moved to the mental backburner as the travel season leapt to the forefront. During those longest days of the year Gregg's admonition not to walk unaccompanied into the woods after dark had been all but forgotten. His admonishment about not going anywhere alone seemed a huge overreaction.

It was certainly wishful thinking on everyone's part, but with the murder investigation having been drawn out for so long, the locals were beginning to carry on as if nothing unusual had happened.

"Did you hear about Bonnie's Bakery?" I was asked one afternoon. By the next day Bonnie's had become the most frequent topic of conversation. The owners, a young couple who were relatively new to town, (neither of them named Bonnie, by the way) had opened a coffee shop called *Bonnie's Brews* on the massive deck behind their house. The deck had a spectacular view of the lake and was an ideal spot to relax with coffee and pastry. It was an immediate success.

Unfortunately the owners had neglected to consult the town board or the local zoning commission before their new endeavor. Their sales permit was limited to their retail bakery location alone, not to their home; and their home itself was not zoned for commercial business. Several local business owners were up in arms over their apparent ignorance of the law.

Despite the overwhelming popularity of Bonnie's Brews, its future wasn't guaranteed.

"I've been hoping a coffee house would open in town; I'm thrilled," was a popular opinion, but so was, "If they can't follow the rules they should be closed down." There was disagreement about whether the owners had been unaware of the regulations, or if they'd deliberately disregarded them. No one was neutral in the discussion, and Zachary's Lounge once again saw an uptick in business due to a local dispute.

Small town politics is amazing. The Milwaukee Journal's headlines all week had dealt with an alarming increase in violent crime and the city's recently released horrific murder statistics. The Gazette's banner headline that week was, "Can the Coffee House Survive?"

My status as a relative newcomer allowed me to refrain from taking sides. Frankly, it was nice to have any topic of conversation other than murder. People were much happier when they were discussing coffee!

We didn't see much of Detective Milton during that period. He'd gone back to Madison's forensics labs and was examining the crime scene evidence, leaving our sheriff's department in charge of the local details. Along with having access to the crime labs, there were other advantages to his stage of the investigation being conducted from headquarters.

"From there he can easily monitor homicides around the state," Gregg explained. "If similar incidents occur elsewhere we'll know about it immediately. Should that be the case our investigation attains an entirely different level of intensity.

"There's no real reason to anticipate a crime spree, or serial killings, but he's watching for similarities in any stabbings, especially further anonymous notes. Stabbings are common in certain low-income neighborhoods, but there's usually not as much finesse involved."

I was uncomfortable with the topics that were being introduced. "Somehow I never thought of murder as involving finesse...and I certainly never considered that this could be part of a serial situation. What a strange world we live in...and *you* work in!"

I'd become accustomed to the rhythm of running a restaurant. It was a constant flow of setting up for guests, taking care of guests, cleaning up after guests, and trying to balance the books and pay the bills in between.

Uncle Al had been right (no surprise there). His long-time employees were excellent at their jobs, and dealt with the challenge of training new staffers with no help from me. Brad kept things flowing smoothly in the kitchen, ruling his staff with an iron hand. The only person he continued being outright rude to was me, and I'd elected to stay out of his way whenever possible. His moments of semi-civility were few and far between, so confusing as to seem awkward.

Savoring a cup of coffee at my desk one afternoon (by the way, the coffee at Unincorporated surpasses that at Bonnie's Brews), I called Al to discuss food inventory. I was still apprehensive about ordering perishables in advance, so Al had continued to handle that job throughout his recovery. Again that day he patiently talked me through the process, offering to let me take on the challenge when I felt ready.

"My old friend Margaret called yesterday," he went on after completing the order, "and told me how very kind you've been to her. I knew you were the right person for the job; you have a knack for dealing with people. You understand them."

"Speaking of understanding people, there's something I'm curious about," I started. "Was there a specific reason you asked me to take over as your manager instead of Brad? Did you know that he wanted the job?"

"I knew he wanted it. I just didn't think he was the right person," Al said hesitantly.

"It's really none of my business, I know. But Officer Gregg asked how completely you trusted Brad, and it made me wonder."

"Brad is a terrific chef. I'd trust his judgment over anyone's when it comes to food preparation. And I believe he's an honest man. But he's not a *people person*, and I don't want him dealing with the public. He wouldn't be good at customer relations; he'd be horrible with personnel problems; and I can't imagine him dealing with time-off requests!" Al was right about that, no argument from me.

"He's most valuable to me in the back of the house," he continued. "That's all there was to it. You're good with people, you relate to people and Brad can't. I actually told him that, which didn't make him happy."

"Thanks for answering that question for me; I was uncomfortable asking it."

Now I understood Brad's dislike of me; he'd actually been told that I was better for the job than he was. That's not a comment he'd accept without rancor. Okay, I would have to accept that he'd never relax his animosity toward me. Al hadn't intentionally created a rift between us, but he'd created it nonetheless.

"Todd, I want to thank you for your help after the storm," I said on the phone one morning. "The new flowering plants on our patio look amazing; guests are constantly taking photos. We tell everyone that The Village Flower Shoppe deserves the credit; hopefully it's helped you gain some additional business."

"Thanks, Ashley; I appreciate you mentioning The Shoppe. Yes, I've had people come in after seeing your patio. That's not why I did it, of course; I felt like I owed you something because of that wonderful spread you put out after Mark's service. He would have been impressed."

"We were happy to do it. It's a shame no one can be around to see their own memorial and realize how much their life meant."

"Amen to that. I just wish they'd hurry up and find Mark's killer. Sometimes I can't believe it happened. I get angry every time I think about it!" Hearing Todd's words reminded me that he'd known Mark for years; I wondered if many people had properly expressed their condolences to this long-time friend. I know I hadn't.

"I feel guilty for bringing him here," he said quietly.

"Don't give that a thought," I said, although it sounded inadequate. "You had no control over what happened. But since we're talking about it….I have a question…" I paused, not sure how to phrase my query.

"Oh? What?" Todd sounded defensive, as if I were possibly going to lay blame on him.

"Do you have keys to Mark's apartment?" I asked quickly. "Or does his landlady have the only set?"

"I have a set of keys. Mark's parents asked me to go through his things, get stuff ready to donate, and decide what should be sent to them. The officers have finished with his apartment and said I can clean it out, but I can't bring myself to start. Things are pretty much the way they were when he…died. Why?"

"Well, this might sound strange, but I've been wondering if there might be some clue that was missed. I know they're thorough, but the local officers are all *guys*. I don't think they had any women go through Mark's things, and it could really make a difference. Women notice different details you know."

Careful, Ashley. Don't make yourself sound ignorant. The officers are trained to notice everything. "Anyway, I just want to help."

"Hmm…you could be right. So you want to look things over?" He said it hesitantly, unsure if it was a good idea.

"I don't want to impose, but, yes, I'd really like to take a quick look around. Not alone, of course, I'd want you to stay with me so you'll know I haven't disturbed anything." Even to myself I sounded like a nosy busybody. I can't imagine what Todd thought of me.

"Well, I have a free hour this afternoon. I could be there around two o'clock." He didn't sound very enthusiastic; I quickly took him up on his offer, before he could change his mind.

"Thanks Todd, I'd really appreciate it. I'll see you at two." I said goodbye, hurried through the day's paperwork, worked the podium during lunch, and did the banking on my way to Mark's apartment.

My heart beat faster as we climbed the exterior staircase to the apartment above Lillian Walker's house. I needed to be observant; this was my one chance. I'd convinced myself there was something to be learned, and I was stubborn enough to believe that I was the one who could learn it.

Tall and gangly, in his mid-20's, Todd Braun had short reddish hair, thick-rimmed glasses, and a thin mustache which accentuated his angular face. He'd arrived in a Village Flower Shoppe van, the odor of cut flowers wafting from his vehicle and surrounding him.

We'd never interacted before, and I was suddenly apprehensive about entering Mark's apartment. I'd impulsively planned this visit, without considering that I'd be alone with a man I knew almost nothing about, a man who was on my suspect list. *Error.* Not the smartest thing I've ever done.

Todd unlocked the door and stepped back, wordlessly motioning for me to enter first. I moved forward cautiously, determined to remain alert. What if I'd been so ignorant that I'd impetuously made an appointment to be alone with a killer? I was ashamed for thinking of Todd that way, but I had to remember that this wasn't a game.

The air in the small apartment was stale and stuffy, with the stagnant odor of rooms that have been closed up for too long. Todd's nose twitched as we entered, and we quickly opened a few windows to let fresh air in. Dirty dishes in the sink and the unmade bed most likely contributed to the mustiness. They gave a clear picture of someone who left home one morning and never returned.

We silently looked things over; there was nothing to be said. I didn't know what I was looking for, but it was fascinating to get some insight into how Mark had lived. My expectations dimmed as I realized I was incompetent at this search. The apartment didn't seem any different than dozens of others I'd been in, impersonal, a bit shabby, nothing out of the ordinary.

Mark's living room was simple, but comfortable. A well-worn couch and chair in a green plaid, two small tables with lamps, a large flat screen TV and a bookcase made up the furniture. There were a few framed photos depicting family, high school teams, and friends partying.

A charger sat on an end-table, but there was no other electronic equipment. I knew the officers had searched Mark's phone and computer. Had his electronics been taken to Madison? Would they be returned? It was increasingly evident that I knew nothing about investigations. *What was I thinking, trying to play cop? I wouldn't know a clue if I found one.*

Several issues of the Indianapolis Star lay on the floor next to the easy chair, the top one opened to the local sports page. An alumni newsletter from Indiana University, Mark's alma mater, lay over the arm of that chair. A copy of Indiana Weekly was on an end table, along with a pile of unopened mail.

"Has someone been picking up Mark's mail?" I asked.

"No, it's being forwarded to his parent's house," Todd said.

No one had bothered to open the envelopes on the table. I paged through them, they all appeared to be junk mail, so I joined the ranks of people who'd ignored them.

The bookshelves held several novels everyone reads in school, a few battered textbooks, and high school yearbooks, as if Mark had filled the space with whatever books he owned. There was even a college yearbook. (People actually have college yearbooks?) A jackknife adorned with a Boy Scout logo lay next to a set of unidentified keys.

Walls were unadorned except for a few sports posters and a calendar featuring historic buildings. The calendar had been marked with an appointment for a haircut, and a date two months back said "Mom's b-day". No help there.

The bedroom was utilitarian, with bed, nightstand and dresser. I moved quickly through the room, feeling like I was invading private space. A nightstand drawer contained appliance manuals and random other paperwork. I flipped through travel brochures and credit card agreements, then came to a stack of envelopes hand-addressed to Mark. I wondered if I dared to read them.

"What did you find?" said a voice in my ear. I jumped a foot. Todd was right behind me looking over my shoulder.

"Oh, nothing. Nothing." I shoved the papers back in the drawer, closing it with the envelopes at the bottom. I badly wanted to read the letters, but they were none of my business, and I was too uncomfortable to invade Mark's privacy in front of Todd.

Wholesale Wholegrains uniforms made up the majority of the clothes in his closet. Neatly folded but discolored and threadbare tee-shirts along with frayed well-worn jeans occupied his dresser. *What a boring wardrobe.*

His bathroom was even more utilitarian; beyond toothpaste and brush, a comb, and shaving things, there was nothing to see.

What was I looking for? I really didn't know. "Todd, did you know Mark's girlfriend, the one he broke up with?"

"I never met her. I was already in Windsor Grove when they started dating." His voice was quiet. "He was totally infatuated; for months he couldn't talk about anything but her. I felt sorry for him when she broke it off; he was so devastated I wasn't sure he'd make it. That's why I suggested he come here. What a stupid idea that was!"

"No, it wasn't. You were being a good friend," I said, trying to encourage conversation. "I was only wondering if there was anyone who would recognize her if she came to town. I guess not."

"But why would she come?" He looked concerned. "You don't think she had anything to do with it?"

"I really don't. I'm grasping at straws."

"But he didn't break up with her, she broke up with him. She would have no reason to come here, or to be angry."

"You're right. It's unlikely she's a factor."

I looked through the kitchen cabinets; Mark had stocked up on canned goods and pasta. I checked the fridge; any perishables had been removed. I wondered if the officers had done that; or maybe Mark's landlady. I found some dish detergent, and quickly washed the dishes and scrubbed the sink; it seemed important that someone should clean Mark's things.

While I did those domestic chores Todd wandered around looking bored and checking his watch. His patience wasn't going to hold out much longer; I knew I'd better get moving. He'd been opening cupboards and drawers, sighing at the thought of dealing with Mark's belongings. Or possibly sighing in frustration at the length of my visit.

At one point I realized that Todd was looking over my shoulder. When I quickly turned around he was intently studying a spot on the counter. Or was he staring at the knife rack? *Don't think about knives, Ashley. Keep moving and get this over with.*

"Here's a mug from Indiana University. It seems like it should become yours," I offered.

"Not sure I want it. Bad memories, you know?"

I nodded. I wouldn't have wanted it either.

"There'll be a lot to donate to the church rummage sale," he mumbled, peering into a shallow drawer. I had to agree. Other than the framed pictures and the yearbooks nothing seemed worth sending to Mark's family. It was puzzling to me that such an outgoing guy had so few personal belongings.

Considering the scarcity of possessions, Mark certainly had an impressive collection of utensils. Especially cutlery. Steak knives, carving knives, paring knives…he had them all. There seemed to be a knife theme surrounding his memory. I shivered at the thought.

We left shortly after that, not having found anything interesting. Todd seemed annoyed with me, as if I'd wasted his afternoon. Well, okay, maybe I had. But I'd wasted my own afternoon, too. Back in my Beetle, I inhaled deeply, willing my shoulders and spine to relax. The air was thick with the floral aroma of the flower shop van, which is unfortunately a scent that reminds me of funerals.

I'd been at a high stress level the entire time I was alone with Todd. I hadn't been able to relax; there'd been no feeling of camaraderie, only an uncomfortable stiffness.

I had to become less impulsive; I know better than to go anywhere with a stranger, and Todd was basically just that. A stranger who'd become an acquaintance through a shared connection to cold-blooded murder. I'd been thoughtless to set up that meeting.

And despite that lack of judgment, I'd learned nothing worthwhile. I felt disappointed and empty, as if I'd missed some clue right in front of me. I did have a better understanding of the person Mark had been; maybe now something would occur to me that would make sense of his death. I wished I'd had a chance to read those letters in the nightstand.

I'd come away with two major impressions. First was the surprising austerity of Mark's living space; second was the absence of anything related to Windsor Grove; no Grove Gazette, no Concert Calendar, no Community Guide. It seemed odd for someone so curious about his new hometown to have possessed no local information.

It was as if Mark had been physically present in Windsor Grove, but emotionally still resided in Plainfield. His hometown paper, college newsletter, photos of old friends and collegiate mug spoke of a man who hadn't let go of the past.

Was it possible that his seemingly sincere curiosity was only an act? But why? To make people like him? Or was he deluding himself into believing he'd successfully left the past behind? I'd have to give that some thought.

As a concept, it made me sad. It was disturbing to think that Mark hadn't emotionally moved forward, couldn't let go of memories. Was this scenario occurring only in my mind? Or did it have basis in reality?

Had Mark been uncomfortable in his new life? Was the answer in his past? Was everyone wrong to study the present? His belongings were almost exclusively connections to his prior life; that may have been important.

What had I missed? Something could have been right in front of me, calling my name, and I'd been oblivious to its importance. I felt overwhelmed by the task I'd set for myself. STOP HELPING THE COPS the note had read. Well I wasn't doing this to help the cops; I was doing it for myself, to regain what had once been my frantic but controlled existence.

One thing I knew for certain; I wasn't going to tell Gregg where I'd just been. I didn't want to hear what he'd have to say about my impulsive actions. I'd ignored his command, "Don't go anywhere alone." Sort of. Being alone with a stranger had been foolishly risky. Would I ever learn?

During those longest days of the year it wasn't unusual for tour busses to drop off throngs of passengers at Unincorporated. The majority of them called ahead; even those that arrived unannounced generally showed up at fully-staffed meal times. Maybe I was just becoming more comfortable in my position, but I was no longer annoyed when groups showed up unexpectedly.

I was beginning to enjoy meeting these travelers, learning about their vacations and plans. They brought another dimension to what I'd started to think of as The Windsor Experience. A person could grow accustomed to this laid-back-in-winter, rush-like-crazy-in-summer lifestyle.

"Why do you call this place a *supper club*, if it's open at noon too?" I couldn't count the number of times I'd been asked that.

This was a frequent question, and everyone working in the front of the house had a ready answer. The short response was that we served at noon only during the few busy months; the rest of the year we served strictly in the evenings. The longer explanation had to do with the definition of a Wisconsin Supper Club.

The concept of a supper club is a holdover from the prohibition era; it was the average person's answer to a private club, Everyman's Country Club. Originating in Wisconsin, the concept spread to other Midwestern states. And, no, there's no membership involved.

In a supper club the guest visits the bar for cocktails before dinner, joining in conversations, chatting with the owner. The supper club is more about a sense of community than about the menu, but traditionally there will be generously portioned steaks, fresh seafood, a relish tray and a basket of breads, with homemade desserts available.

In the tradition of expecting a full evening's entertainment in one stop, the guests often return to the bar after their meal to enjoy alcohol-based ice-cream drinks, intense conversation, and of course more brandy old-fashioneds. The regulars all know each other, and the staff calls them by name. Many of the original supper clubs still exist in rural areas of Wisconsin.

Zachary's Supper Club was founded during the golden era of Wisconsin supper clubs, and as Unincorporated the genre continues. The popularity of the restaurant gives witness to the fact that people still love the friendly atmosphere and the steak-house menu. Zachary's Lounge is an integral part of the experience, as is the old-world decorating scheme.

Our regulars love to tell how generations of their families spent long evenings at this location. World problems have been solved in the Lounge. Our regulars know how to coach every sports team, how to achieve peace in foreign lands, what to do about the value of the dollar, and what's wrong with the younger generation. They also know, of course, every detail of everyone else's lives.

An interesting topic had recently taken its place among the normal town chatter. I frequently overheard groups of locals talking about Man-in-Brown, although obviously no one else called him that. I learned he'd arrived in town around Memorial Day, and had been staying at the Hillside Motel, south of town, with tiny inexpensive rooms.

I tried frantically to think of some excuse I could use to get a look inside his room (you never know where you might find a vital clue), but my imagination wasn't good enough to come up with any feasible request.

Was I butting in where I didn't belong? Maybe. But I only wanted to help. I'd been inadvertently involved, and I might as well continue to follow my instincts.

During the storm and the days that followed Man-in-Brown hadn't been seen; the motel housekeeping staff reported that he hadn't occupied his room for almost a week. Toiletries and clothing still occupied the space, but the bed had been untouched for days. Word of this spread quickly, of course, increasing speculation about this visitor.

Housekeeping staffs being what they are, it had been confirmed that no electronic devices had been left behind. Paperwork and briefcase were also absent; any personal information left when he did. His empty luggage, occupying the closet floor, had no I.D. tags, no airline labels, no information of any kind.

The man was definitely attracting attention, even as he seemed to try avoiding it. I suspected that there was an important purpose behind all his secrecy; I sure wished I understood why this uncommunicative man had taken up temporary residence in Windsor Grove.

CHAPTER 25

The Independence Day fireworks display over Windsor Lake went off without a hitch, garnering *oohs* and *ahhs* from young and old alike, while the smells of charcoal, lighter fluid, and bratwurst permeated the area.

It was a slow day at Unincorporated, but tables near our windows had a tremendous view of the fireworks, and were in demand as darkness descended. Seats on the patio remained full throughout the evening, and outdoor beverage sales were exceptional. Several locals told me apologetically that Uncle Al had always let them spend the evening there, seemingly afraid I wouldn't let them stay if they didn't dine.

As midnight neared and the last of our guests prepared to leave, Gregg walked sheepishly in our front door.

"Are you still open for business?" he inquired. "I don't need food, but I sure could use a beer. What a day!"

I assured him that a beer was possible. The rest of the staff could finish their side work and leave; I would serve Gregg, then lock up. Under ordinary circumstances a lone female staffer was never to be left alone with a guest after closing, but I knew I was safe in this case.

Perching himself on a barstool in the Lounge, he requested a draught Guinness. I was oddly proud that I'd been taught the proper procedure to draw his pint.

"Summer holidays are a nightmare for us," he commented once he'd made a dent in his beer. I raised an eyebrow; what could be so bad about July 4th? His explanation surprised me.

"People are so careless on holidays that we deal with one emergency after another. When a 911 call comes in, the sheriff's department is usually the first responder available. So today I've been called to boating accidents, home fireworks emergencies, a road rage incident, sports injuries, even a first-degree burn from a barbecue grill. I sure feel sorry for anyone working in an ER today." He laughed as he said it, but his frustration was obvious.

"I never thought of holidays as being dangerous." I'd been surprised by his explanation.

"They always are; people never change. They know better, but they ignore their instincts." He sat silently for a moment, concentrating on his beer. Then he continued with is narrative.

"Right in the middle of all the holiday hoopla, I got a call from Officer Collins saying another knife was found in a car. Some family found it a week ago, and thought it belonged to a kid in their carpool. Seriously? A soccer kid with a knife that sharp? They've been asking all the team parents if they're missing a good knife. Finally one of those parents called the department.

"After all our warnings to stay alert, people find a dangerously sharp knife and attribute it to a careless kid. I guess now we have to get the word out for everyone to watch for stolen knives. We'd hoped to avoid adding to the local stress level." He shook his head. "We should have known better."

Finally, sighing, he stood up and smiled.

"Thanks for letting me vent. I needed someone to talk to as much as I needed the beer. Can I help you lock up, and walk you home?"

"Yes to both," I answered, and we made quick work of securing the building and leaving for the cottage.

"I'm glad you're spending the summer here. I always feel good when I'm around you," he told me as he unlocked my door. I was surprised when he kissed my forehead, but more surprised when he said, "I'm so tired I almost forgot how pretty you are. It's therapeutic to look at a gorgeous gal at the end of a chaotic day. It brings back a sense of perspective. Take care of yourself; I don't want anything to happen to you."

He brushed a strand of hair away from my face, and ran strong fingers gently under my chin. His huge dark eyes were mesmerizing in the moonlight, even as he sighed with exhaustion. Once he left, after a long lazy hug, I realized that a different kind of fireworks were going off in my head.

Night after night, when the world was sleeping, when darkness was complete, when the only sounds were the sounds of nature, silent footsteps circled the cottage. Listening, watching, and speculating with anticipation, leaving before dawn without taking action, plotting to eliminate another potential enemy.

There were so many things to consider, but there was little risk.

What fools these people were. Not one of them understood the feeling of power, the absolute rush it brought, to end a life in a satisfyingly brutal manner. It could be accomplished again, it would *be accomplished again, and it would be easier the second time.*

There was little to fear; the so-called "authorities" were pathetic and clueless. No one could doubt the level of intensity and the superb planning exhibited in this manipulation of the community. It was indeed a marvelous undertaking.

A killing was perfectly natural, in keeping with the ebb and flow of nature. God gives life, and God takes it away. Occasionally humans embark on activities that help move things along. That's the way of the world.

The time had to be right; there was no urgency. The message, Stop Helping the Cops, had been ignored. A lesson must be taught. Action must be successfully taken. When taken, it must be lethal. And it must be spectacular, a brilliant achievement.

The planning itself was a pleasurable experience. To carry out the act would bring immeasurable pride.

Summer tourism was in full swing, and the days flew by.

Lynette and John quietly returned to The Pottery Studio. Everyone assumed they'd had a wonderful, relaxing vacation. If there was speculation that it was an odd time for tourism-dependent business owners to travel, no one said so. The locals were adamant about supporting locally-owned businesses, and wouldn't openly criticize other's decisions. Well, actually they would, and frequently, but only to other locals.

I'd grown accustomed to Brad's ranting. If I walked into the kitchen and he wasn't having a conniption about something I wondered what was wrong. If a day went by without him yelling at me I became concerned. Thankfully his artistry with food overshadowed his explosive personality. It was all beginning to seem normal.

Margaret Hunter, my frail new friend, had become a regular lunchtime guest. Her alert eyes would twinkle at me from across the room, acknowledging our special connection. I felt like I had a guardian angel watching over me.

A recent text from Bekah told me she'd met "the most incredible guy" at the gym. I knew better than to expect it to last, but as always she was euphoric.

Carrie, our server, returned to work at Unincorporated with little fanfare. She called one night, saying she was back in town; could I please put her on the schedule? If any of the staff were surprised at her return they never mentioned it. I assume that she'd contacted several of them herself; she was popular among the group and had no doubt kept in touch with a few. I never asked if she'd had official approval to return, or if she'd just decided on her own. It was none of my business, but I was curious all the same.

I wanted to know everything about the investigation. I also wanted to know about every activity in Windsor Grove; it was starting to feel like home, as odd as that seemed. I was enjoying this temporary stop in my career path more than I'd expected to.

"Let's try to get an evening off together. We could go see that Cheesehead play." Gregg was referring to a local comedy production "You Might Be a Cheesehead..." Based on the Wisconsin traditions of brats, cheese, fishing, beer and deer hunting, it had become so popular that additional performances had been scheduled.

"Great! I don't want to be the only one who hasn't seen it."

Every visitor was encouraged to attend ("I've never laughed so hard! You don't want to miss it!"), and residents of nearby communities were coming by the carful. I'd learned to schedule for a quick dinner rush before each performance and a leisurely dessert rush afterward. A dose of comedy was exactly what Windsor Grove needed after a summer so far noted for drought, murder, and a damaging storm.

Long days spent indoors can make a person lose sight of what an amazing place Windsor Grove is, myself included. I made a point of getting out to enjoy nature whenever possible, even if only for a few minutes. The spiritual effects of still water, the stability of mature oak and maple trees, the riotous colors of everyone's flower beds, the decades old buildings lining Main Street, and the friendly greetings from everyone you meet, these are the things that give this town its personality. Local shopkeepers and innkeepers work hard to keep things fresh and interesting so visitors get unique experiences even after numerous visits.

I gave myself constant reminders of why everyone loves it here, why they keep coming back for more, why it is important that Unincorporated remain a first-rate destination. It would have been too easy to become discouraged in the wake of recent events. I couldn't let that happen now; I'd become attached, it had become part of me.

Heading to the post office one day, I decided to park along a side street and spend a few minutes strolling through a picturesque neighborhood. As I exited my Beetle I heard my name.

"Ashley! What a pleasure to see you," I heard a well-bred but squeaky voice from behind a row of shrubbery.

Craning my neck to see the source, I saw Mr. Horner polishing the hood of an expensive looking car. Knowing little about vehicles, I studied the hood ornament, meaning to research that symbol when I got home.

"Hi, Mr. Horner! What a lovely neighborhood. I decided to spend a few minutes exploring Windsor Grove, and this is a really cute area for a walk." Cute? Did I really say *cute*? I must have sounded like a twelve-year old. Thankfully Mr. Horner didn't seem to notice.

Precisely trimmed shrubs bordered his yard. A thick carpet of grass gave testament to constant, almost compulsive care. Tidy flowerbeds added a touch of color. As I should have expected given his seeming paranoia about things occurring behind his back, his home was situated toward the rear of his property, with a high fence defining his lot line.

"Such a nice surprise, having an attractive young lady come to visit. Would you like to come in?" He put the lid on a tin of polish, and wiped his hands on a damp cloth.

Hadn't I just said that I wanted to go for a walk? Oh, well, he seemed lonely, and it couldn't hurt to spend a few polite minutes. We crossed his front porch, proceeding through an elaborately embellished doorway into a surprisingly elegant, but overcrowded, room. With marble-topped tables, an intricately carved settee upholstered in a floral tapestry, two velvet wing chairs, Tiffany lamps and framed photos of someone's ancestors, the room was reminiscent of a Victorian novel. Was this the parlor? I wasn't certain what the term actually meant.

"Have a seat, Ashley. Can I bring you some tea?" It had been more expected when the grey-attired woman at The Marys' house had offered tea. Here it seemed incongruous, as if Mr. Horner were pretending to be someone he wasn't. Perhaps tea wasn't unusual for a man who lived among antique furniture and had, maybe, a parlor.

Either way, tea didn't appeal to me one bit; on a warm summer day I'd much rather have a diet soda. I refused his offer (hoping that wasn't impolite), trying to cut my visit short.

In the back of my mind I again heard my mother's voice saying, "Don't go into a house with strangers, and never, *ever*, take food from strangers." Was Mr. Horner a stranger? Well, yes, sort of.

Then there was Gregg's "Don't go anywhere alone." I may have made another huge error in judgment. *Stay alert, Ashley*! Since when was he so outgoing? At Unincorporated he always seemed withdrawn, almost antisocial. It was as if this was an entirely different person, a person I didn't know. A person I shouldn't be alone with.

Mr. Horner started to educate me about some of the artifacts and memorabilia that filled glass-fronted display cabinets. He was conversant on every item, each piece acquired during past travels. This surprising man told stories of elegant events, famous celebrities, and international expeditions. He showed me ceremonial masks and Indian blowguns.

Precisely arranged, his collections told of a life I would have never expected.

"That's an authentic samurai sword," he said, pointing to a weapon displayed above the fireplace. "The samurai culture is fascinating. I much admire the stamina of their warriors." He reached up to tenderly caress the hilt.

It was then that I noticed a pile of books on an end table. Well-worn, each book dealt with the history of military weapons. Not exactly my idea of casual reading material.

I have to get away from here, I thought. *This is creeping me out.*

"Everything you have is so unique. And wonderful. I really appreciate you showing me your things, but I really do have to go now," I babbled. I felt a bit rude, and was certainly being abrupt, but I'd realized that once again I was alone with someone on my suspect list. What did I really know about his man? Nothing. Why had I ever agreed to enter his house?

"I wish you could stay longer. It was such a short visit." He'd moved closer to me; too close really. For a man who seemed to value his own personal space, he seemed oddly oblivious to the fact that he'd invaded mine.

His manner was kind and friendly, and he seemed hungry for companionship, but I was increasingly uncomfortable. My ever-present tension was again making my spine tingle. I rose and moved toward the door.

"Thank you so much for dropping in. Come back any time. You will come back, won't you? I have many more things to show you," Mr. Horner grinned broadly, his eyes boring into mine.

Reaching the sidewalk I took a deep breath, trying to ease the tension I'd been feeling. There had been something unsettling about my visit with Mr. Horner. Was it all in my head?

I hurried through my post office visit, ran a few errands, and felt an amazing sense of relief when I again reached the refuge of Unincorporated.

"Hi Ashley'" said the grey-haired woman waiting at the podium. I recognized her and her husband as regulars who came to dine on weekends when they stayed at their condo. They were a demanding couple who had servers continually scurrying about.

"This is my sister from Colorado and her husband. They'll be staying with us for two weeks, so you'll probably see a lot of us. I told them about the lovely view from your patio; can we wait out there?"

"The lake is beautiful today. I'll put you at one of our most popular tables." I showed them to seats with a world-class view, and took their beverage order. They were fidgeting when I returned a few minutes later.

"The breeze is too chilly here in the shade," said the Colorado sister in a voice as shrill as nails on a chalk board. "Can't we sit in the sun?"

"Certainly. I'll put your drinks at that table over there." A request easily dealt with.

Moments later Dawn came to me and said, "The foursome that you seated outdoors asked to see you."

As I approached their table the heavyset woman called out, "I don't want the sun shining right on me. Can you move an umbrella to this table?"

"But will we be warm enough?" asked Colorado sister.

"We could all just go inside," one of the men commented.

"Oh, but it's so pretty out here."

"Well, then could we be satisfied with the table we're at?"

"No, we should be able to sit anywhere we want." Her words were becoming louder, and even more grating.

"But you don't know what you want!"

Thankfully at that point Dawn motioned to me that their dining table was ready. It seemed to me that it was going to be a long two weeks in that condo.

I found myself hoping they'd find somewhere else to eat when they wanted to admire the view.

Gregg stood in my office that afternoon looking serious, and apprehensive.

"Ashley...um...there's something I want to tell you...actually I'm not supposed to talk about it; but I feel like I should...I think there's something you should know."

"What's up?" I'd never seen him so nervous.

"Detective Milton compiled a list of prime suspects, based on the evidence, and...uh...you're near the top of the list." His final words were rushed, as if he had to hurry to get them out.

"You're kidding! Me? Why?"

Gregg shook his head. "It's all circumstantial, obviously. But...you were right on the spot...you had the means...and the opportunity. So far no motive, but we haven't found a motive for any other suspects, either."

I was stunned. I couldn't think, couldn't talk. I was numb. I'd never before been suspected of anything. And now, murder? I felt like I was going to be sick.

I stared, unseeingly, at Gregg. After a few moments he said softly, "I'm sorry. I thought you should know. I have to go now." He touched my hand, then turned and walked away. It all seemed unreal. *Please don't let Mom and Dad find out I'm a suspect. They'd be so humiliated.*

As was I.

An overwhelming dinner rush that evening had everyone struggling to keep up when one of our youngest hosts motioned for me to take a phone call.

"Someone with a really funny voice is asking for you," he said.

'Hello, Ashley speaking. May I help you?"

"I could be your best friend right now, or your worst enemy," a hoarse whispering voice said, emphasizing the last four words.

"What? Who is this?"

"Your best friend. Or your worst enemy. An enemy beyond comprehension. Your choice. You were warned. Stop helping the cops. Or you'll be very sorry. Very, very sorry."

Click. End of conversation.

In one sense it had seemed like something from a bad movie, but the overwhelming effect had been terrifying.

Could I identify that rasping voice? No, I wasn't even certain if it was male or female. The cadence had been stilted, giving no clue about speech patterns. One thing, however, was certain; the menace behind the message had been very real.

I stood looking off into space, feeling as if I'd seen a demon. I couldn't keep my hands from trembling.

I was growing increasingly closer to my breaking point. *One of these days I'm just going to quit, say goodbye, and leave Unincorporated and Windsor Grove behind forever. I can't handle much more of this.*

But what about Uncle Al? I'd feel like I'd deserted the guy I'd looked up to forever. I didn't seem to have any good options; my life felt like a constant downward spiral.

A further disconcerting issue occurred a few hours later when I opened my desk drawer, moved aside a phone list, and realized that my pathetic attempt at creating a *suspects and motives* list was no longer there. I knew exactly where I'd put it, and was certain I'd seen it just a day or two earlier. Why anyone would want to take it was beyond me, it was a list anyone could have made; I didn't have any facts beyond common knowledge. But it was definitely gone.

This constant drama was exasperating. I looked forward to the day when I could pack up and head home. Murder, threatening anonymous notes, knives under car seats, severe weather, a chef who bullied me, and now this. Sometimes I really hated this place. Even my personal space wasn't secure.

Any number of people had access to my office; it wasn't locked during working hours. Staffers put time-off requests into my in-basket and searched my cupboards for supplies, delivery drivers tossed invoices in a bin on the desk, but I'd never seen anyone looking inside the desk. I'd have to be careful what I stored in there. I'd always been a trusting person, maybe too trusting. In Windsor Grove I was *supposed* to be able to trust everyone. What was happening to this small town?

Who would have wanted my suspects list? And why? Everyone in town probably had a similar list, and many lists could have been more detailed than mine. I wondered how many of the lists had my name on them.

What about the threatening phone call? How did that fit into this mess? That caller, at least, was one person who knew I wasn't the guilty party. But I was no closer to figuring out who was.

CHAPTER 26

Returning to work one evening I could tell, difficult as it might seem, that Brad was in an even worse mood than usual.

"If you think that steak's medium rare you're even dumber than I thought!" was directed to our most experienced fry cook. When a new dishwasher dropped a dinner plate, which shattered spectacularly, he sent her home, saying, "Come back when you can do something right."

As she stumbled out the door in tears he muttered, "...wish I'd never come to this Godforsaken hole..." *Way to be a team leader, Brad.*

The tension surrounding him was alarming; he was overwrought, near the breaking point. I was determined that somehow the night would go smoothly, but of course that didn't happen. No one can control a tsunami.

"Ashley!" he bellowed later through the pick-up window, "What do you think you're doing out there? Don't you know anything about timing? We don't get a single order for twenty minutes, and then we get freakin' slammed! What good are you if you can't set the pace in the dining room? You don't know a damn thing about this business, do you?"

"Um," I stammered, "Uh...I've been seating people at intervals. But they all seem to make up their minds at once..."

"That's a load of crap. It never happened when Al was here. I'm gonna have a talk with him; you're two steps from useless!" Understanding the origin of his issues didn't make them any easier to accept.

As he stormed away from the window, I turned and realized that much of the staff, and several guests, had been listening intently. They quickly turned away and started nervous, animated conversations. If there were a few smirks I tried not to notice.

Great. Just great. Way to cement your reputation, Ashley.

The next day I held my breath every time the phone rang, expecting to hear from Uncle Al that Brad had been filling his ear, complaining about his favorite niece. But the call didn't come. I never learned whether or not Brad had actually contacted Al. If he did, Al obviously took his ranting with a grain of salt.

Summer days settled into a consistent pattern, and Gregg and I fell into the habit of spending our free time together. Afternoons we would eat ice cream as we walked along the beach, evenings we shared dessert and coffee in front of my fireplace. There'd also been a late night pizza or two. Food seemed to always factor into our time together; if I spent much more time with Gregg it was going to start affecting my waistline!

It was fascinating to share time with a guy who was familiar with everything that happened in Windsor Grove. It satisfied my curiosity, and added an additional element to conversations with guests. Gregg never divulged anything confidential, but in a small town very little happens that isn't immediately common knowledge. When area teens were arrested for jumping a fence into a private pool area, I learned about it at work, and Gregg filled in the details later that evening.

When a local farmer was arrested for chopping down his neighbor's apple trees I was able to answer our guests' questions before The Gazette was delivered. Gregg's inside information became popular in Zachary's Lounge.

"How much was the bracelet worth that was stolen from Silversmith's yesterday?" I inquired the day after a theft.

"Where did you hear about that? We haven't released any information yet."

"Oh, sorry," I shrugged. "I thought everyone knew about it."

"What a place this is; we can't keep anything quiet."

"Well," I explained, "Amanda, our pastry chef, heard about it at the post office, from her friend whose cousin was washing windows across the street from Silversmith's. He saw the police activity and went over afterward to ask questions."

Gregg laughed at that. "We'll have to talk to that window washer. Considering how intently people around here watch their neighbors you may have found an eyewitness." He continued, "I don't know what's happening to our quiet little community. There's usually a slight uptick in crime during the summer months, but it's never been like this. We're earning our pay this summer, that's for sure."

"Last night was really something," he commented another day. "You heard about the bar fight at Rick's Tap? Rick and his customers had it broken up before I got there. They had the two men on the floor, arms tied behind their backs, ready for arrest. One lady filmed the episode on her phone. Another woman made a list of all the witnesses. They had my job done for me," he laughed. "They were so proud of themselves; they said they felt like characters in a TV drama."

He shook his head. "It's okay, as long as no one gets hurt when they play cop. I warned them that they'd involved themselves in a dangerous situation, but they'd had just enough to imbibe that they were mighty pleased with themselves. Now they think my job is a breeze!" He shrugged, "I hate to admit it, but until recently my job *was* a cakewalk. Believe me; even as stressful as it's become I much prefer the intensity of serious police work."

Weeks earlier, the evening after the storm, Gregg had helped me relax after a traumatic day. After my threatening phone call I'd unloaded my concerns onto him. He'd willingly taken my problems on as his own.

The tables were now turned; I'd become the sounding board for *his* anxieties. The unsolved case was wearing on him, with pressure coming from the public and from his superiors, but mostly from inside himself. Rather than needing companionship to help him forget, he needed someone supportive, an impartial listener as he verbalized his thoughts.

"The biggest sticking point is lack of motive," he mused over coffee at my cottage. "We know what the weapon was, and hundreds of people could potentially have gotten their hands on it. Those same hundreds of people had the opportunity to commit the crime, especially if exact timing wasn't a factor. But why? Why?

"Without any witnesses," he went on, "and we're assuming there were none or we'd have heard rumblings by now, we have little to work with until we can figure out the motive. Mark seems to have had no enemies at all; not here and not back in Indiana."

"Crimes of passion are the most common, which leads us back to his recent breakup, but there's absolutely nothing there. It seems to have been amicable, leaving sadness, but not animosity. If there was anyone who felt wounded and held a grudge it would have been Mark himself, so that gets us nowhere."

He shook his head. "No one plans a homicide, works out the minutest details, and patiently waits for their victim with no reason. Unless they're deranged, and there's no indication of insanity in this crime. It was a cool clear-headed person who carried it out. There was no momentary out of control fury, therefore no insanity. Not legal insanity, anyway."

During strolls along the water's edge Gregg would become pensive. "There's a theory that frustration always produces aggression, and aggression is always a consequence of frustration. We may be looking for someone with intense built-up frustration, as simple as someone who felt insulted, or as complex as someone suffering extreme tension when the air pressure changes. Anger can build to a violent stage quickly, or over a long period. If frustration was the cause, it could be anyone, for any reason."

"...anyone...for any reason...that's awful..." I murmured. Our chats may have decreased Gregg's stress level, but mine was increasing exponentially. Watching a Styrofoam container bob gently along the water, I wondered if my life would ever again feel calm and casual.

"And what's the connection to the knives in the vehicles and the threatening notes?" Gregg asked. "It's possible the killer is trying to incriminate someone from Unincorporated. There doesn't seem to be any rhyme or reason behind who's targeted, but there could be some connection we haven't figured out yet.

"We're now assuming that the notes are definitely being left by the killer, since two of the three were anchored by Kellam knives. It would be too much of a coincidence if a random person had knives identical to those stolen by a murderer. The vehicle knives are certainly being left by the killer, too.

"The killer may get a thrill by harassing people. If that's the case, the notes and knives are just muddying the waters. Anonymous letters are a coward's tool. It's been known for a perpetrator to try diverting attention away from his or herself by making it look as if they are also a victim. That points directly to Lynette and John, and Carrie, and you."

"Me? Me again? This all seems ridiculous."

"I don't believe it for a minute, but I'm sure you understand that we have to consider everyone. Even our own trusted intelligent, attractive friends." He reached over to hold my hand, stroking the back and tracing swirly patterns in my palm.

His actions softened his words, but I was unsure how to take it. I was a suspect, and it made me uncomfortable. Gregg didn't seem to be bothered by it, but I hadn't fully relaxed since the first time it was mentioned.

The fact that I'd received a threatening phone call hadn't removed me as a suspect. Why? Because there was no proof of what had been said; I could have invented the conversation completely. The whole thing was ridiculously frustrating.

When Gregg and I discussed possible scenarios, I would mention people I found suspicious. Most of my suspects, however, had an alibi for at least one of the notes' delivery times, and none of them had any clear reason to have disliked Mark.

Even I had to admit that you couldn't just randomly arrest people because they acted suspiciously. Or because the new restaurant manager thought they were a bit odd.

Nothing I'd learned in sociology classes related to brutal murder; now if only the crime had been committed over a disagreement about social planning...or crowd control...

When Gregg and I would enjoy ice cream at the Sundae Parlor our imaginations ran wild dreaming up motives, most so farfetched they seemed positively outrageous. Occasionally we'd get giddy at our own suggestions; the comic relief seemed to help Gregg's attitude, at least temporarily.

I found myself tending toward denial. It was easier to view the entire homicide debacle as if I were an uninvolved spectator. As if it were a performance on a stage.

Only the sheriff's officers knew about my own threatening note, or about the firewood against the cottage; I hadn't even told Al. I'd mentioned my anonymous phone call to Gregg, and my missing suspects list, so the officers were probably aware of those factors, too.

I didn't want to play a part in this drama. Unable or unwilling to deal with the reality of constant personal danger, I let Gregg verbalize his thoughts as if I were a child listening to a fairy tale. Removed. Uninvolved. A simple bystander.

Gregg continued to caution me about safety procedures. I stubbornly tuned his warnings out. Naïve, I know, but I felt calmer that way.

I'd learned Gregg's mannerisms enough to recognize when his tension level was high; he rubbed his neck a lot, and rolled his pen between his fingers. Sometimes the thing that seemed to relax Gregg the most was silence. I made a point of creating pauses in our conversation to allow him time for reflection.

When he silently organized his thoughts, I'd find myself admiring his strong shoulders, determined expression, and the classic angles of his cheekbones. But when he'd look directly at me with his huge dark eyes I found it unsettling, and would quickly turn away.

There was nothing I could do to alleviate the cause behind his stress, other than listen. But that seemed to be what he needed; it was gratifying that I'd become the recipient of his speculations. At the same time it satisfied my curiosity about what was being done toward putting this whole episode to rest.

Chatting by the water's edge one evening, Gregg said, "I'm sorry that I'm so stressed out all the time."

He moved behind me, placing his hands on my shoulders, then around my waist.

"I enjoy being around you, look forward to us spending time together, but I won't be able to truly relax until this homicide is solved. I feel like it's taken over my life." His head lay gently on mine; the warmth of his body felt good against my back.

"Thank you for being here for me. I need someone like you in my life." The tension in his body seemed to ease a bit as he moved his hands to caress the curve of my back and the lines of my hips. I felt myself relaxing against his strong torso. The intimacy was unexpected, but certainly pleasurable.

It was disconcerting to think I was becoming attached to this man. I enjoyed my time with Gregg, even though I suspected he needed my companionship mostly due to the burden of his job. I didn't know if I'd welcome a relationship; I didn't feel prepared to deal with an officer's constant anxiety. That was the last thing I needed.

What I did need was a life of my own. Would I ever have time to develop more Windsor Grove friendships? Spur-of-the-moment sessions so Gregg could download were fine. But I longed for the days when large groups of friends met spontaneously in a dimly lit spot filled with loud music, laughing crowds, and fun. I seemed to have left that life behind. Even though my current life was hectic, enjoyable fun-filled times were few and far between.

Even more discouraging was the state of my career. I'd received an ecstatic email from my college roomie. A senior-year internship had earned her a job offer with a national firm. Her future couldn't be brighter. *Sure. Great. Good for her. Everyone else is going to interviews and fielding job offers. I'm stuck in this never-ending Windsor Grove debacle.*

Since Bekah's visit I'd become increasingly disillusioned, developing a nagging feeling of dissatisfaction. I wasn't depressed, exactly; it was more a constant sense of unhappiness. Jealousy over her job prospects and sadness over the state of things in Windsor Grove had me resigned to a life I hadn't chosen. Constant turmoil made me edgy and indignant, and I didn't like myself when I acted that way.

I'd wake in the morning wanting to pull the blankets over my head and stay in bed all day. When warm rays of sunshine would caress my face they seemed to taunt me with a reminder of days when summer was meant for outdoor activity, not indoor employment. Hearing about someone with a new job made me want to cry. I felt as if my immediate future was a jumbled mess.

I wanted to break out of that funk I was in, but a few dates with a handsome man weren't enough to do the trick. Maybe, just maybe, someday I'd have a date with a guy who didn't want to discuss murder. That would be refreshing, as if I had a normal life.

I needed something to raise my spirits. A favorite online retailer was holding a Shoe Spectacular, and I decided to indulge. Where did I expect to go that I'd need those elegant evening sandals and those cherry-red pumps? And when was I going there? During my afternoon break? It didn't matter...an exciting addition to my shoe collection might do something to improve my attitude...I had to try.

It had become increasingly difficult to remain upbeat.

Unseasonably warm weather continued, with temperatures in the 90's and humidity almost as high. The air pressure was contributing to high levels of impatience, and there were days when it was hard to keep tempers under control among our usually easy-going staff.

The guests, too, were irritable; a break in the weather would be welcomed all around. Anxieties were magnified, everyone's patience was wearing thin, and once again people were looking over their shoulders wondering if there was a killer among them.

"The killer probably works at Unincorporated, that's what I think. I'm not eating there anymore, what if our murderer is a poisoner, too?" I overheard as I entered the post office one day.

Was this ongoing investigation a detriment to our business? It seemed like this insanity would never end. Who decided that Unincorporated was the culprit? I could only hope that most residents didn't buy into that rumor.

I'd learned to take much in stride over the last few months. Certain people, however, had continually rubbed me the wrong way, and I was becoming increasingly less accomodating.

"I have a wonderful opportunity for Unincorporated," shrilled a female voice on the phone. I was already skeptical; Uncle Al had warned me about "wonderful opportunities".

"My name is Harriet Pucker, and I represent the WCDCA, the Wisconsin Classic Doll Collectors Association. There will be over one hundred members coming to your town for a doll collector's conference in a few weeks. They'll need to be fed, and we think it would be wonderful publicity for you if you'd donate our meals."

My hackles went up. Unincorporated has a fairly simple donation policy: we prefer to donate gift certificates over cash, we are more generous toward groups our regular guests are affiliated with, and the recipient *must* be an actual charity. No way was I giving several hundred free meals to out-of-town doll collectors.

"I'm sorry, but we don't have a budget for anything like that. I could send you a few gift certificates that you can use as door prizes or in a raffle, if that will be helpful," I offered.

"Oh, no, that won't do," Harriet said sharply. "They wouldn't get used. Our conference will take place at the St. Francis Church meeting hall. The collectors shouldn't have to leave the site; going out into the community would be too costly. We don't want them to spend any funds beyond the cost of the conference."

So the WCDCA wasn't planning to support our tourist economy at all, were expecting local businesses to provide free food, and somehow this was a "wonderful opportunity" for me? This group didn't understand economics at all. I politely (I hope) said goodbye, and went to my desk to send gift certificates to the legitimate charitable organizations who'd submitted requests that week.

I speculated that Mary Lou, with her porcelain-faced baby doll, might be a member of this group. That could explain the choice of Windsor Grove as a meeting site for attendees who didn't care to enjoy the community...

I've always wondered if Harriet convinced anyone to donate the meals for her collectors.

CHAPTER 27

"Shut up! Everybody just shut up! I can't deal with you right now. I'm trying to figure out why my mango lime chutney doesn't compliment Chilean sea bass, and you're carrying on like this is the school cafeteria! If you value your jobs you'll just fuck off!" Brad's staff, no dummies, immediately got down to work.

I backed out of the kitchen, hoping Brad didn't realize I'd witnessed his tantrum. It could be a long day if he decided I was part of the problem.

Later that afternoon, as I fought my way through a pile of annoying paperwork, Brad showed up at my office door looking down at me as if I were an unwelcome furry rodent. "Hey Ashley," he began, "I got a question for you."

"What can I do for you?" It sounded silly and formal when I said it, but I couldn't think of any better response.

"When you're with that boyfriend of yours, that cop, does he tell you secrets and stuff?"

"First, he's not my boyfriend, just a friend. And, no, he never tells me anything I'm not authorized to know." I wondered what this conversation was actually about.

"That's what you say, but how do I know? You might know all kinds of things about me."

"I guess you'll have to take my word for it. Gregg doesn't tell me anything confidential, even though I sometimes ask him to." I laughed at that, but he didn't seem to see the humor.

"You're sure he never told you nothing about me? About my background? And how about your uncle? Does he ever talk about me?" He was talking faster, and starting to sound stressed. It occurred to me that there was a serious reason for his questions; something was upsetting Brad, and I felt even more uncomfortable conversing with him than usual.

"Really, you can take my word for it," I replied. "Neither Gregg or Uncle Al ever told me anything about you except how good you are in the kitchen. Is there something you want to talk about?" I added quietly.

"It's just that there's some stuff I don't want everyone to know. Stuff about me. And you're spending an awful lot of time with that cop."

"Brad, no one has told me anything about you, or your background. All I know about you is what's written on your resume. And some details from Al about your kitchen talents. Nothing else. Trust me."

"Your uncle was the first person to ever be really nice to me." His voice became quieter, and he spoke slowly. "He's a great guy. I wish there were more people like him." His tone was so wistful that I was shocked. His forlorn expression made him look like a lost little boy.

I felt a stab of sorrow; I'd spent my life surrounded by people who loved me and treated me like someone special. I almost wanted to cry at the thought of a man who would believe that his post tech school boss was the first person who'd been kind to him. I impulsively stood, reaching out to offer Brad a hug. Brad turned away as if human touch was alien.

He sighed, shook his head, and looked at the floor. "I have some issues; some anger stuff; some bad people skills. I guess you know that. I've been in trouble because of it, but I'm not a bad guy, I'm really not. And I don't dislike you, exactly, but I sure wish Al was here."

"I understand. You're right that Al is a great guy; he's always been my favorite uncle. Believe me, I wish he was here too!"

Brad smiled at that, and seemed to relax.

"Would you like to sit down and talk sometime, just about Unincorporated, and the industry, and the community, and life in general?" I asked. "You seem really tense and that might help...maybe Al can get together with us, too."

"Wow. That would be amazing. You'd do that? For me? It would be great, having someone to talk to." Brad seemed so excited at the prospect of having a casual conversation that it was almost pathetic.

I might have disliked him, and been almost afraid of him, but I can't begin to explain how very sorry I felt for my chef at that moment. What would I be like without my parents and my friends? I'd no doubt be a different person, possibly an angry person.

That could explain a lot. I promised to talk to Al and try to arrange a time to get together. But what with Al's recovery constraints, and Brad's and my work schedules, the opportunity for that casual chat could be a long time coming.

Late on a picture-perfect afternoon the front door at Unincorporated burst open and in strode a broad-shouldered, ruddy-cheeked man in a bright patterned aloha shirt with cargo shorts and loafers.

"I am havin' the best day ever!" he announced in a booming voice. "How many people are in the house? Drinks are on me; I'm buyin' the next round!"

Well, that got the attention of everyone in Zachary's, who perked up and decided to enjoy some top-shelf brands.

"Ya got customers in the dining room? I meant them, too. Don't want anyone missin' out. Tell 'em their new pal Jerry's buying!"

Once everyone had been served, including some fancy non-alcoholic Margaritas for a few teens, Jerry took a seat at the bar and told us his story.

"There I was, drivin' along the road, doin' a little over the speed limit…well, actually a lot over the limit…and sure enough, all of a sudden I hear sirens and see red lights flashin' in my rear view. I say to myself, 'Great, this cop sees out-of-state plates and he's gonna throw the book at me!' Well, I guess I deserved it, but it doesn't make me happy."

He threw back his head and laughed. "Ya know what that officer said? He said he didn't want to ruin my vacation by writin' a ticket, so he'd appreciate it if I'd try to obey the speed limit! Ya hear that? He'd appreciate it if I'd obey the speed limit! Don't that beat all? Not only does this place have the best fishin', you've also got the best cops!"

Settling in at the bar, he ordered Raw Oysters on the Half Shell and a Wisconsin Cheese Lovers' Platter which he shared with the patrons around him while they chatted.

As he polished off his 18-year scotch and got ready to leave he said, "I don't know that cop's name, but I'm writin' a letter to your paper about him. You do have a local paper, don't ya? Anybody know the name of a guy from the sheriff's department, young guy, tall, brown hair, real friendly?"

Several locals immediately said, "That's Gregg," and glanced over toward me.

I felt myself blushing (Why? He was just a friend), proud of knowing this kind officer, proud to be his confidante, proud that he was more than a casual acquaintance. But I also felt a bit melancholy; Gregg had spent his time in the limelight, had his chance to demonstrate his criminology skills, and was now back to setting speed traps, answering nuisance calls, and directing traffic.

"Gotta go," Jerry announced as he walked out the door. "I dropped the wife off at some stores, told her to warm up her credit cards while I'm in a good mood. I'm afraid to find out what the damage is!"

I peered out the window and saw him climb into a school-bus-yellow Ferrari. How much money had been spread throughout Windsor Grove that day because of Gregg's kind nature? Financially Jerry would have doubtless been better off paying a speeding ticket. The good feelings that were spread, however, were priceless. I'd be sure to thank Gregg next time we talked.

"You'll never guess who I saw yesterday," Bekah challenged when she called late one afternoon.

"Who?"

"Remember Miss Pennyworth? Seventh grade math?"

"The one who cackled when she laughed?"

"That's the one. I was jogging along the lakefront, down by the Calatrava Art Museum, and I heard that cackle. I knew it had to be her; I looked around, and there she was. From the side her face looked the same as ever. But it was odd; when she turned and I saw her from the front she looked totally different."

"Is she still so frumpy?"

"No, that's the odd thing. She's lost tons of weight and has a really cute haircut, and she was dressed nice, too."

"Clunky shoes?"

"I couldn't tell. But she was with a good-looking guy, and they got into a red convertible. Who'd have ever thought?"

"Did she see you?"

"She looked right at me, but not like she noticed me. I guess I look a lot different than when I was twelve!"

"We all do. And it's a good thing!"

From there we moved on to topics of universal interest (friends, fashion, celebrities), with much time dedicated to Jacob, Bekah's newest heartthrob, and to her ongoing job search. After some hesitation I broached a subject that had been hovering in my brain: Gregg.

"We've been spending lots of time together; I see him almost every day. When he can completely relax he's really kind and funny, and we enjoy all the same things. But so often he's really tense and just needs someone to listen, to be a friendly ear. I know it helps him when he can talk things out, but I end up absorbing his anxiety. He feels better, but it makes me feel awful, and I don't like it one bit. Do you think that's always what it's like when you hang out with an officer?"

"Maybe. But just remember how interesting it is, knowing what someone who's right in the thick of things is thinking. And doing."

"I know you're right. I really do like him, and I know I'm helping by listening. But it makes me uneasy. He carries a *gun* for a living! This is way beyond my comfort zone. I'm afraid I'm becoming too attached."

"Don't worry about it, girlfriend, you'll know what to do."

But would I?

Later, after we'd said goodbye, I reflected on our conversation. It had been great to finally have someone to share my feelings with. My relationship with Gregg was conflicting; discussing it with Bekah had clarified it in my mind, at least a bit.

One thing that stuck in my mine, however, was the topic that had begun our conversation. Bekah only recognized Miss Pennyworth because of her laugh; Miss Pennyworth hadn't recognized Bekah at all. People can change a lot in a few years, especially children; but some adults never change at all.

Might Mark have recognized someone, or may someone who hadn't wanted their identity known have recognized him? Was someone in town trying to go incognito? Could that have any bearing on Mark's murder?

Mark had looked like a kid to me, even in his 20's, so it was hard to imagine he'd changed much. Maybe there was someone in Windsor Grove who'd recognized him, but he hadn't recognized...I was confusing myself. Maybe I needed another category on my list, *people who don't want to be recognized*. But I wouldn't know who to put in that category.

I knew I was becoming too consumed with the idea of solving this murder; I couldn't even hear about an old teacher without considering it a clue. I had to stop obsessing; I was supposed to be in the hospitality industry, not on a homicide squad.

That, however, would be difficult; obsessing had become part of my life.

In my quiet time I began speculating that Mark's curiosity may have led him to learn some incriminating tidbit about Man-in-Brown, or the haunted Mary, or the combined Marys. Or perhaps he knew something about his long-time friend Todd from the past. Mark had constant contact with the bakery staff, and employees at restaurants, delis and resorts. There were hundreds of people whose paths may have crossed his.

Mark could have recognized town board president Ron Barber from when he'd lived in Plainfield. Or he may have learned that Mr. Horner's wife, with the maiden name Fischer, was a distant relative. But so what? So Mark recognized someone from the past, or learned somebody's secrets. That kind of thing doesn't get you killed. Not in real life.

Why would anyone hate Mark enough to kill him? Maybe Mark's relationship breakup hadn't been as amicable as we'd been told. For all anyone in Windsor Grove knew, if Mark's old girlfriend felt animosity toward him, she could have spent time in the area pretending to be a visitor; so could any member of her family. That would certainly complicate the situation

The number of possible scenarios was multiplying in my imagination. I felt like I needed a diagram to chart my various trains of thought. Things were becoming more and more convoluted, as if I were swimming in murky water and couldn't see my way. Would things ever become clear?

The number of suspects seemed to increase every time I thought about them. A variety of people could have been in the woods the morning Mark had been killed; almost anyone could have gained access to our knives and placemats; the warning notes could have been left whenever and wherever an opportunity arose; Al's unlocked restaurant doors may or may not have had any significance; anyone could have piled firewood against my cottage unseen.

The only incident that would have required perfect timing was my episode in the freezer, and it certainly hadn't been premeditated. No one could orchestrate a downpour and a thawing box of tuna. It was a spur-of-the-moment act if there ever was one.

Round and round the details went, and got more muddled with each twist and turn. Was there something obvious everyone was missing? I felt inadequate trying to figure out the answer, but it had definitely become an obsession.

This isn't your job, girl. Get a grip, Ashley, get a grip!

In mid-July I had a phone call from Mom. We were in constant touch via social media, but it was a pleasant surprise to hear her voice. That is, until I learned the reason for her call.

"I just heard from Al, and I wanted to call you right away," she began. "His last appointment with the doctor didn't go as well as he'd hoped."

I gasped for air. My stomach did flip flops. I wanted Uncle Al to be healthy again, not just because of Unincorporated, but because he was special to me. I grabbed the edge of my desk and sat down.

"Oh, no, it's not anything serious; at least not *too* serious." Mom had made it sound more urgent than it was. "It's just that he needs further surgery, this time at University Hospital in Madison, and this recuperation time might be even longer."

Okay, my stomach could get back to normal, but I felt shell-shocked. Now my tenure in Windsor Grove had been extended. I was happy to do what I could for Al, but I'd been hoping to resume my job search sometime soon. Not to mention that certain members of the staff might be less than enthused to hear I'd be sticking around.

"Did Al ask you to be the one who gave me the news?" I teased. "Was he afraid I'd turn him down if he was the one asking me to stay?"

"He did say it might be better if the news came from me," she agreed. "You know, he's really thrilled with the job you're doing. He said he definitely made the right choice when he chose you. The whole family is proud of you, honey."

I'd never found the right time to ask Al about the unlocked doors, or any missing belongings. I was glad now that I hadn't. What difference would it have made at this point anyway? I never wanted this treasured man to feel that I'd accused him of carelessness.

Mom continued to fill me in on some other things that she thought I'd want to know. One of my cousins was dating a high school dropout; a neighbor changed her hair color and it was horrid; Dad was looking for a new car; her favorite TV show had been cancelled. All the things that we loved to gab about. We finally said goodbye, with her promising to visit soon.

"Your dad and I love you and miss you. A lot. But we're glad you're having such a great summer!" she finished.

Was this a great summer? Maybe. Probably not. The jury was still out.

Mom seems sort of clueless much of the time. She's not, really. She's very sweet and kind and actually pretty smart. My high school friends spent tons of time hanging out at our house because she made them feel welcome; she made them feel welcome so she'd always know where I was and who I was with. Definitely not clueless.

Dad and I think Mom has turned a classic case of selective hearing into an art form. She can repeat almost verbatim a complicated news story about feverish trading in the stock market, while seeming unaware of the death toll in a foreign air strike. If something makes her uncomfortable or unhappy, it simply doesn't get absorbed into her brain. She only retains the feel-good parts.

Some people consider her a ditz. But she's a friendly, intelligent, happy ditz. And she's *my* ditz. And I love her, although sometimes the clueless act is hard to take.

It had taken far too long, what with homicide being the news topic of the summer, but, excitement was finally building for the upcoming Windsor Day celebration. I'd attended a few more planning sessions; The Marys gave comprehensive reports on how things were progressing. Posters appeared all over town; the number of volunteers was growing by the day; and people were clearing their calendars in order to fully enjoy the festivities.

The walk-in freezer at Unincorporated (which I was still refusing to enter, by the way, even though the latch had been repaired) was packed to the gills with deliveries for food stands. Anticipation was building everywhere.

I ignored any anxieties I felt, passing them off as insecurities relating to unaccustomed responsibility. I was determined to shake off my apprehension and thoroughly enjoy the event. I owed it to myself.

CHAPTER 28

A light drizzling rain fell during the night preceding Windsor Day, and the town awoke to a cool, gloomy, overcast Saturday. The humidity remained oppressive, not unusual for early August, but the break in temperature was welcome after weeks of heat.

Earlier that week, after Brad snarled, "I suppose you're taking the whole day off and everyone else will have to work," I'd adjusted the schedules so all of the staff could attend part of the festivities. I guessed there wouldn't be many guests at Unincorporated during the day, so I cut the lunch shift to the bare minimum, and scheduled heavily after dusk when food stands would have closed.

The Marys hadn't assigned me any specific duties for the day, so I offered to fill an early morning shift. I'd been assigned to help at a water station during the walk/run, which was expected to end long before Unincorporated opened for lunch. I could fulfill my obligation, without neglecting my actual job.

"We've hired RunWisconsin, a firm that organizes run/walk events," MaryBeth had said. "We never take risks with an activity that should be professionally organized." Hearing that, I felt confident that I'd be helping at a properly organized event; I'm uncomfortable helping with disorganized activities.

Arriving for my shift in the hazy dampness that greeted participants that chilly morning wasn't my idea of fun. I envisioned one of those unfortunate events in which the expenses are greater than the proceeds. If Windsor Day was a failure a lot of work and effort had been for naught. I stood shivering in the breeze, glad that I'd worn a fleece hoodie over my black shorts and flowered tank.

Not being a runner myself, I'm always impressed by the dedication of those who take it seriously. The number of registrants for the Windsor Run far surpassed the population of the town. Working the station, I could feel the intensity of the elite runners and the enthusiasm of the casual joggers out for their morning exercise. It felt good to cheer the runners along, and to see the smiling faces of the walkers, some of them pushing strollers or keeping pace with their children.

Once we'd closed our station I realized that during the run the sun had come out, the foggy patches had lifted, the humidity had dissipated, and it was going to be an absolutely gorgeous day.

I followed the spectators toward the finish line, and stood in amazement when I saw the festival area, the Town Hall grounds and Veteran's Park. Brightly colored pennants sat atop the numerous tents and booths; a steady breeze sending them snapping to attention, as if in formal greeting. Feeling euphoric at what I saw, I found myself rushing to take it all in.

Colorful signage directed attendees to food stands, art displays, games booths, and entertainment stages. The Windsor Community Band played Sousa marches in the historic bandstand, with an impressive number of lawn chairs set up in a circle around the area. Banners featuring drawings of the future playground thanked everyone for attending.

Volunteer parking attendants directed streams of vehicles to nearby lots. Pedestrians were everywhere, as were children, dogs on leashes, even senior citizens in wheelchairs. The locals had come out in full force, but even so were outnumbered by visitors.

The day was expected to become a warm one, and casual dress was the attire of the day. Men in Bermuda shorts and casual shirts stood with women in sundresses or capris. Children wore brightly colored clothing and smelled of sunblock. Sunglasses might have covered most of the eyes, but every face wore a smile, and shouted greetings filled the air.

The sights and sounds washed over me. I felt happier and more lighthearted than I'd felt since arriving in Windsor Grove. In the past this had been my normal frame of mind, my normal outlook on life. This enthusiastic person was the old Ashley, the real Ashley. I welcomed the return of this attitude. *Enjoy it while you can; for a few hours you have no worries, no responsibilities.*

I wondered if I'd ever feel this calm and free while at work…at my current job or any other. The enthusiastic crowd engulfed me, making me feel an accepted part of the community, a true local. I vowed to make the most of this wonderful day

"Hi Ashley, how's it going?"

"Ashley, we had a great meal last night. Your steaks are the best."

"Ashley, it's great to see you somewhere besides at work!" It made me feel good to be greeted by name. I was able to remember most of their names in return, which was gratifying. I smiled to think I was becoming a local.

Familiar faces were everywhere; even Man-in-Brown was there, giving me his unenthusiastic version of a greeting as he carried his lawn chair to a shaded area beyond Town Hall.

I wasn't positive, but I thought I recognized my first really angry customer, the guy who'd announced he'd never return to Unincorporated again. Again he looked annoyed, as if it were a permanent condition. As long as he wasn't annoyed with *me*, I didn't care.

For the first time in weeks I fully relaxed. I looked around at the enthusiastic faces of generous supporters and thought, "Today is going to be a wonderful day."

I removed my hoodie, wishing I'd worn something more upbeat and festive. In the early morning gloom my black shorts had seemed totally appropriate. Now, in the bright sunshine, surrounded by festival attendees in colorful resort wear, they seemed far too utilitarian. As part of the steering committee I should have worn something cheerful and enthusiastic, not basic and boring. No matter, it was something only I would notice; I would just tell myself that my floral tank was the height of fashion.

Several young Unincorporated staffers were in the center of a large boisterous group in front of the dunk tank, and to my surprise I realized they were all trying to dunk Brad, who shouted insults about their pitching ability. When he saw me, there was a new challenge in his voice.

"Hey Ashley, let's see if you can do something right!"

"You don't have to ask twice!" I wasn't one to ignore a challenge, especially when someone tries to humiliate me in front of my employees. I paid for three balls, missed the target by a mile with my first two throws, and had a direct hit with the third. Brad got a dunking, and I earned a round of applause.

"Wow! Way to go Ashley! Great throw!" As unimportant as it was, it felt good to perform well in front of my staff.

Only after it was over did I realize that I'd probably alienated my soaking wet chef even further. It was all in fun, I just hoped that Brad saw it that way. The fact that a reporter from the Grove Gazette had snapped a photo of Brad flailing as he fell was probably not going to help matters.

As early as it was in the festival, there was no longer any doubt in my mind that it would be a huge success. The scent of brats and burgers on the grill mingled with the aromas of corn on the cob, fresh popcorn, and cotton candy. Children's laughter seemed to permeate the atmosphere, while adults shared loud greetings with friends as if they'd not seen them in ages.

A public address announcer kept everyone informed about the results of activities being held nearby. Scores from soccer fields, results of the hole-in-one contest, and constant updates on the activity on softball fields were being conveyed to everyone on the grounds. No carnival barker could have been more enthusiastic about the food options and the children's activities than Ron Barber, Town Board President, as he encouraged the crowd to enjoy every possible venue.

No one seemed to think it was too early in the day for liquid refreshment, and the runners were among the first to visit the beer stand. Contestants for the Well-Dressed Dog competition were gathering beyond the military statues, while a quilting demonstration was being given by the local historical society in front of town hall. Todd Braun was holding flower arranging classes beyond the bandstand for a donation to the cause. Madeline Cleary, Windsor Grove's only centenarian, proudly wore a crown declaring her the Honorary Queen of Windsor Day.

To my surprise, but apparently no one else's, Mr. Horner (for once not in a corner) was recognized as the local expert on vintage vehicles. A small entourage trailed behind him as he wielded a clipboard with authority. He was judging the car show, busily scoring Model A's, classic Corvettes, original VW Beetles (yes, even older than mine), a few rather rusty pickup trucks, and other vehicles I couldn't categorize.

Eager expressions on vehicle owners' faces spoke to how important this judging was to them. Mr. Horner's word seemed to be law among the area car buffs; they seemed unaware of, or unconcerned by, his habitual glances over his shoulder. He loudly hummed a familiar tune as he took notes, which I was amazed to recognize as the theme from Sesame Street. He never fails to surprise me.

Passing the crowded face-painting booth I considered how the guests at Unincorporated would respond to a decorated face on the manager; probably not well. I kept walking, heading over to the town hall to encourage The Marys to call me if the food stands ran out of anything.

Mary Rose and Marybeth were situated under a brightly-colored canopy, dressed in period costumes with large sunbonnets. A banner above the canopy read "No donation too small, or too LARGE!" A constant stream of festival attendees wandered over to drop cash into a large container decorated to resemble the nearby bandstand. Mary Rose, standing at the front of the canopy, greeted each and every one of them, acquaintances with hugs and kisses, strangers with a smile and handshake.

"Ashley!" she cried, wrapping me in a huge bear hug. I tried not to display my shock; I'd only known her for a short time and I was being treated like a long-lost friend.

"Isn't it great? The weather is perfect, the crowd is enormous, and we're going to meet our goal; I can just feel it!" If enthusiasm is indeed contagious I can understand why everything she organizes becomes a success. She won't allow anything else.

Marybeth, however, was getting right to the heart of the issue, seated at a table surrounded by donation envelopes, with paperwork available for those interested in pledging a larger amount. Based on the number of forms already filed in the briefcase at her feet, she was doing a great job of lining up major donors. The smiling faces surrounding her table spoke of the generosity of Windsor Grove residents and visitors.

Brightly colored buttons worn by attendees leaving the tent designated each of them as a DONOR. An impressive number of those buttons could already be seen on the grounds; they were becoming the fashion trend of the day, a local badge of honor.

I was overwhelmed at the organizational skills of The Marys. I'd seldom seen anyone able to create crowd enthusiasm the way they could. Curiously, Mary Lou was nowhere to be seen; the sisters were never far from each other. There were any number of things she could be doing, but I wondered if perhaps her eerie attitude and prying questions would have turned potential donors away. The two Marys might be even savvier than I'd thought.

A larger than usual amount of security was evident throughout the festival area. Gregg was there in uniform, along with several other local officers. They were assisted by officers from various nearby towns, and even Detective Rob Milton was there representing the State Department of Criminal Investigation and keeping an eye on things. I was glad to see the obvious presence of so much authority; it should keep anyone from getting ideas.

I knew there were also plainclothes security officers on hand. Hopefully they wouldn't be needed, but I felt better knowing they were there.

After enjoying a hot dog with jalapeno mustard, a container of buttery popcorn, and some amazingly sour lemonade, I headed back toward my car. It was time to think about getting to work. I couldn't help but be proud of the part I'd played, no matter how small, in planning the amazing event. This is what small town life is all about,

I thought to myself, everyone coming together to work for a common good.

And then I heard it.

"Let's play behind those trees. You be the dead guy in the truck!" Several energetic young children went running past me, ready for their version of excitement.

"No, you have to be the dead guy this time. I was dead last time! I wish we could go into the woods and play. That would be cool!"

"I have a pretend knife I could bring..."

"When I played with Annie we used a real knife from her mom's cupboard...but not a sharp one..."

Oh no. Not again! I cringed, and my lighthearted mood vanished. Would it never stop? This mess had to be solved soon, or no one would ever be able to totally relax. What I heard next was even worse.

"Did you hear that Jeff was actually in the woods when the murder happened? He saw it all; he's helping the cops solve the crime." This bit of information came from a teenager, who chose to share his questionable knowledge with a group of children in soccer uniforms. The soccer players were wide-eyed and full of questions, giving the teen the audience he craved.

Glancing toward a cluster of teenage boys, smirking nearby, I realized that the Jeff in question was our former dishwasher, fired for attendance issues. I knew this story was concocted for the benefit of a captive audience; Gregg himself had interrogated every one of our staffers, finding no eyewitnesses, at least none who were willing to own up to it.

I could easily believe that Jeff spent time hanging out in the woods. He'd been among the group I'd reprimanded for smoking behind Unincorporated, and his lack of discipline would fit in with my idea of someone who'd meet friends for illicit activity in the forest. However, hanging around a murder site for unsavory activity was entirely different than actually seeing a murder in progress.

Didn't kids realize that it was dangerous to claim they'd witnessed a murder while the killer was still on the loose? No; teens think they're invincible. They don't comprehend that having other kids think you're *cool* is too high a price to pay when a murderer could be listening. The whole thing made me queasy. The community awareness program didn't seem to be accomplishing its goals.

I hoped the sheriff's department would get things solved soon. Or the state crime lab. Or someone. Anyone. I hadn't been able to give Gregg any help; listening in on conversations at Unincorporated made me an expert on local goings-on, but hadn't brought any useful clues to light.

Back at work it was clear that the success of Windsor Day negatively impacted business at Unincorporated. I cut staffing levels even further for the afternoon, then spent time catching up on paperwork while listening to silence from the dining room, hoping paying customers would show up later.

When the noise level finally increased, it did so with a vengeance. An influx of excited chatter and general commotion caught my attention late in the afternoon, and I followed the noise to the Lounge. I was gratified to see that the majority of the arriving guests sported the bright DONOR buttons.

"I don't understand what just happened."

"...and then the officers all ran into the building..."

"The Mary's were in a panic!"

"...so much excitement! Maybe Ashley knows what that was all about!" Everyone turned questioning eyes toward me, waiting for me to reply.

"What happened? Something at Windsor Day?" I stared blankly; I had no idea what they were asking about.

Everyone started talking at once. I managed to ascertain that officers had taken someone away in a squad car, and Windsor Day had shut down early.

The number of guests arriving at our door made it clear that rather than go home, the festival participants were now intent on dissecting what they'd just witnessed. Patronizing businesses where they might learn details had become the preferred activity of the afternoon.

This was verified when the next person in the door demanded, "Hey Ashley, what have you heard from Gregg? What's going on?"

No one took me seriously when I said I didn't know; it didn't diminish the frenzied conversations occurring throughout the building.

I heard that, "It didn't seem like a normal arrest," whatever that meant.

And, "I've never seen that many officers in one place at one time. Especially not in Windsor Grove. Where did they all come from? It happened so fast."

I wasn't about to call Gregg while he was working, so I resigned myself to the fact that I knew even less than everyone else, and went to work trying to get these guests all seated. The Lounge had a good crowd; only beer, wine and soda had been served at the festival and there seemed to be a need for stronger stuff. The crowd continued to grow, with several groups admitting that they hadn't bothered to eat at the festival and were "starving." That worked for me, I had a dining room ready and waiting. It looked like this was going to be a good day for Unincorporated after all.

My staffers who'd been at Windsor Day were arriving for their shifts, along with other staff members who hadn't been scheduled at all. Based on the clamor coming from the kitchen, I could tell they were coming in full of chatter, more interested in conversation than work. Determined to quiet things down, I headed to the kitchen, wondering why Brad wasn't keeping things under control.

I found out soon enough. As I walked through the door Brad slammed his fist down on a chopping block.

"Ashley! You have to do something about this! It has to be a mistake!" *Now what? And what made it my responsibility?*

"It's all so unfair! They frisked him right there in front of everyone and put him in handcuffs. Like a serious criminal! It's all wrong! Can't you do something?" This came from our normally calm server Carrie, blue eyes flashing indignantly.

"During the festival? Really? Who?" I was confused. "*Who* was arrested? Will someone please tell me what's going on? Why are you all so upset?"

The answer came from Brad, who turned toward me to announce, "It's Roger!" Roger was the fry cook who'd admitted to lying about his criminal record, but who was an exemplary employee who'd earned everyone's respect.

"Apparently he's been arrested for murdering Mark! What kind of crap have you been telling that boyfriend of yours, anyway?"

CHAPTER 29

S tunned, I stammered, "He's not my boyfriend! He's just a friend."
It was an unimportant point, but I felt compelled to clarify.

"And I don't tell him anything about employees' backgrounds.
Even if I know something incriminating I can't, there are confidentiality
laws!" As I tried to justify my position, my anger grew. How dare anyone,
especially Brad, accuse me of divulging confidential information!

No one believed me, I could tell. They were all aware of Roger's
previous transgressions, and it was clear they were ready to blame me if
that information led to his arrest.

"You know perfectly well that the officers did background checks
on everyone here. For Christ's sake, they even did a background check
on Uncle Al!" I informed them more loudly than necessary. *Oh no, I'm
starting to sound like Brad. Calm down, Ashley.*

"Anything they learned didn't come from me. They've seen criminal
records, traffic records, probably even school records." This seemed to
be a revelation to them; they knew they'd all been questioned, but didn't
seem to realize just how thorough the investigation had been. They
become slightly more quiet and thoughtful, but continued to whisper
and mutter amongst themselves.

"We need Roger here! Right here. In this kitchen", Brad announced.
"He's no God-damned good to us if he's locked up!" I totally agreed,
but there wasn't much I could do about it.

"I need a cigarette, and I don't even smoke! Outta my way," he barked at a fry cook who was standing at the grill exactly where he belonged.

"Some idiot forgot to put last night's jambalaya in the blast chiller!" was the next thing out of his mouth. It seemed to me that it was probably Brad himself who'd forgotten that detail.

"I don't know how in hell I'm supposed to run a kitchen when cops take away my best worker!" It was definitely not going to be a pleasant evening in the kitchen.

The sheer number of guests arriving simultaneously led me to ask the unscheduled staffers if they'd like to punch in and help. They weren't properly dressed, but that really only mattered in the front of the house. A few servers went home to change, and numerous kitchen staff immediately pitched in and got to work. Nervous energy can create a great work team.

Out front, the questions were non-stop.

"Do you have any details about the arrest?"

"What happened? Did you hear that shots were fired?"

"Who got arrested? Was it a local?"

"Did they catch the killer?"

"Was there another murder?"

"I heard it was a young kid. How could a young kid do something like that?"

The questions continued, as if everyone was certain I knew more than I was telling. It took a lot of patience to answer calmly.

I could honestly say, "I've been here all afternoon; I wasn't at the festival when it happened." I could also say, "No, I haven't talked to Gregg all day." What I really wanted to do was scream, *"No, Roger didn't do it!"*

As long as I kept moving I could evade many of the questions. I didn't want to get into discussions about who, or why. Thankfully we remained busy enough that this was easy.

It wasn't long before word passed through the Lounge that the suspect, arrested for Mark's murder, was an Unincorporated staffer. This caused even more buzz as everyone's curiosity was piqued. Being a relative newcomer to Windsor Grove, Roger was unknown to most of our guests. People were disturbed to learn that a local man had been arrested; however the main reaction seemed to be relief that there'd been a solution.

Not so amongst the staff, who'd all liked Roger and were struggling to control their emotions. I sympathized with the servers, being questioned at every table regarding a friend of theirs who was under arrest. I tried to maintain order by visiting tables myself if the diners seemed overly intrusive. This, of course, made my evening a nightmare, their questions having no answers.

The tension-filled dining room was made even more insufferable by families whose children, overtired from festival activities, were out of control. Parents who allowed outdoor voices to be used indoors and considered banging on a highchair tray with a spoon to be entertaining created an uncomfortable atmosphere. The anger among my staff threatened to boil over.

As the evening wore on the Lounge filled time and again with curiosity seekers who made no secret of the fact that they'd come just to get information. I'd sent Mike home from his position at the dish machine to come back dressed to help out front, and had Renata call in a few people who tended bar for us on an as-needed basis. Believe me, they were needed that night!

The Unintimidated softball team arrived during the evening, looking glum. Tournaments had continued even after the festival had closed, and our team had advanced to the finals only to suffer a resounding defeat. Somehow that seemed fitting given the circumstances. Another loss for Unincorporated.

"I suppose you heard the news," Gregg said when he finally called. It was almost laughable. I explained the restaurant atmosphere to him, and he remarked, "So I guess I shouldn't come in to see you tonight."

"Not unless you want to be inundated with questions, and have the staff yelling at you," I said. I smiled to myself; I would have loved to see him deal with the kind of discourteous questioning that was part of my daily routine.

"Seriously, though," I continued, "What's with the arrest of Roger? It doesn't make any sense."

"Ashley, we've got convincing evidence. We don't like to risk false arrest."

"But Gregg…."

"No buts'. He's being booked at the station in Oak Landing right now; once that's done the basic details become a matter of public record. Then I can tell you what we have against him. It's pretty damaging."

My heart fell. I realized I'd been assuming the arrest was a mistake. But I knew Gregg better than to think he'd do anything rash. It still seemed impossible that Roger could be guilty, but there must be more behind it than I'd thought. What evidence could they possibly have, unless Roger truly was the culprit?

"Gregg, you just don't know Roger. He couldn't do anything like that!" I was determined that there was information out there that no one had unearthed.

"Remember, you don't know him all that well yourself. You know what he's like at work, you know nothing about his private life. Now you'll just have to trust the justice system to do its job." Gregg's tone of voice indicated that the conversation was over.

"Will you at least give me whatever information can be released? As soon as you can?"

"That, I'll do. But don't go getting ideas and thinking you're going to prove us wrong. We feel confident that we've finally caught the perpetrator. We're professionals, after all," he said curtly.

For the remainder of the evening my stomach churned. I tried to keep a smiling face for our guests, but I was every bit as upset as the other staffers. The evening wore on, and the guests' constant discussion about Roger became almost too much to endure.

The normal clatter coming from the back of the house was magnified several times over; emotions from anguish to rage controlled the kitchen, making food production seem disjointed and disorganized. Pans were being slapped onto burners, utensils were roughly thrown into the scullery sink, and cooler doors were being slammed.

Those who'd worked side-by-side with Roger were angry, and were taking their frustrations out on our equipment. I was thankful that these kind people who'd watched a friend being taken away by authorities didn't have to listen to the comments of that evening's guests.

"What else would you expect from a kid with a pierced nose? We should have known he was guilty." A middle-aged man who spent weekends in an area condo was making his opinions known.

"I heard he also has a pierced tongue. Is that true?" His dining companion was wide-eyed.

"And an eyebrow, and his lip. Haven't you seen him around town?"

"No! I'm sure I would have noticed someone like that!"

"And his arms are completely covered with ugly tattoos. Why did he ever come to Windsor Grove? That's what I want to know. Totally obvious that he'd be trouble. Totally obvious!"

"We're all better off with him locked up!"

My stomach felt sick from listening to ignorant comments about a quiet hard-working guy they'd never met.

When the phone rang around closing time and I again heard Gregg's voice I put him on hold to take the call in my office. My nerves were strained, it was difficult to continue being pleasant, and I was afraid I might start crying at any moment. I needed answers, not questions.

"I haven't had a bite to eat all day. Want to go with me to get some food?" Gregg asked when I got back on the line.

"Alright, provided that before we go anywhere we have a chat. Someplace where we won't be overheard." I wasn't about to attempt polite conversation until I'd asked all the questions rolling around in my brain.

"I'll pick you up in about thirty minutes. I'm not allowed to disclose all the details yet, but I'll tell you what I can. And after that we won't discuss Roger, or Mark, or any police business whatsoever, alright?"

He needed a break from dealing with the arrest as much as I needed to learn about it.

"Don't hurry to get here," I instructed. "I have some things to finish up, and a few calls to make, and I want to change. Can you give me little longer?"

"Alright. Well, I'll see you in a while. Maybe an hour."

I said goodbye to Gregg, and before doing anything else I made a few important phone calls.

Uncle Al's most recent surgery was a success, but Mom had reported that his recuperation time would be "extended". I'd chatted with him casually, but tried not to bug him with Unincorporated's daily minutia. A positive attitude is beneficial in the recovery process, and I felt compelled to stop running to him with every little distraction. My recent reports to him had been short and upbeat; easy during the busy tourist season.

This time I had to be the bearer of bad tidings. He needed to learn about Roger from me before he heard the news from someone else, or worse yet, on the radio. I decided there was no time like the present, and made the call.

Al's voice sounded weak over the phone, but his attitude was upbeat and he wanted to hear all about Windsor Day. Describing the day brought back the feeling of excitement and accomplishment I'd felt, along with my pride in the overwhelming commitment from Windsor Grove's residents. It was easy to make the event sound magical, because that's exactly what it had been.

"I can tell by your voice how wonderful it all was. You did a great job. I knew you would."

"Thanks, but the praise goes to The Marys. They're amazing."

"They won't consider it a success until final numbers are in. Any idea how much money was raised?"

I couldn't answer Al's question about profitability, but I promised to keep him in the loop as soon as I learned anything.

"But now I have some bad news," I began.

"You're calling to tell me about Roger, aren't you?" was his reply.

"How did you hear about it?" Why was I surprised that he already knew? Windsor Grove's grapevine had been hard at work, and Al has hundreds of friends. I should have known I wouldn't be the first to call.

"I've been on the phone all evening. I've never felt so popular; I think I've talked to everyone I know. But no one has any details." This last sentence inflected upward, making it more question than statement. Unfortunately I had nothing to add, but promised I'd fill him in once I'd spoken with Gregg.

"I just can't understand it," he said. "It's very upsetting."

"I know. It seems like there has to be a huge mistake." We said melancholy goodbyes, and I assured Al that I'd give him a report on anything I learned.

After talking with Uncle Al, I called to check up on Margaret Hunter.

"You heard about the arrest, I'm sure."

"Yes, dearie, I sure did. I didn't go to Windsor Day, and now I wish I'd been there. I missed all the excitement!" Her voice sounded younger, somehow, steadier and less hesitant.

"I can't tell you how relieved I am, the arrest is such a load off my mind. Sleep will come much easier now. You're a sweet thing to worry about me." She proceeded to ask questions about the arrest, many that I couldn't begin to answer.

"I feel bad for you honey, that you had to work with that horrible person. He must be a wicked, wicked man. I'm so relieved that he's been locked up!"

I gritted my teeth, but thanked her for her concern.

CHAPTER 30

I turned the remainder of the night's business over to my staff, who were keyed up and didn't want to leave anyway, and went home to change. I have no idea what I wore, for all I know I may have looked like a bad trip to a thrift store. Normally I put thought into my clothing choice when I go out in the evening, but not that night.

Gregg showed up quickly, as if he'd been hovering in the neighborhood waiting until he could politely arrive. When he walked in the door his haggard face told me I'd never seen this side of him before. His selection of clothing was as poorly put together as mine. Again, I don't remember the details, but a combination of plaids and stripes comes to mind.

"Might as well get right to it," he said, parking himself on a huge sofa. "I know Roger is a key member of your staff, so this could be hard to take."

He looked up at me and hesitated. "Sit down, you're making me nervous." He'd taken his pen from his pocket and was worrying it between his fingers. I sat across the room so I could look directly at him, and he continued.

"We've been watching Roger for some time now. As soon as we learned about his prison time we did a further background check. He told us he'd never seen Mark until he came to Windsor Grove, but that wasn't true. The time Detective Milton put into verifying statements paid off.

"We learned that Roger met Mark previously, when Mark worked on a research program. Roger had been in a minimum security facility, and certified college students, including Mark, traveled the Midwest with some developmental rehab programs. Once we learned they'd met, we kept a close eye on Roger.

"We had a search warrant for his apartment early in our investigation and found, you guessed it, some knives and other things that belong to Unincorporated. We didn't make an arrest at the time; all it proved was that he was pilfering from work. But it was certainly a red flag. We took the items to the station, and have been holding them as evidence. He knew the stolen items had been confiscated from his apartment, he signed a receipt. From then on, he knew he was a suspect."

This was even worse than I'd anticipated. Once again I was having trouble breathing, and could feel my heart beating at an abnormal pace.

"We've known all along that he'd lied about his whereabouts the night before Mark's murder. He'd been out partying in the woods with friends. We have beer cans and cigarette butts with his DNA, and the same items with the DNA of those friends. But his friends all have someone who can vouch for the time they got home that night, and no one actually saw Roger until he arrived at work the next noon."

I rolled my eyes. I might not be any expert detective, but I'd read enough novels to know that the word of a family member about what time a teenager got home was not considered corroborative evidence; certainly not in a criminal investigation.

"I know what you're thinking; that's not evidence we can use in court. You're right, but we still take it into consideration." He could see the skepticism in my face. "There were other Unincorporated staffers in the woods that night too; we've also been keeping an eye on them. But none of them had your knives in their bedrooms."

"And," he added quietly, "None of the others have done prison time."

This wasn't getting any better. For a split second I wondered if Gregg's growing attention toward me had been merely a way for him to study my staff. But, no. He'd been practically haunting the place since the day after the murder; we hadn't spent our down time together 'til after the storm, so that wasn't the case. I had to erase that from my mind if I wanted to maintain our friendship.

"Obviously, the people who were most likely to have access to your knives and placemats are your staff. Most of the county may have been in the building over the last six months, but your employees are there on a daily basis, and would have no trouble taking a few small things without being noticed."

"Yes, but so would most customers. Especially the regulars."

He ignored my comment and continued. "So even though we've been following numerous leads, our investigation kept pointing us back to Unincorporated. We've also had to keep in mind that no matter who actually committed the crime, there may have been an accomplice, and that accomplice was very possibly one of your staffers. We've investigated them all thoroughly. Even you."

Even me? There it was again; *even me*. It was a blow to hear him say it. I preferred to be considered an innocent bystander.

"Now, for the details of Roger's arrest...as you know, we had several officers, both uniformed and plainclothes, on duty at the festival. We were trying to keep an eye on everyone, but especially anyone who'd aroused our suspicions. We couldn't be everywhere, and we missed an opportunity to have indisputable evidence.

"You remember Lisa that works at the Sheriff's Office?" I nodded numbly, recalling the girl who'd driven me home during the storm.

"Well, she was on duty today, using a spare room in Town Hall, coordinating the security teams. Around three-thirty this afternoon she walked into a vacant office, and found one of those threatening notes, slid under the door. At first she thought it was a piece of garbage, and almost threw it away. Before she dropped it in the trash she glanced down and read what it said. LEAVE ME ALONE OR YOUR IN TROUBLE was printed in the same childish scribble we've seen before.

"Lisa called for help, and an officer was with her almost immediately. That's where we'd missed our chance; no one working security had seen anyone slip the note under the door. Town Hall has security cameras in a few locations, but none were aimed at that particular spot. We did, however, have a tape showing everyone who'd walked down that hall all afternoon, and sure enough, there was Roger walking down the hallway about an hour before. Other people had been there too, of course, it was on the way to the public restrooms. But no one else who'd been a 'person of interest' was in that hallway during the day.

"When we confronted Roger he tried to run, which was foolish with so much security around. We caught him before he'd gotten more than a few yards, and had to handcuff him because he started swinging at us. If he'd come quietly our plan had been to make it seem like a friendly chat because of the festival, but he was belligerent so we took him into custody the hard way.

"Unfortunately for Roger and his relatives, the Gazette photographer saw the activity and came running. On Wednesday everyone will be treated to several clear photos of Roger struggling with officers, and of a handcuffed Roger being forced into a squad car."

"So that's when you shut down the festival."

"Closing the event was a decision made by The Marys, not the officers. With the arrest occurring in such a public area, there was much pandemonium and confusion. Young children were shrieking in terror; elderly ladies were in tears; and boys of a certain age were hurling insults as the squad cars drove away.

"People started picking up lawn chairs, gathering families together, and heading to their vehicles. It was as if there was an abrupt unscheduled end to the enjoyment. Rather than risk the humiliation of a festival that ended with barely a few dozen people standing about, The Marys closed the food stands and ended the contests. Athletic events continued as planned. It was probably a wise decision."

"So, now what? I demanded. "What happens next?"

"Roger's been taken to the jail in Oak Landing, the county seat. He's been booked on suspicion of first degree intentional homicide, and will certainly be held on bail, possibly as much as $500,000. We had probable cause, and we've had an arrest warrant since finding the pilfered goods in his closet.

"All these details are part of the criminal complaint and will be released to area media in the morning. We're attempting to find some of Roger's DNA on the placemat scraps, but even without it we've got a good case."

Running his fingers through his hair, he continued, "Right now that's all I can tell you. He'll be assigned a public defender to represent him, but until he's released on bail, or is cleared, you're going to be short one fry cook."

"Sure," I said, "You'll get him some court-appointed attorney, some inexperienced and underpaid yahoo just out of college. So kind of you." Again Gregg chose to ignore my comment. "We don't have a clear motive, but once Roger has legal representation we can interrogate him and we'll figure it out. He certainly had the opportunity, which he lied about. He had the method, which he obtained by stealing from his employer. He'd known the victim previously. And he resisted arrest. We're confident that we've got the right guy, Ashley, I hope you understand this."

I understood, sort of. But this all fit the category that in detective novels they call *circumstantial evidence*. It could still be one huge mistake, couldn't it?

Controlling my anger with effort, I stood to pace around the room. I had nothing to say, couldn't think of any questions, and really just wanted to do something else, anything else. I couldn't keep still, and was fidgeting with my hair and the buttons on my shirt and the knick-knacks on a shelf.

Gregg seemed to understand. He got up and headed to the door, calmly holding it open for me.

"Can we go now? I'm famished," he said resignedly. "I know you need time to think this over, but life has to go on, too. He's an employee of yours, and I know this comes as a blow, but right now there's nothing you can do for him. You can't take Roger's problems on as your own, if only for your own sanity. Now let's go, we both need to eat."

He was right; I needed to continue my life as usual. So I went with Gregg, who chose a neighborhood pub near Oak Landing where he hoped not to be recognized. Our evening ended almost as soon as it began, with Gregg feeling stressed and me in a bad mood. Afterward I couldn't remember what I'd eaten, or anything we'd discussed. I felt dazed; I'd never before known anyone who'd been arrested for murder. Traffic violations, underage drinking, of course. But murder? Never.

I should have been relieved that I was no longer a suspect. But nothing about this made me feel any better. The whole thing was unsettling.

If I trusted the sheriff's officers and the state detectives, I had to accept the current state of affairs. Roger had been arrested as a murder suspect, and Unincorporated was connected to it on several levels. Even though there'd been an arrest, this mess wasn't over yet.

By the following day it was apparent that Margaret wasn't the only one whose stress level was lightened by the arrest. As if an invisible cloak of lead were lifted off everyone's shoulders, the atmosphere became almost euphoric. This was great for business; for the next few weeks I was able to report to Al that we were having highly profitable sales numbers.

My own emotions, however, were a mess. It was fortunate that I was busy at work, because when I had time to relax my brain was in a state of turmoil. I knew I had to eventually accept the official solution of Mark's murder. But it seemed inconclusive to me.

It all felt wrong. One more time I called Uncle Al, the one person who would willingly listen to my reasoning.

I filled him in on what I'd learned from Gregg, and realized by his response that he was as saddened by the facts as I was.

"But they can't prove he actually killed Mark, can they? They don't have any real proof." He sounded defensive, mirroring my feelings.

We commiserated over the dilemma of a good employee being accused of a horrendous crime. Al seemed to take it personally, which was explained when he said, "I hired Roger as a favor to the Mitchells. You know them, the older couple who eat their dinner sitting in the Lounge every Friday night, and sit at the window looking over the lake every Sunday noon."

I knew exactly who he meant. A kind couple who are loved by the staff (which probably means they tip well).

"They know Roger's relatives, the ones who took him in when he needed a fresh start. The Mitchells met him and were impressed with his desire to turn his life around. They knew he needed a source of income and a sense of importance, and they came to me. I decided to take a chance; I thought a good steady job was what he needed. I guess I was wrong."

"Not necessarily," I sighed. "In fact I think you were right, this job was exactly what he needed. He's an exceptional fry cook; doesn't get flustered; takes charge of the situation; and gets along great with the rest of the staff. His arrest seems wrong, like there are huge parts of the puzzle still missing.

"His personality doesn't fit the crime," I continued. "His past arrests were all for non-violent crimes. Nothing makes sense. But the officers seem certain they've got the right guy. I don't know what to do."

"Ashley, honey, you can't do anything. You're still young and impressionable enough to think you can change the world. You have to accept that there are things you can't fix. Take a deep breath, say a prayer, continue on with your life, and keep smiling."

It was sound advice, but didn't make me feel any better. Actually, it made me increasingly determined to unearth more facts.

CHAPTER 31

Windsor Grove was again inundated by the media. Intrusive reporters from across the state, scruffy photographers in multi-pocketed vests, and on-air talent made up like runway models descended on our quiet little town like swarm of bees, and were just as welcome.

"Can you tell our readers how it feels to know a murderer?"

"Do you feel safer with alleged criminal behind bars?"

"Did he have any friends in town?"

"Tell us your feelings…"

Windsor Grove residents may have been relieved by the arrest, but were increasingly annoyed by the statewide publicity, with strangers bustling about importantly, getting in everyone's way.

Sadly the very successful fundraiser received almost no coverage in comparison; The Marys were reported to be highly annoyed. As people's lives slowly returned to normal, everyone's most prominent memory of the festival was related to Roger's arrest.

Working the podium one evening I recognized a loud voice reverberating from the Lounge. It was the overbearing man who'd given everyone the benefit of his views on weather patterns, this time making a pronouncement about how "…innate criminal tendencies cannot be overcome without extreme intervention." His demeanor indicated his amplified sense of self-importance, my dislike for the man grew exponentially the more he talked.

"Al should have never hired that kid," he announced in his grandiose manner, chin held high. "It was a supreme error in judgment. I could have told him that unprincipled and unethical inclinations cannot be disseminated by the good intentions of untrained citizens. Al's naiveté created a judgmental weakness where caution would have been advisable. It was an astonishing detriment to wise business practices."

How dare he! How dare he insinuate that Uncle Al was anything less than an accomplished professional! I had to walk away before I gave this *expert* a piece of my mind. Many of Al's friends were present at the bar, and this guy's comments were not exactly adding to his popularity.

More determined now than ever to avenge Roger's reputation, along with Al's, I stormed fuming and sputtering into the kitchen, and barged right into Brad.

"Hey there, I'm the one who gets that fired up. You're ready to explode! What happened? What's up, girl?" His strong hands steadied my shoulders; my fists were clenched and I trembled with rage.

I managed to blurt out an explanation, and quickly realized I'd vented to the wrong person.

"Let me at him! Nobody talks about Al like that! I'll break his fuckin' neck!" The expression on Brad's face was terrifying. He'd gone from questioning to confrontational so quickly I had trouble processing what had happened. His fury made my anger seem like something from a schoolyard tiff.

I grabbed his arm in an attempt to calm him, or just slow his reactions. Physically restraining him from charging into the Lounge wasn't possible, but I planted myself firmly between him and the doorway, determined to keep him from causing a scene. If anything, Brad was even more protective of Al than I, and his feelings at that moment were on display for all to see.

It took time and patience, some calm words and serious eye contact, but I did manage to convince Brad that the words of a pompous ignorant man meant nothing.

Nothing, that is, except as fuel to a fire; fuel to my determination to learn the truth. Anger is a great motivator, and my motivation had never been stronger.

I needed time for concentration. With most of my waking hours being spent at work, I had to find *thinking time* whenever I could. I'd identified a few regular opportunities to relax with my thoughts.

The biggest disadvantage to staying in Uncle Al's cottage was the lack of laundry facilities. Relatives who stayed here on vacations just packed up their dirty clothes and lugged them home. Al took his things to his home in Oak Landing. I endured the indignity and visited the local laundromat.

Patronized mostly by area campers, the laundromat was utilitarian and unwelcoming. Vending machines, a TV with fuzzy reception, and ancient magazines were meant to occupy one's time while waiting. I tried to use my laundry time to ponder alternative solutions to Mark's murder, but every time I felt as if I was nearing a breakthrough, the surrounding noise level increased by a few decibels.

It was hard to think creatively when distracted by screaming campground kids. Useful ideas just wouldn't develop. Ear buds and familiar music helped my creative thinking, but I stopped using them at laundry-time after I unwittingly sat in the middle of a children's football game. A sore sport on my head was the result of tuning out the commotion.

In the past my imagination had flowed most freely in the shower, especially during shampoo time. But this summer I never showered long enough for my thoughts to arrange themselves into definitive solutions. The cottage didn't have enough hot water!

I started going for long afternoon walks. Walking calmed me, and cleared my brain. The multitude of available walking trails made it easy to avoid the fire lane through the woods; I wasn't ready to consider that a comforting route. Continuing beautiful weather made my wanderings fairly pleasant. I hoped that somehow things would become clear when I could relax and let facts rearrange themselves.

Designating those specific situations as *thinking time* had sounded like a good plan, but they didn't help to clarify things at all. Whether at the laundromat, or in the shower, or on a long walk, the harder I tried to make sense of things, the more muddled my thoughts became. If anything, the facts occupying my brain were growing increasingly complex. My imagination would create one theory, then another, none of them showing much promise. But I held to my opinion that there was one elusive but definitive solution, someone just had to continue the search.

I considered myself a good judge of character, and Roger had never given off dangerous vibes. There was no sense of wickedness about him. Numerous people around town made me uncomfortable, apprehensive, even panicky, and he was not one of them. His disarming honesty about past transactions gave him an aura of openness that I found believable. He was pleasant to be around, someone I would trust with a secret, someone I felt I could depend on.

Mark's personality had to be the key, or so I decided. It was the only path left to explore.

If no viable motive was ever established, there'd be no logical explanation for the murder. I wasn't willing to accept the official explanation, I just didn't believe it. If the authorities had stopped searching, believing they'd reached the correct conclusion, then I'd continue my quest. I seemed to be the only one still trying; it didn't seem like Roger's second-rate lawyer had lit any fire under the officials.

Any summer traveler who'd known Mark before he moved to Windsor Grove could have been carrying a grudge. And what was it Gregg had said about frustration and aggression? Almost anyone could have been frustrated over something Mark had done; it certainly didn't have to be someone from my staff. In fact, sheer numbers would suggest that statistically it must have been someone else. I just had to figure out who.

"There's a lady here to see you," one of our young hosts announced one noon. "I think she's a friend of yours."

Heading to the lobby I heard, "Hey girlfriend!" in a distinctive voice.

"Bekah! What are you doing here?"

"I'm so stressed waiting for the phone call. I've had two follow-up interviews, but so far no job offer. My parents are making me crazy; I realized that Jacob is a jerk and told him to take a hike; and I needed to be with my BFF. I hopped in the car and headed to Windsor Grove… so can we go someplace to eat, and to talk?"

"Not right now, I have to be here through lunchtime," I leaned closer and whispered, "It's a weak staff today. Our head server had to take her son to a doctor in Oak Landing. It might be an hour before I can leave."

I let my voice return to normal volume. "Why don't you have a seat in the Lounge and check your email or something. Better yet, go over to the cottage. I'll come get you when I can finally leave."

"No way. Today I need some retail therapy, I'm going shopping! Text me when you're ready."

It was mid-afternoon before we left for The Grove Diner where we rehashed our recent life events over crunchy salads. My frustration with Roger's arrest dominated my thoughts and my side of the discussion; Bekah's job search, hers. There were numerous topics I wanted to cover, but there just wasn't time for the complicated details. The discussion was disjointed, but was cathartic for both of us.

As we neared the end of our lunch Bekah displayed her shopping treasures: colorful sandals, a leather clutch, and a silver bracelet. Then she handed me a bag.

"Open it. You need something new, too. My treat." She'd given me an assortment of herbal products; lotions, room sprays, candles. My eyes were suddenly misty; I hadn't realized how badly I needed some special care.

"You're a true friend. What would I do without you?"

"You'd be solving a murder right now instead of hanging out eating lunch!" We both laughed. It was time for me to return to work, so we hugged goodbye, and looked in each other's eyes.

"Don't worry about getting the job, the phone call will come," I assured her. "You know they'll hire you; how could they not?"

"Ashley you're the best. I feel so good when we're together. You can handle anything. You always make me feel better; you'll find the killer; you'll get a job you love; you'll end up with a perfect life…maybe with Gregg! And we'll always have each other. Keep smiling, girl, you can do anything!"

If only I felt as confidant about my life as she did.

There was tension in the air as I entered the cottage one day after a walk. I've never believed in premonitions, but I couldn't explain my reaction any other way. Nothing was obviously wrong, but something wasn't right. A familiar tingle down my spine warned me.

Going for a short afternoon stroll hadn't seemed to require that doors be locked. Perhaps I had been naïve. Well, clearly I had been naïve; but there it was, the cottage hadn't been locked.

Cautiously, I moved through the building, entered each bedroom, looked in all the closets, even peered under the beds. Nothing was noticeably out of place. Nothing was missing from my purse or wallet. Nothing verified my sense of unease. But there was something alien in the air, like the scent of someone else's lotion, leaving a bad vibe. It was suddenly an unfriendly environment.

I recoiled as I noticed that a few books on a shelf seemed askew. It was hard to be certain. I didn't usually pay a lot of attention to the placement of things, but something seemed different.

I studied the main room thoroughly, looking into cabinets and under furniture, then returned to my bedroom. Had I really folded that sweater with one sleeve sticking out? Hadn't I arranged those shoes more neatly? How many magazines had I tossed on the bedroom floor? I couldn't accurately remember. The building felt alien, uncomfortable, as if danger lurked. I couldn't pin anything down, but I was certain someone had invaded my space.

Then I saw it. That stack of mail on the kitchen counter. To anyone else it might have appeared to be a disorganized heap, but it had been arranged in my own kind of order. I knew, without a doubt, that the renewal notice for People Magazine had been on top. Now I looked down on a flyer for cable service.

With a feeling of dread I quickly checked that doors and windows were locked. I parked my body in a chair, and with a feeling of foreboding, sat staring into space.

My head hurt, the back of my neck was aching, and I could feel the increased pace of my heart. I wasn't sure I'd ever be able to relax again. I'd been threatened over the phone, someone had stolen a list from my desk, and now someone had shuffled through my personal mail. What did that someone think I possessed, what did they want so badly that it was worth theft or illegal entry?

Gregg may have disagreed, but to me this seemed like positive evidence that the wrong person was in custody. A sinister butcher was walking free, and had expertly broken into my home. Okay, it didn't take much of an expert to enter an unlocked door. It had been someone with audacity, not necessarily skill.

Since the day of the arrest, our guests had openly discussed people who'd been on their own "persons of interest" lists and it was fascinating to learn how their minds had been working.

Not only was Mary Lou on everyone's list, with her peering and prying, I was amused to hear that many residents also suspected one or both of her sisters. Evidently being tremendously wealthy and taking charge of every event in town did not endear The Marys to their neighbors.

Man-in-Brown was another person on almost everyone's mind. I hadn't been the only one suspicious about this stranger and his odd behavior.

Also on many lists was the quiet Mr. Horner with his curious mannerisms. Picturing him in our dining room playing tic-tac-toe against himself as he eavesdropped on conversations, I could certainly understand his presence on people's tallies. I wondered how many residents besides me had seen his collection of weaponry.

An amazingly high percentage of residents had made it to one person's list or another. The owner of the weaving studio, a local handyman, several people I'd never heard of, and even the pastor's wife had all been suspected. Everyone in town had seemingly caught someone's attention.

It was unpleasant, but not unexpected, to learn that many locals had been convinced that Mark had been killed by someone employed at Unincorporated. The arrest of Roger made total sense to them; they'd been assuming something similar. There had been particular speculation about Brad with his growly attitude; but even I had made it to some suspect lists. Yes, there it was again. Me.

Someone had also mentioned Uncle Al in conjunction with the crime. Preposterous.

Listening to their justifications while they chatted made me more determined than ever that the investigation was far from complete. It was time to recreate my chart of suspects. This time there was another category. The *Suspects* section was now divided into *Local, Visitors,* and as much as I hated to say it, *Unincorporated staff.*

I added a subsection titled *people who don't want to be recognized,* but it remained empty. Annoyingly, I didn't have much to add beyond what had been on my previous list; surely I must be learning things that mattered, if only I could sort them out in my mind. There had to be an answer, the *real* answer, and it was becoming clear that I was the only one still searching for it.

It was disconcerting. I'd never felt so conflicted, so confused, but so determined. Any thoughts I'd had of giving up and leaving town had given way to a commitment to delve deeper into what I considered an unresolved situation. I was fully involved in the dilemma and wanted to see it through to conclusion; I wouldn't be satisfied until I felt confident that the real killer was behind bars.

My anger had become a motivator, and I longed for aggressive action and solution. I didn't feel like my previous complacent self any longer; I felt strong and tough and powerful How odd.

"Got the job!!" said a text I received from Bekah that week. "Called some friends to go out and celebrate! Wish you could join us."

"Congratulations!" I replied. I couldn't think of anything else to say. I was happy for Bekah, but my brain was so overwhelmed with events in Windsor Grove that everything else seemed insignificant.

I did feel sad, though, that I wasn't there for the celebration. I was envious of friends who still had an easygoing life. It seemed impossible that a few short months ago I'd been one of them.

I talked to Gregg a few times during that period, but our conversations were stilted and uncomfortable. He'd grown accustomed to using me as a sounding board, and I was no longer feeling receptive.

Gregg's demeanor had become stiff and unyielding when we were together, and I'd grown increasingly uncomfortable in his presence. He no longer needed to drop in continually at Unincorporated, and I found that I welcomed his absence.

I needed time to think, and I didn't want his unsubstantiated conclusions complicating my thoughts. Our phone calls became shorter and less frequent, and then stopped altogether.

I did wonder how Gregg was dealing with his inner stress, and wondered who listened while he talked things through. I didn't really care, but still I was curious. Had he found someone else willing to lend an ear? Was it a female ear? But I didn't care. Not one bit.

I intentionally failed to mention to him the prowler in my cottage. I feared that my "intuition" that had told me there'd been an intrusion into my comfortable abode would be ridiculed. Childish, I know, but I felt like my opinions weren't being taken seriously. I refused to accept that Roger was guilty, certain that if I could uncover a motive I'd know who the real killer was. Gregg had disregarded my perceptions, which had only made me more determined; I wasn't about to be dissuaded.

Scuttlebutt heard in the Lounge said that the official investigation had entered an accelerated phase. Resources were being spent creating an iron-clad case against Roger. Was anyone considering other suspects? Or was Roger's guilt accepted as a foregone conclusion? Hopefully those experts were being open-minded in their inquiries. There had to be something that I, and everyone else, was missing.

I felt sure of it.

The complete darkness of deepest night provided welcome cover in the dense forest, offering secrecy and anonymity during nightly wanderings. It created a feeling of serenity, the enchanting mysteries of the night giving rise to silent preparation for angry action.

Stealthy footsteps approached the cottage, circling as always. Once again the doors and windows had been secured when she turned in, draperies drawn to shield any view of activity. It was frustrating that she obscured things so completely; eliminating the opportunity to observe details that might augment well-organized plans.

Those plans had developed slowly, tediously. If the girl would make only one error, one slip-up, the opportunity for action would arise; victory would result. She would get what she deserved, in dramatic emotionally satisfying style. One day the sun would rise upon another deliciously gruesome scene.

Occasion for proper attack had not presented itself, but with patience would come triumph. The superior planning would guarantee success, would verify who held the power position. Foolish girl. No one should challenge the skills of an expert.

Branches bowed in the gentle breeze, affirming the patience required. Patience is a virtue; the virtuous will attain their goals; the threat posed by this girl would be eliminated. It was just a matter of time.

The hours devoted to planning had been deliciously pleasing, like a gift from the Creator. How ironic.

CHAPTER 32

"I hope you can make yourself available on Saturday morning," Mary Rose said. "The invoices have been paid, and the final numbers are in. We'll have our Windsor Day wrap-up meeting while details are still fresh in everyone's mind."

So twenty-one days after the event I was back at the mansion home of The Marys. This time I'd worn a sleeveless dress in tones that reminded me of seashells; it seemed correct for the setting.

There were fourteen of us; the three Marys, eight local employers who'd helped with one aspect or another and one representative each from three local service clubs.

Once we'd all arrived and were seated in the vast library, the woman who'd been working at their home on my previous visit appeared again. The silver tray she carried was filled with crystal glasses of champagne, strawberries adorning the rims. Once we each held a glass of bubbly, Mary Rose proposed a toast.

"Here's to the exceptional committee who planned the inaugural Windsor Day celebration!"

We raised our glasses, and could tell by the flush on Mary's Rose's face and the smile she couldn't contain that the event had been successful. When Marybeth handed out spreadsheets with final totals I was flabbergasted. We broke out in spontaneous applause, and raised our glasses again.

"I have another exciting announcement," Mary Rose revealed. "We've received a state grant that will allow us to add an additional feature to the playground. Windsor Grove will have the only completely handicapped and wheelchair accessible playground in the county!"

Diagrams and photos were passed around as glasses were refilled, and trays of fruits and cheeses were placed on tables throughout the room. Mary Lou (Scary Mary), who'd remained silent throughout, was quick to heap her plate, and was equally quick to request a third glass of champagne. She studied each volunteer intently, as if peering directly into our psyches.

"Our heartfelt thanks go to every one of you for what you've done to make this playground a reality," Mary Rose started, "and I have a favor to ask.

"The overwhelming response we received indicates that Windsor Day is destined to become an annual event. Even with the unscheduled and abrupt end, we seem to have generated nothing but goodwill. In a way it seems fitting that our felon would be captured at a community gathering." I flinched when she called Roger a felon. I'd never get used to that idea. Scary Mary smiled broadly at the mention of the arrest.

"With that in mind," Mary Rose continued in her taking-charge voice, "we need a steering committee to begin making plans for next year's festivities, and to select the next worthy cause. I'd like each of you to be among the key players." This plan was met with resounding affirmation from all present. Except me.

"I'd love to, but I'll have to respectfully decline. As you know, I'm only here temporarily, until Uncle Al can get back to work. I won't be available for the planning, but I will come back for the festival, of course," I said, trying to graciously refuse the request.

"I thought you were staying on at Unincorporated; someone at the bar told me that," the owner of Rick's Tap said.

"That's what I heard. Everyone at the post office says you're staying." This from a woman I'd just met that afternoon. *Nice of other people to make my decisions for me.*

"Al said he was sure you'd love to remain involved," Mary Rose said. "He was thrilled to hear how helpful you'd been with food purchasing."

I should have known Al would be in touch with The Marys. But why would he tell them I'd continue to help? He knew I'd be gone by then, didn't he?

"Please consider it, we'd love to have you back," Marybeth emphasized. "Your purchasing skills were a huge help in our profitability."

What was wrong with this picture? Hadn't I just said I was leaving town? I agreed to consider it, just to close the conversation.

We began sharing our thoughts about the event; those parts that were satisfying, elements that could have been better, ideas for additional activities. We discussed feedback and publicity, finishing with a discussion of a bad-weather fallback plan. The gathering ended soon after, with much back slapping and handshaking, and congratulations all around.

As we left, Marybeth handed out cards listing upcoming meeting dates. I was puzzled, and felt slightly manipulated at the turn things had taken. It was as if my life was no longer my own.

As I drove slowly and thoughtfully to the restaurant my spirits were lifted by the sheer size of the crowds that seemed to be everywhere. *No Vacancy* signs hung outside every inn, and swarms of people wandered the streets. Traffic crawled as drivers gazed at storefronts and scenery, stopping for pedestrians in crosswalks.

Locals mingled with tourists along the sidewalks, pausing to chat with friends, giving directions and recommendations to strangers. That's what Windsor Grove is all about; acquaintances and hospitality…the human element at its best.

The same people who make me want to tear my hair out when they order me around at work give me a deep sense of pride by the way they interact with visitors. Windsor Grove residents have many layers.

Glancing toward the shops I saw Gregg, looking tanned and fit, wearing pressed black shorts and a red polo shirt, leaving The Sundae Parlor, ice cream cone in hand. I considered stopping to say "Hi", but changed my mind when I realized he wasn't alone. As he left the building he turned to hold the door for someone behind him.

She had the confidant stride of a model. Her long-legged slender figure, shoulder-length blond hair and brilliant smile drew admiring glances from strangers. A simple green dress accentuated her tiny waist, and strappy sandals showed off a recent pedicure. I knew she wasn't a local, but she certainly seemed comfortable around Gregg. They smiled and laughed and sampled each other's ice cream as they walked down the street.

Sure. Acquaintances. Windsor Grove hospitality. *Crap!*

For a moment Gregg glanced toward the street and looked directly at my Beetle. It was the only red one in town; he had to know it was mine, but he looked away so quickly that I didn't have a chance to wave. Had he not seen me? Or did he not care? He was probably so distracted by his cute blonde friend that he didn't notice anything at all.

Well, good. I was happy to have Gregg out of my hair. He may have been my only real friend in Windsor Grove, but that was just too bad. I didn't need friends like him. I really didn't. I could make other friends. I just needed more free time, that's all there was to it. And I wouldn't be in town much longer anyway.

How did Gregg manage to make friends? He was as busy as I was. Did people crave the companionship of someone in authority? Did gorgeous women gravitate to men in a uniform? I was glad to say that I was no longer one of the women who wanted to be around that particular officer. I'd find myself a new best friend someday soon.

Did I just say *best friend*? No, he wasn't my best friend. Bekah was my best friend. I barely liked Gregg. I could live without him just fine. Except he was so easy to talk to, and so much fun to spend time with, and so kind…but now he was with the stunning blonde and I was alone. But I refused to care. In fact, I couldn't care less. Really. Who needed him, anyway? Not me.

But I couldn't deny the sudden lump in my throat.

Back at work, I was in a daze. Every part of my life seemed to be out of control; I didn't have time to search for a job in my field; I was in a community where I had no close friends; every time I started to relax and enjoy life I was reminded about a murder; and now people assumed

I was going to stay here and keep on running Uncle Al's restaurant. I needed another dose of Bekah's friendship and enthusiasm, and I needed it badly.

I went into my office, moved a pile of mail off the chair so I could sit, and punched Bekah's number into my phone.

"Ashley! I've been meaning to call you!" were the first words out of Bekah's mouth. "It's so exciting! Did you get my text? I got the job! I'll be a marketing assistant for Anderson and Associates! Visiting you must have been good luck, they called the next day!" She went on to tell me about her new position, about the employee benefits, about the professional wardrobe she planned to purchase, and about all the single guys in her department. I'd barely gotten a word in edgewise, and for a moment I wondered why I'd bothered to call.

"So, what's up? How's everything going? How's Gregg?" Bekah inquired when she'd eventually exhausted the topic of her employment. For once she seemed prepared to listen.

I verbalized all the thoughts that still cluttered my brain, even though she'd heard most of them before. Again I left out my own threatening letter, the anonymous phone call and the intruder in my cottage. But I covered storm cleanup, time spent with Gregg, my scarcity of local friends, Windsor Day, Roger's arrest, and finally Gregg's gorgeous new friend.

I couldn't keep my voice from wavering when I talked about it, which gave away more of my true feelings than I cared to admit. He'd been my only real friend in Windsor Grove, and now he was sharing ice cream with that beautiful blonde. I gulped back tears, even while I said I didn't care.

"Oh Ashley, that's so sad. But don't worry, he'll see the error of his ways and come back to you."

"I'm not sure I want him back. And he wasn't *mine*; he was just a good friend. A friend who's trying to convict one of my employees. And who didn't believe me when I told him he'd made a mistake."

"Then you'll just have to prove he's wrong, won't you?"

"That's exactly what I was thinking. But I'm not sure how."

303

"You'll work it out. You're smart; let that brain of your take in all the details, and I'll be that someday you'll magically know the answer. You can figure anything out if you want to badly enough."

Could I really? Maybe so. She was right; it was time for me to accomplish something I could be proud of. Solving this homicide mess would definitely fit the bill.

We spent considerable time dissecting the latest entertainment and fashion news, talked about a few old friends, and said goodbye with me feeling more like my old self.

"You'll have to let me know everything about your new career. Don't worry about it; you'll be great!" I praised.

"You're the best friend anyone could ever have, Ashley. Call me anytime you need to talk. I'm always here for you. Love you!" Then she was gone.

She truly was always there for me. Once we made it past the newest details of her social life, she became my rock, my cheering section, the belief in my abilities that kept me going.

Reaching into my desk drawer, I took out version two of my suspect list, and struggled to find some gap in my thinking, something I'd overlooked that was important. I didn't really know much about Mark, but from everything I'd learned he was a kind and caring individual whose life was too precious to have his killer go free for lack of evidence.

Based on what I'd seen in his apartment, he hadn't separated emotionally from his life in Indiana. Was that relevant? Was Mark's past a key to the solution? If so, any list I could make might be pointless.

There was one thing I'd never seriously considered: was Mark perhaps *not* the thoughtful compassionate person that everyone saw? Was it synthetic kindness, a ruse for some hidden agenda? Was it possible that Mark had deliberately provoked someone with knowledge he had? Was there a vindictive streak within his personality?

Nah, that theory was too farfetched; it would be grasping at straws to take that idea seriously.

He hadn't seemed like a guy who flaunted knowledge, or gloated about uncovered secrets. On the other hand, if there was something he didn't understand he wouldn't hesitate to ask questions. Friendly personal questions, asked innocently without any thought that some questions are best left unasked. But that is exactly the kind of thing that could get a person killed.

So, on with the list. Time to be thorough and get down to business. Organize it differently this time, maybe something will become obvious. First, assume that Roger is not *the culprit. Forget the categories. Just look at the suspects...my suspects...anyone who makes me uneasy, or elicits that spine-tingling sensation. Consider the various personalities; maybe something will become obvious.*

At the top of my list: *Man-in-Brown*. Why was he in town? The officers had investigated him thoroughly and must know why he came, but it is possible to hide things, even from professionals, isn't it? Where was his hometown? Had he ever met Mark?

Scary Mary. Okay, I shouldn't call her that. *Mary Lou*. Her fascination with everything gruesome or morbid was disturbing. Her sisters watched her closely; did they know something troubling about her background? Had she ever had psychiatric treatment? She certainly seemed to be a candidate for it. Where had she been during the festival? Perhaps her prying had unearthed secrets about Mark. Or about the killer. The thought made me shiver. Mary Lou herself might be in danger.

Was it possible that all three Marys had hidden secrets? There was something unnerving about their family dynamic.

Todd. The only local person who'd known Mark in the past. Could he have invited Mark to town in order to kill him? Was Todd better off in any way with Mark out of the picture? Had there been unresolved issues in their previous time together?

Jeff. I realized that I had ingrained prejudice against him because he was the only person I'd ever had to fire. Had the officers figured out the connection between Jeff and Man-in-Brown?

Old Girlfriend. Only a factor if the accounts of an amicable breakup were false. Was there animosity on her part? She could have been any young female tourist; no one would be any the wiser. Gregg had stated that most homicides take place between loved ones. That certainly brought her into the picture.

Town Board President *Ron Barber*. He'd lived in Mark's hometown. He couldn't meet my eyes in the woods. But so what? That's hardly suspicious. What brought him to Windsor Grove? Why had he become so involved in local government? Aren't small town officials usually home-grown?

Mr. Horner. His oddities and mannerisms were hard to categorize. He had a background in restaurants, his wife's last name was Fischer, and he seemed to have no real friends. Was there something in his past that explained his apprehension about things behind his back? And then there was his fascination with weaponry. Suspicious? Perhaps.

Brad. I didn't want anyone from Unincorporated to be involved, but I had to include him because of his hostile attitude. This obnoxious man might be capable of almost anything. On the other hand, he worshipped Uncle Al, so he couldn't be really bad, could he? Wait…he rescued me from the freezer. That certainly clears him as the culprit, doesn't it?

There were many more potential suspects: Lady Elizabeth's irate owner; any one of the employees at Wholesale Wholegrains; an employee at any restaurant or inn on Mark's route; anyone who'd come to central Wisconsin to escape their past. The possibilities seemed endless, but unfortunately that wasn't particularly helpful.

I considered all the people I'd been assuming innocent: the local shopkeepers, the numerous property owners who were only here on weekends, local farmers, gallery volunteers…literally hundreds of people supposedly without motive. Were any of these people innately wicked? Psychologically unstable? Harboring hidden anxieties?

What about the Angry Diner, the guy who'd hated his pesto burger? I had no real reason to suspect him, but now that I knew he was still in the area…well, it was *my* list, I could put anyone on it I wanted to, couldn't I? He certainly was a man with anger issues.

The more I thought about it, the more complicated my list became. I felt a sense of emptiness when I was done. There was a void in my brain where there should have been insights and answers.

"You can figure anything out if you want to badly enough," Bekah had said, much like Madame Isabella's, "You can do anything if you really want to. Just try, try, try, and you'll get it right."

How ironic that a dear friend and a hated instructor would mirror the same opinion. Was there really something about me that would inspire this kind of confidence? It was an amusing thought.

CHAPTER 33

Facts that exist in a person's subconscious often move to the foreground during REM sleep cycles. I've always slept with a pad of paper on my nightstand so I can jot down revelations that surface overnight.

Unfortunately, for every time that I've had a brainstorm about completing a school project or understanding a disagreement between friends, I would wake up a dozen mornings to notes saying things like "at a soccer match" or "purple balloon". I'm sure the notes all made perfect sense in a dream-like state, but in daylight they left a lot to be desired.

A notebook and pen were handy in my current bedroom for just such deductions (the good ones, not the weird ones), but I hadn't penned any useful insights since Mark's murder. I was thinking of almost nothing else these days when I fell asleep, I assumed that sooner or later my "aha!" moment would arrive. Teddy Maxwell spent his days guarding the notebook, just in case I'd jotted down anything vital.

I tossed and turned well into Sunday morning. My brain was overflowing, and several times I woke and jotted down what was on my mind. The next morning I looked at the pad and read "dead flowers", "on the moon" (that one might have been "on the menu", my nighttime handwriting is dreadful), "what you know", "winking", and "brown sweater". Not exactly profound stuff. Not only were my notes useless, I didn't feel one bit rested, and my eyes had dark circles.

I spent more time than usual on makeup and hair that day, wearing coral jewelry to complement a navy skirt and top. Coral ballet flats with navy bows pulled the outfit together; somehow I hoped that the perky outfit made up for a face that looked like I hadn't been to bed.

It was a hectic Sunday, with a good mixture of locals and visitors enjoying brunch. A full Lounge and dining room kept my staff hustling for most of the day.

As the day wore on I realized that I recognized many locals not by their names, but by what we knew about them: the lady who filled her shoulder bag with dinner rolls when she thought we weren't looking, the man who detoured to the Lounge for a shot of whiskey on his way to the men's room, the family whose kids run screaming through the dining room. I recognized the woman who'd complained about painful shoes after the memorial, and her friend who'd made some complicated comments pretending they were very profound. What were they again? Something about not knowing what you know...

What you know! A light went on in my head, and I stood dumbfounded, staring at the wall. That was it! My note from last night. Her comment the other day, "It's not always what you've done that matters. It's what you know, even if you don't realize you know it."

That was my dream! That was the answer. Or part of it anyway. Mark, with all his curiosity and questions, knew something about someone and didn't realize its importance. He knew something, and he didn't know that he knew it. Or at least someone *thought* he knew something. Someone felt threatened and desperate, and Mark lost his life.

Who would have something to hide that was so serious that murder would seem like a solution? Who had Mark unwittingly made a discovery about? Who had something in their background that they would kill rather than have it revealed?

I'd found the motivation. I was horrified. But I was confident that I was correct. Everything finally fit together.

Everyone has secrets; but whose could be so damaging that they'd commit murder to keep it concealed? Man-in-Brown? Mary Lou? Mr. Horner? All three seemed to have questionable backgrounds. But it could be anyone. Anyone from Windsor Grove or anyone from Mark's home in Indiana. Someone from our staff, or a summer visitor. Unfortunately, as far as I knew, Roger was the most likely person to have something to hide, and he was the one I was determined to clear.

"Ma'am, ma'am," a nearby voice demanded my attention, "Can I get some more coffee?"

I'd been oblivious to things going on around me, and I quickly snapped back to reality. I felt like I was finally zeroing in on an answer. I mulled the idea of personal secrets over in my head while I worked, speculating on ideas that I wanted to bring to Gregg's attention. Not that I wanted to see Gregg. Of course not. But I hoped he would at least listen to me. Now it was my turn to need a sounding board.

Later in the day, when I could finally take a break, I did some online research. Tense and disturbed by what I learned, I left an urgent message on Gregg's phone asking him to check into a few details that weren't available to the public.

If I was right...and I felt certain that I was...a dangerous killer was still amongst us and was likely to kill again, possibly soon.

It was clear to me that Mark's good-natured curiosity had cost him his life.

I spent another restless night, but I was restless with anticipation, not the previous sense of helplessness. I could sense I was on the right track; I felt confident that something decisive was going to happen soon. There was apprehension involved, only because I was unsure if anyone was following through on my ideas. I was keyed up, and wanted swift action.

Gregg hadn't called back; that worried me. I knew I could depend on him to be thorough. Even if our friendship was disintegrating he would never neglect anything related to his job.

But what if he thought my ideas were pointless, or irrational? Would he ignore an idea if he thought it had no merit? Or put it off until he had spare time? I tensed at the thought; I needed to know he was making strides.

It had been a like a weight lifted off my shoulders when I'd turned my information over to him; I definitely didn't want to be the only one possessing critical knowledge. My immediate concern was whether Gregg could prove my theory. Was there enough evidence to make an arrest? Would the final piece of the puzzle fall into place?

Hopefully Gregg had understood my message and was busy verifying details. Maybe he'd been up all night doing research. But perhaps he'd been occupied with his new blonde friend. Had he listened to my message at all? Or were my messages no longer considered a priority?

Maybe I should have called the sheriff's department, not Gregg's private cell phone. Had that been a fateful error? If I didn't hear from him by noon would it be impertinent to call again? I'd make that decision when the time came.

I felt certain that I knew who our adversary was. How would I react if I bumped into the killer in a social setting? I didn't know if I could hide my feelings, I prayed there wouldn't be any sudden encounters that would make my thoughts transparent. If my conclusions became obvious my life could be in danger.

I was preoccupied and panicky that morning. I had trouble concentrating. The harder I tried to focus the more agitated I became. My breathing was shallow. When I walked I felt off balance. With Brad's help I wrote food orders for the week and called them in. I checked the weekend tills, opened mail, and paid a few invoices. I put together a deposit and called the bank with a change order. I kept my phone next to me and waited for it to ring. But it remained silent.

Activity could be heard from every area of the restaurant. Amanda was humming as she rolled her pastry dough. Brad grumbled his way through his morning routine. An electrician on a ladder was trying to figure out why some dining room lights were suddenly dim. Someone from our coffee supplier was installing a new coffee maker. A carpenter was replacing hinges on a restroom door.

It was a typical Monday, with the kitchen and Lounge being readied for another week, and repairs being completed on everything that had broken down over the weekend. It should have been calming in its normalcy; it's usually reassuring when things follow their customary pattern, no matter how hectic that pattern may be. I did some deep breathing and tried to stay calm.

Leaving Unincorporated, I made my usual short drive to the bank, stopping at the post office and the local printer. There'd been a break in the monotonously beautiful weather. Lawns had again been stressed from lack of moisture, so we welcomed an overcast day that promised to provide much-needed precipitation.

A steady light rain had begun falling at dawn, and was now accompanied by a mounting background of thunder. The air pressure added to my increasing stress level. Memories of the recent damaging storm made it difficult to accept a summer rain as the commonplace event that it was.

The roads had little traffic; on lazy summer days things don't start to happen in town until almost noon. I finished my errands quickly, making it back to work with an hour to spare before opening. The repair trucks had gone, which I took to be a good sign. I entered through the kitchen, arms filled with heavy bags of change.

Reaching my office, I was immediately on alert. The light, which was always left on during the work day, had been turned off. Perhaps the electrician had been in there; anyone on my staff would have left it lit.

But something wasn't right. An eerie atmosphere permeated the room. The air felt stagnant.

No. Oh no. That elusive scent…from my cottage after the break-in… now it was in my office. Oh God. Someone's been here.

With trepidation I moved forward, unable to reach the light switch with full hands. Shuffling toward my desk in the semi-darkness I stumbled over a box of Visitor's Guides that someone, probably me, had left on the floor.

I never had a chance to turn the light on. As I tried to regain my balance strong hands reached from the darkness behind me, seizing my shoulders, spinning me around.

Accompanied by rolling thunder came a hoarse whisper, "Stay quiet or you're dead. Right here. Right now!" It was *that* voice, the voice from my phone call.

My office door was kicked shut creating total darkness. The lock clicked, and with awakening terror I realized I was on my own to fend off this enemy.

There was no question about who held me; I knew. I'd always felt uneasy in the presence of this person; my apprehension was based on a gut instinct I should have trusted.

The picture became clear. My hunch had been right; my call to Gregg had been accurate. The current situation verified my conclusions; not that it did any good at the moment. I'd taken precautions at home to lock doors and windows; I'd tried to be cautious when going places alone.

I had naively remained oblivious to dangers at work.

Something stung the side of my neck, razor-sharp, grazing my skin with deliberate, controlled scraping motions. The burning sensation that resulted was more torturous than anything I'd ever experienced.

My mind went blank. I forget to breathe. My face became blazingly hot, things started to go black, there was a loud buzzing in my head, I could feel blood rushing through my veins. I was about to faint; I'd be at the mercy of a killer.

A rush of adrenaline surged through my body, my thinking cleared, and I did something I never thought I'd be fearless enough to do. Dropping several bank bags to the floor, I swung the heaviest bag, filled with hundreds of dollars in quarters, toward my assailant's head. It wasn't a direct hit; the darkness made accuracy impossible. I think the heavy bag made contact with a shoulder.

My attacker seemed astonished that I'd fight back; for a moment I felt the hold on myself loosen as we both stumbled backwards. That distraction didn't last for long. I was again yanked upright, painfully, viciously.

There was another menacing whisper, "You couldn't leave well enough alone. You had to interfere; you had to keep asking questions. I warned you, but you were too stupid to back off. Now you get what you deserve!" A crack of thunder emphasized the threat.

The darkness was suffocating. I'd never been claustrophobic, but I felt the walls closing in. For the first time in my life I knew acute panic. My heart pounded, my breath came in uneasy spurts.

The sharp-edged tool pricked my neck once more; I knew this person would show no mercy. I had no more weapons at hand; the things I recalled from one self-defense class were woefully inadequate. I tried in vain to remember Suzy's tips. No thoughts came.

The cutting edge against my neck was scraping vertically, like an ultra-sharp razor being used improperly. Searing pain said that layers of skin were being sadistically removed. Was I being peeled like an onion? Was it one of our knives doing the peeling? Was it near an artery? I felt drops of blood on my neck. For a split second I was angry that there might be permanent stains on my white silk blouse.

That thought was wiped out of my mind when I heard the chilling words, "Say goodbye."

CHAPTER 34

closed my eyes and held my breath, preparing for the worst. This was a nightmare. Things like this don't happen to me. Things like this don't happen in Windsor Grove.

I wanted to awaken and find myself lying in bed, listening to the sounds of nature. But the blade continued to shave my neck, slowly, methodically. The fiery pain was almost unbearable; this was a new kind of reality.

"You're going to die, meddling bitch. But first you'll suffer!" The whispered words filled the room.

They say that in the face of tragedy your life flashes before your eyes. They're right. I thought of my parents, I thought of Bekah, I thought of Uncle Al. Oddly, I thought of childhood tea parties. But mostly I thought of myself. Things I'd done, things I still wanted to do. Tableaus floated through my consciousness like a fast-moving newsreel.

A few words from Suzy Warren's self-defense class flashed into my brain. "Engage your attacker in conversation, the fury may dissipate." At this point I'd try anything.

"The state crime lab has proof that you murdered Mark," I lied. "Killing me won't help; you're going to prison anyway. We've got an alarm system, and officers are on their way. They'll go easier on you if you release me."

That comment resulted in me being brutally slammed into the wall. *Okay, not the best topic for creating calm. Try again.*

"I should have known it was you, you have such a complex personality," I expressed admiration for my foe's repugnant actions; a pure farce. "How did you keep it secret? You're very good at fooling people."

Heavy breathing and a vicious growl were the only answer.

"Did you send the anonymous notes, too?"

"What do you think?" was the whispered response, almost drowned out by the clamor of the storm.

"That was very clever. You sure kept everyone confused," I gushed.

"Quiet! No more talking!" The knife blade was relocated to pierce a so-far-untouched section of neck.

Don't be foolish Ashley…give up on the conversation.

Intense emotion created a reckless burst of energy. My anger had been building for weeks. Rage over what happened to Mark had combined with fury about the disrupted lifestyle in Windsor Grove. They were brought to a peak by the indignation of sheer terror.

I lashed out, frantically shoving against the knife-wielding arm. I kicked my assailant's legs, wishing for a better sense of balance. I considered spitting at that hateful human. I wanted to inflict injury and pain and humiliation and punishment.

Remembering a tip from the self-defense course, I tried to jab my enemy's eyes with outstretched fingers. In the darkness I couldn't make contact. Twisting to kick a shin I lost my balance and kicked at thin air. Where were all those workers who'd been here? Did no one notice the sounds of a struggle? If I screamed would anyone hear? Or would I meet the same fate as Mark?

I tried to remember any available weapon, but came up blank. In movies there's always a convenient lamp, or golf club, or paperweight. In my office there were catalogs, invoices, menus and schedules. Useless. Not even a letter opener within reach. There was a stapler somewhere amid the flotsam and jetsam, but any creative stapler action would beg for lethal damage by that stinging knife.

My fight was ineffectual; when you're overpowered you're overpowered. My attacker had an insane irrational brutality I couldn't match, even in terror.

An inhuman growl filled the room, turning into the savage yowl of an animal attacking its prey. I was roughly shaken from side to side, the knife blade bouncing painfully along.

I did what I could, kicking and punching, mostly at air; my shorter arms couldn't make contact. Knowing how to inflict pain didn't help when there was a blade at my throat. Any moves I made resulted in more sustained motion against my raw burning flesh.

It was urgent that I take immediate action, but options were limited. The malice and loathing in the room were palpable. As heightened as my sense of self-preservation was, my adversary surpassed my strength with sheer evil. It was possible that these were my last moments on earth. *Well then, Ashley, go down fighting.*

My heartbeat increased in intensity; my breathing accelerated. I forgot about pain, acting in desperation. With renewed determination I reached behind me, grabbed a pile of paperwork, and flung it toward my assailant. It gained me a few seconds; the blade was pulled away from my neck while invoices flew around our heads.

A high-pitched howl reminded me that I'd neglected to completely close the lid on that silly floor safe. For once my carelessness had been advantageous; the ankle being twisted was not my own. *Score one for me.*

In that moment of confusion, I lunged forward, scraping my nails across my attacker's cheeks. This was met with another inhuman screech, the howl of a wild animal, this time a tortured animal. *Good, you deserve it.*

With the heel of my hand I aimed an upward thrust toward the culprit's face, making crunching contact with a nose. Finally there would be blood that wasn't mine. *Score two.*

My terror was second only to my pure hatred, my desire to extract revenge. I was vaguely aware that the noise from the storm had become a constant din, masking the commotion from our struggle.

Another hostile growl announced an escalation in fervor. The weapon was now being thrust toward my chest; only the darkness had prevented a direct hit. My attacker was enjoying this, the more I fought, the worse my position became. *If I survive this I'm signing up for a much more in-depth self-defense course. If I survive.*

Please, please, someone, help me. Where did everyone go? Can't anyone hear the wailing of this creature?

Feeling trapped, I envisioned the beautiful waters of the lake rising to engulf me, with myself unable to react, falling deep into an abyss. It seemed inevitable. Another life lost. Nature taking its course, reclaiming one of its creatures. *Say goodbye.*

Suddenly a different type of clamor broke through the din.

Pounding footsteps and a thunderous crash, accompanied by the unmistakable sound of splintering wood, abruptly changed the scene.

A tall figure hurtled into the room. I was flung roughly aside, sent sprawling across my desk. Now two people frantically struggled in the tiny office, and thankfully neither of them was me.

Momentarily I thought Gregg had arrived in the nick in time, but a shaft of light through the damaged doorway told me the newcomer had a bulkier silhouette, and a street-smart style of aggression.

"Get your filthy hands off my boss!" With overwhelming relief I realized that Brad had broken down the door and was battling Mark's killer.

"How dare you kill people with my knives? Those are chefs' knives, for serious business, not meant for mother-fuckers like you!" It would have been hilarious if I hadn't been terrified.

I extricated myself from my desk, reached toward the door, flipped the light switch, and joined the struggle, attempting to keep the razor-sharp knife (yes, it was one of ours) from slashing into my chef's muscular body. My brain felt too fuzzy to recall any self-defense tips; I tried to assist Brad, but I was useless in the battle.

Clinging to the knife-wielding arm, I pried at the clenched white knuckles. For this I was flung into the wall. I lurched forward to grab the arm again, earning an elbow in the face and some obscene language. Flailing backward, I slid on a pile of loose papers, landing on one hip, my left shoulder and cheek making sudden sharp contact with the side of a metal filing cabinet.

Brad has overpowering physical strength, and he needed every ounce of it just to remain upright. Natural athletic ability is no match for maniacal brutality. The demonic eyes of the attacker gave witness to a psyche that had lost touch with reality.

The struggle continued, with tremendous grunting and groaning. The ridiculously small area of clear floor space inhibited the ability of anyone to gain an advantage; movements were minimized, making for a rather bizarre fight. My impulses urged me to forge ahead, but a sense of self-preservation convinced me to stay on the floor avoiding the fray.

Reluctant as I was to do nothing, I cowered in the corner, trying to develop a strategy that would be more help than hindrance. It was hard to focus; I felt beaten. I could hear Suzy in her self-defense class saying, "Never risk your life trying to be a hero." Made sense to me.

I was light-headed; dizzy and confused. I could feel blood dripping from the scrapes on my neck. How much blood had I lost?

There was a desperate need for effective action; the shining knife blade would slice Brad's flesh any second, but I was trembling and doubted if I could stand. I debated whether I could crawl out of the room unnoticed and get to a phone, when a tall brown-clad figure exploded through the broken door, and the amount of tension increased dramatically.

"Stop right there! Drop the knife or I'll shoot!" I heard in a familiar voice. "Drop the knife to the floor and put your hands in the air!" And there was indeed a service revolver aimed directly at my attacker's head, and the struggle ended, then and there. The relief I felt cannot be described. An elephant had been lifted from my shoulders.

"It's about time!" Brad announced as he assisted Gregg in wrenching the knife from the intruder's hand, dropping it to the floor. Brad gleefully detained the criminal as Gregg pulled handcuffs from his belt, and slapped them roughly on the struggling suspect.

My feelings cannot be described; I wanted to just sit and cry, but was too weak to make the effort.

"You're under arrest for first degree intentional homicide, attempted homicide, and physical assault." Then he began to recite, "You have the right to remain silent. Anything you say can and will be used against you in a court of law…"

Silence, however, was not what we got. Instead we received a loud, indignant, obscenity-laced tirade. "You can't do this to me! No God-damned way will you bastards interfere with my plans! My life has importance; I'm superior to the rest of you losers. Get your fucking hands off me! This is an obstruction of justice; I'm filing a lawsuit!"

And then, more to the point, "My life will be ruined if this gets out!"

"That's exactly what I had planned," Gregg nodded satisfactorily, as we all stared at Mark's killer. At that moment, Rupert, Candidate for State Senate, red-faced, snarling, trembling with rage, was a sad caricature of the respected leader he'd plotted to become. There's some quote about the mighty when they fall, and if I could remember it, I'm sure it would be appropriate.

The next hours were a blur. Rupert had been hustled through the storm, kicking, struggling and bellowing threats, thrust into a squad car and taken away.

Paramedics worked quickly, applying dressings to stem rivulets of blood dripping down my neck. An oxygen mask was placed over my nose and mouth; a blood pressure cuff, a stethoscope and a clip on my finger were used to check vital signs. I was assured that I wasn't in any immediate danger, and was asked if I needed a painkiller. I happily accepted.

I was subjected to an embarrassing ambulance ride to an area hospital where more cuts, scratches, scrapes and bruises were treated. From there I was driven to the sheriff's station for questioning. It says a lot about my state of mind, and state of exhaustion, that I don't recall who it was who drove me.

I was interviewed once again, and learned that Brad had been interviewed separately. Eventually we both signed statements, and were released. Thankfully it was a Monday, typically a slow restaurant day; we obviously weren't being any help to our staff. I knew they could handle things without us; they were an expert crew, after all.

Brad, however, had been frantic to get back to the kitchen. He'd made several phone calls to the restaurant, having been in the middle of preparing that night's French onion and minestrone soups when he rushed to my rescue. His diligence was admirable, but his nervous energy drained everyone around him.

Having literally saved the day, he paced like a caged lion until he was released to go back to Unincorporated.

"I gotta leave, the place needs me," he announced, taking off the minute he was dismissed.

I'd made an effort to thank him; if not for him I may have been another tragic statistic. But he grumbled, "It's my job, taking care of things. And people," and turned away.

For all his churlishness, he'd saved my life twice in as many months. I couldn't ask for more in a friend.

It seemed to take forever before Gregg came to see me, but eventually he entered the room. I'd remained reasonably calm, proud of myself for how well I'd held it all together. But one look at Gregg's face was all it took, and my tears started flowing. The other Sheriff's Department employees immediately remembered things they had to do in other parts of the building.

"I'm so sorry I wasn't there sooner." His voice was quiet as he put his arms around me in a not-at-all-professional way.

"At first I didn't understand your message. We thought we'd investigated Rupert as thoroughly as we investigated everyone else. When you said, 'Check his college records', it didn't make sense.

"Everyone knows he has a law degree; he's been practicing law for years. Even so, we'd checked that his license to practice in Wisconsin is current. It is.

"It's also common knowledge that he went to Harvard; he can't shut up about it. It never occurred to anyone that the credentials on the wall might be forged. Who earns a degree from one college and then hangs a fake diploma from a different one? Officers know better than to assume things, but we assumed he was truthful on that count."

I couldn't control the waterfall from my eyes, and was now gulping and sniffling, but I gratefully heard Gregg's next words.

"When I realized what you meant I made some phone calls, and sure enough, Rupert had been expelled from Harvard, then attended

Indiana University, and Maurer School of Law. Rupert's college exploits were legendary at Indiana U, and Mark recognized him immediately from photos on campus.

"The first time Mark spoke to Rupert in Windsor Grove he actually said, 'I knew right away who you are; kids at Indiana still talk about Rabble-Rouser Rupert.' He intended it to be a compliment. That was the catalyst for Rupert's plot to eliminate Mark.

"Mark thought nothing of it. He considered Rupert's exploits normal student disobedience. He chatted in his friendly way about things Rupert was determined to conceal. Mark never realized that we'd been told Rupert's degree was from Harvard, but as far as Rupert was concerned the truth had become too close to the surface."

Gregg pulled me closer, so that my right cheek (the side that wasn't swollen and throbbing) was against his shoulder.

"Rupert feared that Mark would innocently divulge his secret, and the world would know he'd lied about his alma mater. That impressively engraved fake diploma was his prized possession. Law degree or no, he defined himself by his Harvard connection."

"Did he think he could maintain the lie if he won the election?"

"Who knows? It was so important to him to succeed in politics that he took a chance on murder rather than admit deception. It's crazy. But I guess Rupert was exactly that, crazy. Savagely crazy. Or just plain nuts, take your pick.

"Once I knew the truth, I rushed to Unincorporated. You were right, Mark knew something, and was oblivious to its importance. Once I realized that you knew it too, I was terrified...panicked...I couldn't move fast enough." I felt his body shudder. Gregg's normal steady composure was gone.

"I feel like I failed you, big time," he gulped. I lifted my head, ready to remind him that he had, after all, arrived in time. But words didn't come. His eyes were tear-filled, and he looked miserable.

His voice broke as he added, "Your intuition was right. I should have trusted your instincts. From now on, when you say 'go', I go!"

I put my arms around his waist, clutching the fabric of his shirt.

"I was scared...so...scared...just...*really* scared." My words came out in a squeak. My body continued to tremble, with the occasional tear still escaping to decorate my face.

"It's alright now. It's over. You're safe. I've got you."

I relaxed into Gregg's arms. It felt like I was where I belonged, tight against his strong chest. I hadn't realized how much I'd missed him. I closed my eyes and concentrated on breathing; in and out, in and out, until finally my breath came more naturally. The nightmare was over.

CHAPTER 35

The Windsor Grove grapevine works at a fevered pace when there's scandal involved, and this was considered the scandal to end all scandals. By evening all the RUPERT FOR STATE SENATE signs had disappeared; Roger had been released from custody and had immediately been added to our kitchen schedule, and the locals were out in full force hoping to learn every delicious detail. Business was hopping at Unincorporated with guests anxious to weigh in on the now universally reviled political candidate.

Gregg had generously given me full credit for determining who the culprit was, telling everyone he spoke with that it was my insight that revealed the motive.

I was being treated like a local hero; very embarrassing. The staff seemed to hold me in higher esteem than before, which was gratifying. Except Brad, of course, who grumbled about, "All the bullshit since you got here…"

Some things never change.

CHAPTER 36

Early on Tuesday Gregg picked me up in his squad car, and we rode to the courthouse in Oak Landing for Rupert's initial arraignment. It was a cut and dried affair and my presence wasn't necessary, but I wanted to be there; partly due to curiosity, but mostly for the sense of closure.

It was a dark, damp, gloomy day that made my skin feel clammy and created a frizzy mess of my hair. I wore a casual teal dress with white trim, black pumps and a white cuff bracelet. I thought I appeared businesslike and serious in that outfit (if you ignored the hair). I definitely didn't want to appear frivolous, or younger than I am.

I could have covered the bruising on my face with thick makeup, but it was considered better to show up in court with obvious injuries, if only to emphasize the degree of trauma for the benefit of attorneys and judge.

They couldn't overlook the left side of my face, an unnatural shade of purplish blue, like some ghastly Halloween creature. The black stitches, open sores and scrapes on my neck were positively alarming, and defined the most terrorizing part of my ordeal.

Word about town was that Rupert's lawyer (hopefully a more ethical lawyer than he was himself) would propose an insanity defense. Gregg explained that in this case insanity was a legal term, not a psychological term, and the insanity defense requires the defendant be wholly or partially irrational when the crime occurs. That defense is only successful about two percent of the time, so it was unlikely to work in this case.

Rupert's obvious deliberate planning gave testament to a methodical, clear-thinking mind.

Watching Rupert being hustled into the district court in handcuffs, wearing an ugly orange jumpsuit, shielding his face from photographers, felt incredibly satisfying. For once I was pleased to see the swarm of reporters, photographers, and a television crew. Rupert deserved every bit of coverage he received, and then some. Like everyone else, I'd been blinded by his stature in the community. I'd assumed that political aspirations would demand a law-abiding lifestyle. How wrong we had all been.

It was gratifying to assume he'd pay the consequences well into the future.

After the judge formally charged Rupert with everything from first degree intentional homicide to resisting arrest, from breaking and entering to inflicting bodily harm, had denied bail and set a date for a pretrial hearing, Gregg drove me home.

I expected him to leave me at the door, but he followed me inside, saying quietly, "Ashley, there's something I need to say." I wasn't sure what to expect, but his next words were music to my ears.

"First, I've really missed you. I hated the wall that grew up between us, but I didn't know what to do about it. I had to do my job, but I felt awful most of the time." His intent gaze made me tremble, and I moved toward him as if drawn to a magnet.

He pulled me to him and put his arms around me. "I owe you a huge apology. I should have listened to your instincts from the start; but it's hard for officers to admit that our investigation could lead in the wrong direction."

"That's alright," I whispered into his shoulder.

"No, it's not. You have better natural intuition about human behavior than I have about criminal behavior. I realize that now," he said with a laugh. "Since this is my first murder investigation I shouldn't be surprised!"

His arms tightened around me. His fingers played with my hair as he pulled my face toward his. His lips touched my forehead, then my cheek. His eyes bore into mine, with such mesmerizing intensity that it took my breath away. His lips brushed mine briefly, and then returned for a longer visit. They were softer than I expected, and warm. I relaxed into his strong comforting arms.

Knock! Knock! Tap...tap...tap... The sound of familiar laughter accompanied the knocking. I pulled myself reluctantly from Gregg's arms, hurried to the door and opened it wide, to find my parents standing there grinning.

"Surprise!" Mom shouted as she walked into the cottage, turning to me for a hug.

"Hi Honey! How's my girl?" Dad bellowed, following her in carrying several pieces of luggage.

They both stopped short when they realized I wasn't alone. Gregg wore his Sheriff's uniform, pressed and official, but his wide-brimmed hat was across the room, his hair was rumpled, and he struggled to conceal his annoyance at the interruption. To their credit, my parents did a good job of hiding their surprise.

"Oh...oh...um...Ashley...no..." Mom had focused on me, and was staring at my face and neck, looking stunned.

Dad hadn't yet looked in my direction; he was busy scrutinizing Gregg. I blurted out something about Gregg driving me to a court appearance, which increased the skepticism on Dad's face. I couldn't tell if he was displeased because he thought I should be at work, or if he felt obligated to intimidate any male who visited his daughter.

Mostly I hoped that Dad didn't think I was being arrested (after a summer spent in the midst of a murder investigation it was the first thing that came to mind).

Mom continued sputtering and stammering, unable to form words. It took a few moments longer for my very visible wounds to register with Dad, who had finally turned his attention toward me and was upset with what he saw.

"Your face! Honey, your face!" Mom had found her voice.

"My God, what happened to your neck? Who did this to you?" Dad got right to the point.

"It's a long story," I didn't know how else to begin.

They both glared at Gregg, jumping to unwarranted conclusions, ready to place the blame on whoever was at hand. I stammered over introductions and made it clear that Gregg wasn't to blame. There was polite handshaking all around and Gregg wisely announced that he had to get back to work.

After he'd gone, I gave my parents the hugs, kisses, and warm welcome they deserved, followed by an abbreviated explanation of how I'd been injured. (It's possible that in my version I came across as being a bit more heroic than I'd been in reality).

It truly was great to have them visit, although some advance warning would have been appreciated. I hadn't planned on them seeing their daughter looking quite so bruised and beaten.

"It's been an overwhelming summer. I have so much to tell you!" I felt an adrenaline rush and I knew Mom and Dad would be an attentive audience. "Right now I need to head over to Unincorporated and get everything ready for opening. Unpack and make yourselves at home. I'll be back by noon; we'll go somewhere for lunch so I can explain everything."

Mom smiled, having filed the horrors into storage in her subconscious, and commented kindly, "That sounds great, dear. It's been a long time since we've had time to chat; we have a lot to get caught up on. We're just happy that you're having such an entertaining summer!"

Right.

AFTERWARD

Mom, Dad, and I spent several relaxing days together, occasionally accompanied by Uncle Al, even including Gregg when available; my key staffers willingly put in extra hours to make it possible.

It was great to have family time, but it was equally great when Mom and Dad left. I needed time to organize my thoughts; hovering parents were definitely not conducive to quiet reflection.

My cottage had never looked so welcoming; flowers had never seemed so gorgeous; a blue sky had never before brought joy to my heart. It's amazing how a solution to the homicide had changed my perception of reality. Even Teddy Maxwell was more content; his crooked smile seeming more amused, less apprehensive.

"Of course you solved it," Bekah said when I called her. "I knew you would; who knows more about human behavior than you? Now I think you own yourself an online shopping spree!" *Hmmm...not a bad idea...*

The summer became more predictable after Rupert's arrest. Work, sleep, work, sleep...the pattern of a restaurant manager during the busy season. Gregg kept me updated on developments in the court system. Some details made me feel vindicated; some made me feel foolish.

Having committed cold-blooded murder with a knife he'd confiscated during a kitchen tour, Rupert decided to cast suspicion on my staff. Grabbing placemats was easy as he wandered through the dining room greeting the public. Depositing notes and knives throughout the area was simple, since recipients could be chosen at random. Time spent in the courtroom had taught him the importance of avoiding fingerprints and footprints, and having an alibi.

When he learned I'd become friendly with Gregg, Rupert watched for an opportunity to get me alone, smiling and shaking hands all the while.

It was common knowledge that the employee entrance was left unlocked during daytime hours. All Rupert had to do was watch for an opportunity to eliminate me, while directing suspicion to my staff. When locking me in the freezer didn't work, he waited for his next chance.

Rupert had deluded himself into believing that if he wanted something badly enough he was invincible. He hadn't thoroughly planned the details of his final assault, which turned out to be his downfall. And my salvation. If I'd been alone in the building when he made that violent attack in the office I wouldn't have lived to tell about it.

Having pled "not guilty by reason of insanity" Rupert was headed to trial. Predictions from the courthouse (and from our guests who held an ongoing trial in Zachary's Lounge) were that he would spend many years, perhaps the rest of his life, behind bars.

Needless to say, Rupert's opponent won the election handily. It's awful to realize how close we came to being represented by a vindictive egomaniac with homicidal tendencies (terminology learned in all those sociology classes had suddenly become relevant).

"Downfall of a Politician" blared a front-page article in the Milwaukee Journal which chronicled the case from beginning to end. Gregg was credited with the solution; I was happy to take a back seat when official accolades were handed out. It was surprisingly satisfactory that the final resolution had been reached using exclusively Windsor Grove talent; state investigators received none of the credit.

After all my speculation, it was anticlimactic to learn that Man-in-Brown was a private investigator in town gathering ammunition for a high-dollar divorce case. He'd paid Jeff, the ex-dishwasher, to keep an eye on some local residents. Once the final report had been filed the rest of us were given the salty details by the aggrieved spouse.

Uncle Al's recovery was finally on track, and he filled me in on his plans. He wanted to spend time relaxing and enjoying life; partial retirement sounded appealing. He's asked me to stay on as a full-time supervisor, living in the cottage, keeping an eye on things when he's not around. I haven't made a commitment yet, but Windsor Grove just might become my permanent home. As long as I can finally get some shopping time.

Roger was repentant when I confronted him about workplace theft. He blamed old habits being hard to break, and promised to do better. After his release he became more dedicated to his job than ever. Twenty-plus days in the Oak Landing jail seemed to strengthen his determination to remain law-abiding. Brad is keeping an eye on him, and Brad doesn't miss much, so I feel comfortable putting faith in his resolve.

The weather continued to be idyllic. Weathercasters were positively euphoric in their predictions, and travelers hit the road in record numbers. It was a profitable summer for Windsor Grove businesses, with smiling faces behind every counter. I was proud of the part I played in this tourism economy, and began to thoroughly enjoy my job.

The gorgeous blonde who'd shared ice cream with Gregg? A cousin, his closest friend during childhood, in Windsor Grove visiting family. Gregg thinks that she and I will become good friends; he's promised to introduce us next time she visits.

The best part of it all, as I'm sure you've guessed, is that Bekah was right. Gregg is more than just a friend.

Things are definitely looking up.

www.ingramcontent.com/pod-product-compliance
Lightning Source LLC
Chambersburg PA
CBHW032049020426
42335CB00011B/252